Creating Effective Boards
for
Private Enterprises

John L. Ward

Creating Effective Boards
for
Private Enterprises

Meeting the Challenges
of
Continuity and Competition

FAMILY
ENTERPRISE
PUBLISHERS

Division of The Family Business Consulting Group, Inc.

CREATING EFFECTIVE BOARDS FOR PRIVATE ENTERPRISES
Meeting the Challenges of Continuity and Competition
   by John L. Ward
Original Copyright © 1991 by: Jossey-Bass Inc., Publishers
                                350 Sansome Street
                                San Francisco, California 94104
Copyright © 1997 by: Business Owner Resources, Publishers
                                1220 B Kennestone Circle
                                Marietta, GA 30066

Copyright © 2001 by: Family Enterprise Publishers
                                1220 B Kennestone Circle
                                Marietta, GA 30066

Library of Congress Cataloging-in-Publication Data

Ward, John L.
   Creating effective boards for private enterprises: meeting the
challenges of continuity and competition / John L. Ward. — 1st ed.
   Includes bibliographical references (p. 255) and index.
   ISBN 1-55542-352-3
   1. Directors of corporations — Handbooks, manuals, etc.   2. Private companies
— Management — Handbooks, manuals, etc.   I. Title.
II. Series
HD2745.W37   1991
658.4'22 —dc20

Manufactured in the United States of America

JACKET DESIGN BY WILLI BAUM

FIRST EDITION

HB Printing   10 9 8 7
Reprint   10 9 9 8

To my family, Gail, Jeffrey, and Julie —
for making the future so exciting

CONTENTS

PREFACE

Thousands of small and medium-sized private companies across North America are reaching a crossroads. Many entrepreneurs who founded their businesses after World War II are nearing retirement without any plans for management succession. Other closely held companies are struggling to chart a sound strategic course amid a flurry of fundamental changes in the business environment. Some wrestle with unexpected new competition from other industries or from overseas. Others face rising capital demands and rapid consolidation within their industries. Still others stagnate because of a lack of management confidence in the face of the extraordinary stresses of doing business today.

Perhaps most difficult of all, many owner-managers of these often vital businesses experience a growing sense of isolation in their daily struggle to survive and excel. Many will ultimately sell out under duress or fail, falling victim to a powerful tendency among private companies to fall short of their potential.

Together, these factors pose a fundamental challenge to private ownership and to the freedom it represents. "In American industry today, you have to continuously improve if you're going to compete successfully," says Paul Lehman, a fourth-generation president of Fel-Pro, a family-owned automotive parts manufacturer with more than $235 million in sales. "That's the challenge to us: to be able to maintain the values around which the company was founded, and also to be fully capable of competing."

I believe the resource explored in this book — the active

board of outside directors — is equal to that challenge. It is the
mechanism most often recommended by a rapidly growing group
of family business consultants and speakers to help business
owners with a wide range of issues and problems. The idea of
an active outside board has generated increased media coverage and growing enthusiasm among business owners as well.

Intended Audience

This book is the first handbook on the subject of effective
boards for private companies. It will guide the business owner,
director, or professional step-by-step through the process of establishing and managing an active board. It offers the closest
examination yet of the role of the board and its relationship to
shareholders in the private company environment, including
one of the most comprehensive texts available on the legal liability of private company boards. The book also gives special
treatment to the unique issues faced by family business owners,
showing how an active board can serve as a resource in perpetuating the enterprise.

The book will be of particular value to business owners
with 50 to 2,000 employees and to owners of professional service firms with 20 or more employees. These owners, as well
as the heads of smaller firms, will find the book useful in laying
the groundwork for future corporate growth and ownership or
for management succession. Members of the business owner's
family who might like to learn more about the subject also may
benefit. Owners of family businesses, as well as the sons and
daughters who will succeed them in the business, will find sections of the book designed specifically to meet their needs.

Directors of private companies can use the book to gain
a deeper understanding of their role, as well as practical advice
on dealing with a variety of special issues and situations that
arise in private businesses. The book is also written for advisers
to private businesses — consultants, bankers, accountants, lawyers, and family counselors — who seek a broader understanding of the purpose, role, liability, and management of outside
directors.

Background of the Book

Few other resources on this subject are available. The pioneering book *Outside Directors in the Family-Owned Business* (Danco and Jonovic, 1981) does not cover all the topics included here. While some monographs and a few other books (Vance, 1983; Anderson and Anthony, 1986; and Whisler, 1984) address the topic of boards of directors, most are intended primarily for public company professionals and directors. The business owner is left without an understanding of the rich and varied role an active outside board can play in the private company environment.

For this book, I draw on more than twenty years of business and consulting experience and research, including some unique data gained through surveys of existing private company boards. The material is illustrated by authentic examples drawn from my work with more than twenty boards and from interviews with more than thirty business owners and directors across North America. Names and certain details have been changed or omitted in a few cases to protect the privacy of the business owners who so generously shared their experiences, including many who overcame their natural reluctance to divulge information that might help other business owners.

For many of the business owners who told their stories for this book, an active outside board has been the single most important element in their effort to reach beyond mere subsistence for enduring excellence. "If you're satisfied to say, 'Enough's enough,' and to siphon off profits, then you don't need an outside board," says John Honkamp, president and owner of a chemicals concern with more than $100 million in sales. "But if you're trying to grow and stay that half-step ahead of the competition, you'd better have all the assistance you can get. I don't know why anyone wouldn't want to give himself all the weapons he can to win the advantage."

Overview of the Contents

The chapters of this book are organized to guide readers to a greater understanding of the potential, structure, and management of an active board. The first two chapters will help business owners, directors, professionals, family members, and others appreciate the potential of an effective board in the private company environment. The middle chapters will serve as a guide to defining the role of an active board, as well as to setting up and managing one. The final chapters address the challenges faced by chief executives, business owners, and directors in sustaining a highly effective board, with special attention to family business issues.

Chapter One shows how an active board can improve the quality of corporate decision making and planning without any significant loss of privacy. It illustrates a wide range of potential purposes for directors, such as serving as a sounding board and confidential ally to the chief executive officer (CEO). And it shows how directors can heighten the accountability of the business — not only to the company's various stakeholders but to the business owners' own goals as well.

Chapter One also addresses sources of resistance, both legitimate and unfounded, to naming outside directors. It dispels many of the myths surrounding outside directors, providing practical answers to such questions as these:

- Won't outside directors rob me of control of my company?
- Isn't director liability too big an obstacle to forming an outside board?
- How can outsiders ever understand my business well enough to be helpful?
- Why should I give up any of my privacy to share information with a board?
- Why would anyone want to serve?
- Won't an active board just eat up management time and obstruct decision making?

Chapter Two elaborates on the particular benefits of outside directors to the family-owned business, such as help with management succession and family compensation. It shows how directors can assist the family in laying a firm foundation of strategic, estate, family, and succession plans and, if desired, greatly increase the chances of perpetuating family ownership.

Chapter Three lays out the role of the effective board and shows how good directors can serve far more than mere custodial and fiduciary purposes. It covers both basic responsibilities and special opportunities, such as helping with human resources and strategic planning. It also shows how directors can help private companies avoid the common pitfall of missing their potential.

Chapter Four offers the most comprehensive text available on private company director liability issues and dispels some of the myths surrounding this subject. It includes the results of recent research showing that litigation against directors of private companies is less a threat than is generally believed. The chapter examines the board's legal duties and offers practical advice on avoiding liability problems. It also includes guidance on structuring a panel of advisers as an alternative to a more formal board of directors.

Chapters Five, Six, and Seven cover all aspects of setting up and managing the effective board, from envisioning its purpose and selecting directors to preparing effective background materials and managing committees. Chapter Eight offers suggestions on helping your board meet its potential, including tips on sparking creativity, avoiding rubber-stamp tendencies, promoting honest discussion, brainstorming, and asking good questions. Chapter Nine is addressed to the director, offering practical advice on topics ranging from approaching common board topics to asking good questions.

Chapter Ten presents for the first time some proven methods of fostering a constructive, healthy relationship between shareholders and directors in the family-owned business, with particular attention to issues that arise after a second generation of family ownership. It offers an original analysis of how family, business, and board issues evolve through the generations. It also includes practical guidance on setting up and maintaining a family council. Finally, Chapter Eleven examines the value, to both the individual and society, of drawing on an active board as a primary tool to help perpetuate private ownership of American business.

Acknowledgments

Learning from successful, thoughtful business owners through the years has been a tremendous privilege. I am genuinely grateful to the scores of private company leaders, their directors, and their families, who have taught me so much. Through them, I have come to appreciate better how private companies enrich our society. They have shared with me their pain and joy as they help shape our future. They have enlightened me regarding some of the marvelous complexities of building and continuing an enterprise. This book is possible because of them.

I have also been uniquely fortunate to have as a special friend the true inventor of the idea that private firms need active outside boards. Léon Danco of the Center for Family Business in Cleveland, Ohio, inspired my interest in this subject and influenced me more than anyone.

I am also grateful to Sue Shellenbarger, who helped make this book interesting and pleasant to read and enhanced it with specific examples and clear organization. There is at least as much of her in this book as there is of me. Sue, I have never enjoyed working with anyone more than you.

I particularly want to thank those who have made specific contributions to the book. I appreciate the generous and thoughtful interest of Irving Blackman, Shirley Brinsfield, Ralph Cator, Edward Duda, James Foley, Patricia Frishkoff, David Gallagher, Nan-b de Gaspé Beaubien, Bernie Hale, John Harrison, Charles Hoch, Al Hoffman, John Honkamp, Walter Horwich, Frank Hudetz, William Jentes, John R. "Ted" Kennedy, Richard Kent, Ivan Lansberg, Paul Lehman, Clayton Mathile, Alfred McDougal, Jack Mollenhauer, John Mooney, Allan Muchin, Bill Nance, John Nash, Kenneth Nowak, Richard Payne, Alain Roman, Fred Ruiz, Lew Smith, Tim Stockdale, Jerome Stone, Ronald Taylor, and Kenneth Wollner.

Evanston, Illinois   John L. Ward
June 1991

THE AUTHOR

John L. Ward is Co-Director and Clinical Professor at the Center for Family Enterprises at the Kellogg Graduate School of Management of Northwestern University. Ward received his PhD (1973) and MBA (1969) from the Stanford University Graduate School of Business, where he studied strategic management and leadership. Ward also attended Northwestern University (BS 1967) and the Sorbonne, University of Paris.

John Ward's main research activities are in the field of family business. He has authored or co-authored numerous articles and books on family business continuity, governance and strategic management. (See www.efamilybusiness.com for specific publication and contact information.)

In addition to teaching at the Kellogg Graduate School of Management, Ward is a regular visiting lecturer at several business schools around the world and an endowed professor emeritus from Loyola University of Chicago. He is an active consultant to business owning families and boards of directors. Through the years, he has served on fifteen boards in North America and Europe.

John and his wife, Gail, live in Evanston, Illinois, and are the proud parents of Jefferey and Julie.

Creating Effective Boards
for
Private Enterprises

Part One

THE PURPOSE
AND STRUCTURE
OF BOARDS

1

Truths and Myths
About Boards

The hardest thing for business owners to say is, "I need help." It's doubly hard for an entrepreneur, who is seemingly self-reliant to his peers, employees, and family. Yet every one of them is scared to death.

—Clayton Mathile

By the time he acquired control of the IAMS company in 1982, Clayton Mathile already had scored some impressive wins. As half-owner for eight years of the pet food manufacturer, he had spent a year on the road interviewing customers and distributors and a year in the laboratory remaking the company's dog food. Then he borrowed money and built a new plant, growing the company in the process from $1 million to $10 million in sales. "We put some good foundation in the ground," he says.

But as the company grew, so did Mr. Mathile's nagging sense that he no longer could manage every detail. He knew he needed help. "I had to change the way I was doing things," he says. "I told my wife, Mary, 'I know this business. Now I have to learn to be a manager.'"

Mr. Mathile formed an active board of outside directors in 1986 as part of an overall professionalization of management. Today, he credits his directors with ideas that have returned $1 million to the bottom line, including broadening a product line, expanding into Europe, and introducing an in-house czar of new products.

"Our board has contributed greatly to the success of the company," Mr. Mathile says. His directors, each with experience in human resources, marketing, operations, or finance, help him review major corporate issues and decisions. He keeps a running file of constructive questions raised by his directors. He even asks the board to review his own performance every year.

"Your outside board can be the inside sparring partner who tests your strengths and weaknesses before you get to the main arena — the marketplace," Mr. Mathile says. "Where else can a business owner go to find help from someone he trusts, who is unbiased, and who will help him do the job?"

Meeting the Challenge

Like Mr. Mathile, many owners of private companies wrestle with some of the toughest problems in management. Consider the following examples:

- The founder of a medium-sized publishing concern cherishes his independence. But his industry is consolidating fast, and he can no longer compete with big competitors' lavish spending on new projects. Should he sacrifice management control to affiliate with a deep-pocketed partner?
- The second-generation owner-managers of a fast-growing $40 million printing concern are proud of the company their father founded. But sibling concerns over officer compensation and other matters are mounting, and the CEO worries that the business will soon outstrip the family's ability to manage it. Is selling the company or going public the necessary next step?
- The founder of an office supply concern knows she should retire and hand the reins to her oldest son. But she cannot erase memories of the boy as an irresponsible teenager, and her two younger kids who are working in the business have their doubts too. Increasingly, the company drifts as family tensions drain management energy.

All of the CEOs in the above cases are talented entrepreneurs who have managed their fast-growing companies successfully for decades. Yet the natural evolution of their businesses has brought them face-to-face with problems that could erase their independence, divide the family, or even destroy the company. Similar problems drive thousands of closely held businesses into eclipse or extinction each year.

But one factor sets all of the above cases apart. Each executive led the business through its crisis and sustained it as a thriving, independent, owner-managed concern. And in each case, the business owners identify the same resource as the most important factor in that achievement: an active board of directors including experienced fellow business owners, executives, and entrepreneurs.

The publishing executive's board helped him realize that affiliation with a partner would cost him an unacceptable degree of management control, then offered ideas on alternative capital sources instead. "The board helped me see the problems" that a partnership could cause, the CEO says.

Directors of the printing concern acted as a lightning rod to help resolve family issues, then gave management a resounding vote of confidence and helped chart an ambitious new growth plan. "If it weren't for the board," says the CEO, "we'd be doing the exact opposite of what we are."

And at the office supply concern, directors helped the founder make peace with the succession process, groom her eldest son, and relinquish the management reins at last. "Most of the forward movement we've made in the last few years has been a result of board discussion," says the eldest son.

Outside directors are one of the richest and least-used resources available to private companies today. Only about 5 percent of private companies across the United States have active boards with outside directors. Yet as the examples of research in this book will show, most business owners' fears about outside directors vanish in the light of experience with an effective board.

In interviews for this book, more than twenty business owners with active boards said their outside directors helped them tackle major issues without robbing them of control, independence, or any meaningful measure of privacy. For some, outside directors brought new ideas, perspective, insights, or self-confidence. In some instances, outside directors acted as a catalyst for important strategic, financial, and succession planning.

In others, they served as a confidential ally to the chief executive in grappling with knotty succession or family issues. Almost unanimously, these owners agree that outside directors have improved the quality of decision making at their companies and increased their chances of perpetuating private ownership, should they choose to do so.

Consider the following examples:

- One entrepreneur credits his outside board with helping his specialty baked goods concern develop an upscale image and a new line of brand names for its cookies. "You can see the influence of the board here," says the owner proudly, encompassing an array of attractive products with a sweep of his arm.
- An owner of another family-held concern said its outside directors correctly refocused top management's attention toward strategy and long-term planning, and away from day-to-day operating details. The board "has really helped us to move the company forward," she says.
- The president of a private specialty chemicals concern credits his board with helping him sustain order and management discipline through his company's headlong expansion. "We've been able to handle many aspects of our growth in an orderly fashion — or as orderly as can be expected, when you've got a tiger by the tail," says the CEO.
- The president of a high-tech defense contractor says his outside directors have helped him make crucial government contacts and lay long-range plans. He would advise other high-tech startups to name a board of "outside experts who understand the business," he says, "so you can avoid pitfalls by drawing on their experiences."

Recent research also shows that chief executives with active outside directors report an unusually high level of satisfaction with their boards. In a survey of 147 closely held companies, almost 90 percent of the CEOs with at least two outside directors termed their boards "useful," "very valuable," or "tremendously valuable" to the company—a far higher level of satisfaction than expressed by CEOs with more conventional boards of only shareholders, family, or top managers.

When asked what advice they would offer to other CEOs and what they would do differently if they could, 78 percent of the CEOs said they would increase the number of outsiders on their boards, and 17 percent said they would give outside directors more influence (Ward and Handy, 1988).

When a Board?

An active board can benefit almost any firm with fifty or more employees. For professional service firms, the threshold is even lower, at about twenty employees. Smaller firms can benefit from forming an informal two- or three-member advisory council, including respected peers or the corporate lawyer, accountant, or consultant.

Ideally, the board should be in place before the company reaches major—and sometimes predictable—corporate transitions. Often, for instance, a company hits an "entrepreneurial plateau" at about forty to eighty employees, when the business outstrips the entrepreneur's ability to run it alone and stagnates or loses its strategic focus as a result. At this point, the owner often experiences burnout and badly needs energy from an active board.

A board can also be particularly helpful during a change in corporate leadership. The continuous guidance of trusted, experienced outside directors can provide a kind of insurance policy guaranteeing that the transition will be smooth and orderly. A broadening of ownership, a change in industry structure, or the onset of new forms of competition, technology, or regulation can pose similar challenges, taxing even the most vital and skilled manager.

Where to Begin?

The role, structure, and management of an active outside board are unfamiliar territory for many private business owners. All are treated in detail in this book.

In many ways, the freedom of the private company environment allows the active board to play a uniquely helpful role. Freed from some of the pressures and obligations that burden public company directors, directors can fulfill some special opportunities, from helping the CEO clarify the company's mission and philosophy to improving the quality of strategy.

Family-owned businesses pose special problems. Effective directors can help family business owners with management succession, compensation, planning, and other issues. As the business matures beyond its second generation of family ownership, it poses new challenges, including shareholder relations. But it also offers a special opportunity to perpetuate private ownership.

Liability issues are manageable too, provided that the business owner takes steps to understand and assess the risk (see Chapter Four). In most cases, business owners' fears of liability are overblown. Careful planning and a clear understanding by directors of their obligations under the law are the best safeguard. Other options, including formation of a panel of advisers, are available as well.

Later chapters discuss in detail setting up and managing a board. Often, the benefits begin even before the business owner contacts the first director candidate. Structuring a board requires the CEO to focus intensely on the most important questions and issues facing the company.

Once selection begins, many CEOs are delighted to discover that they are able to attract other entrepreneurs, business owners, and CEOs as directors. As discussed in Chapter Six, these "risk-taking peers," in the words of respected family-business adviser Léon Danco, are often ideal board members (Danco and Jonovic, 1981). Those who have run larger private companies and can draw on their own experience in surmounting hurdles that may still lie ahead for the business are the best candidates of all.

Unlike consultants, attorneys, or other paid advisers, these peers are not jeopardizing a client relationship by offering the CEO honest, unvarnished, objective opinions. Also unlike paid advisers, their advice is not available for a fee. And their experience in running profit-making enterprises is unparalleled.

Once the board is assembled, the book offers practical advice in preparing for and making the most of board meetings. For some business owners, this can be an adventure. An effective board may spark breakthrough thinking, offering fresh new approaches to problems that transcend the capability of any individual director alone. Managing an active board can also require some unaccustomed skills from the CEO, such as learning how to handle feedback.

Whatever the case, many business owners find that using the special talents of directors to the fullest is one of the best investments of time they can make.

Resistance to Active Boards

If an active outside board is such a valuable resource for the private business, why are there not more of them? By most estimates, only a small fraction of private firms in the United States have active boards that include outsiders, according to John Nash, president of the National Association of Corporate Directors. More often, boards are figureheads composed of a few shareholders or family members. Some meet perfunctorily to rubber-stamp required resolutions. In other cases, lawyers write fictional minutes of board meetings that never took place. Some business owners even forget who is on their boards.

In some cases, business owners' resistance to creating an active outside board is well-founded. Sometimes unusual tensions among shareholders weigh against it. In one family business, for instance, the sixty-two-year-old CEO and his wife, the company's financial executive, were eager to hand the business over to their daughter, who was working in the company. But their energy was consumed by struggling to help hold together the daughter's troubled second marriage to a man also employed in the business. Clearly, this was a no-win situation for outside directors. The family needed to resolve some internal problems before it could focus on the problems of the business and deal effectively with a board.

In other cases, a CEO's own position is too tenuous to involve active outside directors. Perhaps he has constructed a tense truce among shareholders who are continually nipping at his heels. (In such a case, the executive could likely benefit instead from a small panel of personal advisers.)

Other business owners are not willing to use outside directors effectively. A CEO may not be open to tackling the tough and time-consuming issues that likely would be raised by an effective board. He or she may be more interested in using directors as a rubber stamp or symbol than as a resource.

Some CEOs are not emotionally prepared to deal with an active board. Some are not receptive to constructive advice. Others are unwilling to put up with the discomfort associated with the process of review and accountability. All of these are valid reasons to avoid forming an active outside board.

More often, though, resistance is rooted in a lack of experience or understanding of the potential benefits of effective directors. Let us take a closer look at some of the reasons most often cited by CEOs for avoiding an active board.

"I Never Met an Outside Board I Liked"

Many business owners' only experience with outside boards is as directors of banks or charitable or civic organizations. Unfortunately, these are often poor examples. Banks tend to pick directors for the wrong reasons, packing their boards with customers. Directors in this heavily regulated industry also tend to become mired in operations, meeting monthly or more to vote on loan approvals and other operating matters. These boards typically have little opportunity or inclination to focus on long-range planning or other ideal board issues.

Similarly, boards of philanthropic or civic organizations are often assembled with political goals in mind: appealing to various constituencies, building alliances, or aiding fund-raising efforts. These boards are often far too big and too social to engender much helpful discussion.

Public company boards are another well-known model. But their operations are influenced by the breadth of the shareholder base and by major public reporting requirements. Directors carry a heavy load of fiduciary responsibilities to diverse and farflung shareholders, who increasingly hold directors accountable for the return on their investment (see Chapter Three). The scope of some public companies' operations also forces directors to spend enormous amounts of time just staying abreast of the business. Another drawback is that public companies often reach into top management to fill directorships, reducing the board's objectivity and preventing it from tackling the most sensitive personnel and strategic issues (see Chapter Five).

While public company boards often function very well despite these obstacles, owners of private businesses typically only hear or read in the media about bad examples: boards hit by liability lawsuits, boards ousting their CEO, boards under attack by special-interest groups, boards that crumble from infighting.

Few private business owners see any reason, based on what they know, to embrace any of these models—the bank, philanthropic, or conflict-ridden public company boards. But as this book will demonstrate, an effective private company board can operate much differently.

While it requires some courage to invite active directors into one's business, says one entrepreneur, "The more you understand their role, the less intimidating the whole idea is."

Fear of the Unknown

With so few good role models, many CEOs harbor a variety of fears about outside directors. Let us take a closer look at a few of the most common ones:

"Why should I give up control of my company?" Thanks in part to the public company model, many business owners suspect outside directors will somehow rob them of control of the business. This fear obscures the fact that *all* directors serve at the pleasure of shareholders. In the private company, the business owner structures the board to meet his or her needs. Few issues need come to a vote.

If a dispute does arise, directors can be removed as quickly as the CEO can call a shareholders' meeting. (And in a private company, that can be very quickly!) "Nothing has ever come to a vote by my board," says one CEO. "Let's face it. In a family-held firm, the family holds all the votes. If my directors were to disagree with me on something I felt strongly about, I'd disband the board, and we'd move on. But frankly, I don't imagine that ever happening. They respect me, and I'd be a fool not to consider their opinion."

Moreover, grabbing power is the farthest thing from the mind of the effective private company director. Most see their role as a sounding board, a guide, a confidential ally, or a resource. And their motivation is usually to offer help when they can and to learn what they can in the process (see Chapter Three).

"The liability risk is too great." As mentioned above, both experience and recent research suggest that this fear is over-blown for private company boards. At least one study suggests that the actual incidence of liability suits against directors of small, privately held companies is low (Wyatt Company, 1990b). And means of alleviating the risks are available, of course, such as shareholder indemnification or director and officer liability insurance. (These issues are treated in detail in Chapter Four.)

Another alternative preferred by many private companies is naming a panel of outside advisers rather than directors. This panel is authorized by the board to exist but not to make any final decisions. Such a panel can be almost as effective as an outside board.

Ultimately, the best defense against legal liability is conscientious and good-faith conduct by the director — a guiding principle routinely embraced by effective board members.

"My lawyer advises against it." Many professional advisers recommend that their clients avoid naming outside directors. "That's a terrible idea," an adviser may say. "Look at the liability risk! No one will want to serve." Such advice is often rooted in self-interest. (When asked to serve on a board, the same consultant may jump at the chance.) Some advisers worry that outside directors will disrupt their relationship with the client. In fact, an outside board can be extremely helpful in evaluating professional advisers.

"I don't want to give up any of my privacy." Many entrepreneurs strongly resist sharing financial information. But as a business grows, financial performance data become a crucial management tool. Some level of disclosure to top managers becomes necessary to set goals, measure progress, and grow. It is a necessary step in the transition from entrepreneurial to professional management.

Revealing selected information to directors is a good place to start. A business owner need not bare all, especially at first. He or she can make clear to directors that the information shared is confidential. And he or she should not have to fear leaks or other indiscretions by the board; confidentiality and integrity are minimal requirements of good directors (see Chapter Six).

"I don't have any idea whom to choose." Many entrepreneurs have been too busy building the business to develop an extensive network of outside contacts. Many worry that qualified people will not want to serve. Some fear making bad choices. But the process can be virtually fail-safe if approached deliberately and thoughtfully. Business owners typically have more resources at hand than they realize to help identify good candidates, and a careful screening can dramatically reduce the risk of making a poor choice (see Chapter Six). To the surprise and gratification of many CEOs, their top candidates usually agree to serve!

"I'm not organized enough to deal with a board. Besides, I don't like making presentations." Many entrepreneurs have neglected organizational and management skills in favor of growing their companies. But these are not just board-room skills. As a company and its work force grow, the CEO's ability to articulate ideas and goals becomes increasingly important to the quality of management.

Managing a board can be a good first step toward developing these professional abilities. Many CEOs say preparing for and conducting board meetings can be a valuable exercise in focusing on and communicating the most important issues facing their businesses.

"Outsiders could never understand my business." No one will ever understand any business as well as its owner-manager. Good outside directors know and respect that fact. Effective directors are not there to run the business, and they will not try (see Chapter Three). Directors will, however, in time develop valuable knowledge of the company. And because good boards tend to focus on broad, long-range issues such as strategy and succession, the directors' diverse experience can be an asset rather than a liability.

As discussed in detail later in this chapter and in Chapter Five, directors chosen from companies in some way analogous to the business can offer valuable new perspectives by examining issues in light of comparable areas of their own experience. This kind of reasoning by analogy can free the business owner from the constraints of a narrow, single-industry perspective and open the door to a wealth of new ideas.

"Outside directors will force me to act more quickly than I want to." Many CEOs fear that raising an issue with an outside board will force them into quick action. Effective boards do not operate this way. The role of an effective private company board is never to force or coerce, but to listen, lend counsel and support, and raise questions. A good board will be patient as well. Directors likely have already faced similar problems and will be sympathetic with the business owner's difficulties.

"An outside board would be a bureaucratic encumbrance." Meeting legal requirements for board actions is easy indeed when mom and dad or a few shareholders are the only directors. In practice, though, a well-managed private company board can deal with its legal duties almost as efficiently, expediting them at one of its quarterly meetings (see Chapter Seven). Although many managers fear an active board will slow operational decision making, this should not occur. The directors' role is not to interfere in operations but to raise and help consider longer-range issues that typically are pending for months at a time, such as strategic or succession planning (see Chapter Three).

"Why Bother?"

Inertia is a deeply entrenched obstacle. Many CEOs say they plan to form an active board but add, "I've got a few things I want to clean up first. I don't have a marketing plan . . . the plant isn't remodeled . . . " or whatever. In fact, the CEO who waits to put his or her business in perfect order will never form an active board. Nor do good directors expect a business to be shipshape in every way.

Other business owners say they already have plenty of trusted people to talk to. However, as will be discussed later in this chapter, the business advice of employees, consultants, friends and family, while valuable, can be easily colored by existing relationships with the CEO, personal interest in the business, or inexperience.

Perhaps most importantly, many business owners find in time that these objections evaporate when weighed against the benefits of a board. Nowhere outside the board room can business owners find such a pure, private, and comprehensive laboratory for testing embryonic ideas, seeking support and advice from respected peers, and weighing such sensitive long-term issues as estate planning, executive compensation, succession planning, and shareholder relations.

As one business owner explains it, "Knowing that I have the board as a resource gives me emotional comfort. I know I'm now doing some things that were long overdue."

Let us take a closer look at how this laboratory works.

Ten Benefits of an Active Board

In-House Experience and Expertise. In the sunny, pleasant board room of Solar Press, directors listened carefully as President Frank C. Hudetz laid his questions before them. The issue was one that worries owner-managers of thousands of private companies: "Will we need to sell out? If so, when?"

Solar Press, a thriving, $40 million specialty printing and mailing concern founded by Mr. Hudetz's father, had won a commanding share of the nationwide direct mail market. Frank Hudetz and other family members in management saw a need for even more expansion, but they feared the company would outstrip the family's ability to manage it. As Mr. Hudetz laid before the board the idea of going public, he explained, "You need to be big to succeed in this business."

Across the table, Director Jerome Stone, co-founder and chairman emeritus of Stone Container Corporation, the $6 billion packaging concern, weighed the talented young CEO's concerns against his own fifty years' experience as an entrepreneur, executive, and director of many companies. "Why can't *you* be big?" he asked. "If owning this company is good for somebody else, why isn't it good for you?"

The exchange and ensuing discussions changed the course of Solar Press. With encouragement from the board, the Hudetzes retained control and began exploring acquisitions to speed growth. "The board gave us a vote of confidence," Mr. Hudetz says. "They told us, 'You guys can do it. You're not lacking in any big way, in any area.' We needed that feedback."

Outside directors can bring a wealth of experience to a business. A board of risk-taking peers — other CEOs, executives, and entrepreneurs who already have passed the milestones that lie ahead for your business — can ease the fear of the unknown and help anticipate new challenges. The value of this can be measured in the unease so many CEOs express about the counsel of professional consultants: "I'd feel a lot more confident if these people had ever run a business."

Many business owners worry that outside directors' experience will work against them, derailing their plans. But in practice, as in the case of Solar Press, directors more often bolster the business owner's self-confidence and raise his or her aspirations. "That's the role of the director: to give vision, as well as perspective — and hopefully, complete objectivity," Mr. Stone says.

Many times, directors simply encourage the CEO to trust his or her risk-taking instincts. The directors' presence can even spur a new sense of competition: "If these guys have done it, I can do it too!" the business owner may tell herself.

One entrepreneur says he found it much easier to share financial information for the first time with the help of one of his outside directors, another entrepreneur who had opened his books many times in the process of selling and repurchasing his business. Another credits directors experienced in international operations with his own overseas expansion strategy. "Without the board, I wouldn't have known where to start," he says.

Often, directors bring a network of personal contacts to the business. At least once in most board meetings, directors offer helpful resources: "If you need advice on this, why don't you talk to so-and-so?"

Other times, they offer special expertise that may be peripheral to operations but valuable to the overall smooth functioning of the business — suggestions for computer or plant security, employee safety training, or data processing, for instance. The CEO of a specialty chemicals concern says one of his outside directors spent a full day before each of several board meetings going over plans for the company's first plant. "He was a sage source of advice," the CEO says. "He came up with thoughts that changed the way we were doing things."

On balance, outside directors can broaden even the most effective CEO's range of knowledge.

Self-Discipline and Accountability. When Fel-Pro decided to establish a panel of outside advisers, the $235 million automotive parts concern had already won national attention for progressive personnel policies that had spawned remarkable loyalty and low turnover among its 2,000 employees. But the firm's three controlling families sought even greater management accountability. "We felt a need to have continuing input from the outside," says Paul Lehman, a Fel-Pro president and a fourth-generation family owner.

The result: improved financial reporting and an intensified management focus on companywide strategy. "In a lot of ways, the advisers have really helped us to move the company forward and to think about the future," Mr. Lehman says. They "essentially hold our feet to the fire. We are paying these people to give us a hard time, and they do."

Accountability is seldom comfortable. Yet the most successful CEOs seek ways to hold themselves accountable. Without it, they often experience a nagging sense of unease and isolation. Worse yet, they may allow the company to drift off course or to stagnate far short of its potential.

As much as many private business owners relish autonomy, many find that accountability is a crucial tool in helping to preserve it. If a CEO goes public with his goals and objectives, the chances of achieving them increase. Many CEOs even ask their boards to review their own performance annually against the goals they have set for themselves. "You don't know how valuable you are," one CEO told his new outside board after several meetings. "You are constantly looking over my shoulder with me as I walk through major problems in my business."

Often, directors help develop the tools business owners need to gauge their own performance and set measurable goals. Many CEOs say their boards have helped them master financial reporting techniques, including key performance ratios.

Ultimately, says one entrepreneur, the reward of such accountability is greater personal satisfaction. "Before [naming an active board], if I had a bad year, I could shrug it off. Now, somebody is going to say, 'Well, how can we help you?'" It's comforting, he says, to know that "you've got five more pulse checkers on your side."

A vigilant board brings another, often unforeseen benefit: organizational accountability. As the discipline encouraged by outside directors trickles down through management, many CEOs see improvement in subordinates' performance. Asking a manager to report to the board on a certain subject can be a powerful incentive to timeliness and professionalism.

Divisional managers of one chemicals concern used to be informal in their board presentations of major capital-spending proposals. But after the business owner named outside directors, they began preparing thorough presentations, complete with charts and graphs, and distributing them to the board a week early. "They have an entirely different air than five years ago," the CEO says. "They know they're going to have to justify their plans, and they do their homework better."

This added step in the review process can be a big help to a CEO seeking to impose discipline and accountability on employees. Once a topic is on the board's agenda, everyone involved knows the CEO cannot change the date. "The whole organization has to toe the mark to meet that deadline," says Richard Kent, an entrepreneur and director.

A Sounding Board. Business owners are full of ideas—good ones, bad ones, and those only partly formed or poorly thought out. What many of them lack is a sounding board to help evaluate the ideas—someone knowledgeable and objective who will listen and react honestly, appropriately, and without unintended consequences.

Airing ideas with employees may confuse them and set them in motion prematurely: "What does the boss really want? Should I react honestly? Or run with the ball?" the employee may wonder. Too much thinking out loud with employees can invite the conclusion that the boss is indecisive or lacks a sense of direction. Other potential listeners, such as consultants, family, and friends, may lack the experience, objectivity, or inclination to act as a sounding board. Powerful ideas may languish and die as a result, or poor ones may be carried out with costly results.

An experienced, active board can serve as a useful sounding board. For the founder of the publishing concern mentioned at the beginning of this chapter, an outside board pointed out the risks of his idea to affiliate with a foreign partner. "It's easy when you're by yourself to get off on a tangent and come up with something you think is a good idea," he says. "But the board helped me see the problem: that the amount of capital I would probably get compared with the independence I would have to give up wouldn't be worth it. As a result of one board discussion, I put it out of my head—after messing around with it for years."

In other cases, a board may give the business owner the confidence he or she needs to charge ahead. "In business, you've always got one foot on the gas and one on the brake," says one business owner. "The directors are the clutch. They let you know which one should take over."

Honest, Objective Opinions. A well-chosen board can provide an excellent forum for gleaning honest, objective opinions. The business owner exerts little power or influence over good board members. The effective director has nothing to prove or gain by promoting his or her own interests; nor is the director's fee enough to make him or her beholden to the company. As discussed later in this book, the honoraria typically paid directors (about $6,000–$8,000 a year for most small to medium-sized private companies) is not enough to sway the opinion of an experienced business owner or executive.

Instead, he or she typically seeks the satisfaction of associating with other directors, providing help, and learning something in the process. That leaves the director truly free to serve the CEO by rendering honest, objective reactions. "The board isn't here to kid around," says one owner-entrepreneur. "They're all very successful people, and their financial needs are met. They're going to tell me what they really think and question me in any way."

Other people in the busines owner's life have their own complex agendas and may for various reasons resist telling the CEO the unvarnished truth. An employee may fear for his or her job. Members of an executive committee may worry about their own fiefdoms or relationships with the CEO. Relying too heavily on a friend can tax the relationship; as many CEOs have learned from experience, directors are easier to find than friends.

Seeking advice from family poses pitfalls as well. "I can't tell my wife I'm worried about how my son-in-law is doing in the business," says one CEO. "She'll just say, 'You'd better keep him working, because he's got three of our grandchildren to support.'"

Consultants may have a different kind of conflict of interest: a fear for the client relationship. "The consultants can dance to my tune, but I'm on the spot before the directors," one entrepreneur says.

Strategic Planning and Counsel. It is management's role to set strategy — not the board's. But many business owners have found outside directors helpful in prompting them to begin strategic planning, in helping with the process, and in monitoring the plan's implementation.

At A. Duda and Sons, a giant Oviedo, Florida, agribusiness concern, directors are helping address long-term strategic questions: "What kind of company is Duda going to be in 2010?" says Edward D. Duda, president. "Right now, we're an agribusiness company in real estate. Maybe twenty years from now, we'll be a real estate company that's in farming."

Many business owners find their boards help focus attention on such important strategic questions. "I wholeheartedly endorse the idea of an outside board," Mr. Duda adds. "It's a mistake not to have one. Without our board, we wouldn't have the professionalism and discipline we have now."

Once a plan is in place, the board can help oversee implementation. "Nine months ago you established these as priorities," a director might say. "How are we doing? Have they shifted?"

Adds Richard Kent, entrepreneur and director: "If a CEO says, 'Our strategy is to make blue widgets,' and then comes to the board with a plan to make red gizmos, he is at least forced to examine the original strategy and not just ignore it."

Insight into Key People. Many business owners are eager for help in evaluating key people. The vice-president for sales, the chief financial officer, the promising new technical chief, the leading candidate for a pivotal job, and even the corporate lawyer, banker, or accountant — all are candidates for formal or informal meetings with the board. This gives directors an opportunity to offer candid reactions and first impressions that can help the business owner make important personnel and management decisions.

Sometimes, directors provide the support a CEO needs to dismiss a chief financial officer or manufacturing manager who is performing poorly. In other cases, the board affirms the business owner's choice for an important post. Often, directors help set up management development and evaluation systems that give the business owner greater overall control over employee performance.

Directors can also help evaluate providers of professional services, such as accountants, attorneys, and bankers. These relationships do not lend themselves to shopping around, and directors can help spot inferior performance or suggest alternatives.

When the second-generation head of one chemicals and wood products concern sought financing for his first acquisition, he was afraid of disrupting the family business's traditional banking relationship. Yet he was stunned by the loan agreement offered by the company's longtime banker. "I couldn't understand most of it. It read like *Webster's Dictionary*. And what I could understand, I didn't like," he recalls.

When he took the agreement to his board, "they were appalled," he says. Directors gave him the courage to apply at a competing bank, where he received much more favorable terms. To his surprise, he says, "our old bank has been treating us even nicer now."

Challenging, Penetrating Questions. After top managers of a medium-sized manufacturing concern proudly laid before their board what they thought was an airtight proposal to build a new plant in City A, they sat back to await the directors' approval. To their surprise, what they got instead was a question: What about City B? Isn't that nearer our eventual goal to enter a new market in the next state?

Glancing uneasily at one another, the executives had to agree that the question was a good one and admit that they had not studied the markets around City B enough to know whether they would be missing a valuable opportunity there. Back to the drawing board!

At an effective board meeting, 80 percent of the sentences end in question marks. Many CEOs find that challenging, penetrating questions help them learn more, and learn it more quickly, than almost any other device. And the outside director, free from office politics, self-interest, and other sources of bias, can unearth good questions that may never even occur to insiders. This process is not always comfortable, and it can mean extra management work. But it almost always improves the quality of decision making.

When another business owner proposed a profit-sharing plan to his board, the directors asked how it fit into the entire benefits program. "My first reaction was, 'Dang it, I'd like to get this thing taken care of.' My second reaction was, 'Yes, that's the right way to do it,'" the CEO recalls. The result was an improved, updated, and less expensive benefits package.

Confidential and Empathic Counsel. Business owners have unusual empathy for each other. On an airplane or at a party, two business owners usually manage to find each other and share stories. This almost instinctive relationship carries through to the board room, and it can be a unique resource to a CEO facing issues too big, too sensitive, or too troubling to discuss with anyone else.

Business owners often develop deep trust in their outside directors. One sought help from his board in deciding whether he should send his two young manager sons on business trips with a woman executive. During a particularly difficult time for another CEO, he unburdened himself at a board meeting, laying all his self-doubts on the table and gathering his directors' empathy and encouragement in return.

One CEO recalls struggling with a decision to terminate an eleven-year employee who was fifty-nine years old. The man was well-intentioned, but "he was in a position of responsibility, and he just couldn't cut it," the executive says. The matter had drifted along unresolved for months, until the CEO presented it to his directors. The response was encouraging—and galvanizing.

"If I look back over my career," one of the directors told him, "the one thing that stands out in my mind as my biggest defect was failing to bite the bullet with people when I should have." Other directors chimed in with similar experiences and then joined in helping the CEO plan a fair termination package. With the directors' support, the CEO was able to remove the employee and fill the post with a more capable person.

Other matters raise so many sensitive issues for shareholders, employees, and managers that they simply cannot be discussed outside the board room. One CEO called on his board to help decide whether to divest a major business. "That's a mental hurdle for us. In the past, we have always grown. But with this, we'd be downsizing," the CEO says. "We've got to have a plan" before revealing any major divestiture, even to top managers. The board helped weigh the matter without upsetting any of the company's other constituencies.

Creative Thinking and Decision Making. To escape the demands of his business, Richard C. Payne, third-generation president of a family-held metal fasteners concern, likes to jump in his boat and sail far out into Lake Michigan. Distant from shore and intent on the winds, he often thinks of fresh new solutions to problems back at the office. For the same reason, Mr. Payne says, his company added outside directors to its board. "In closely held businesses, you really need that perspective," he says. "You've got to step away as often as you can, to ask yourself, 'What are we doing? What's going on here?' and reflect on that."

The unique perspective of the board room can engender creative new approaches to old problems. While the business owner might not hope for sheer brilliance or Van Goghian insight from the board, the forum offers the freedom to brainstorm ideas, invoke different perspectives, and make connections among analogous situations or problems. All are important parts of the creative process.

Effective outside directors bring to the table the ability to see a problem from different points of view. Often, a director will suggest to a CEO wrestling with a problem, "Why don't you look at it this way?" The result is often a fresh and sometimes a liberating perspective.

One food company CEO with a strong production background had laid plans to cut the quality of a product in order to maintain profits. But when he reviewed the plan with directors, they helped him see the problem from a marketing perspective: Any cut in quality would hurt sales. As a result, he changed tactics, reducing the size of the product rather than hurting quality. "We got our margin" and eliminated the marketing pitfalls as well, the CEO says.

The board structure can engender another creative tool:

flexible frames of reference. This can be defined as a good board's ability to think laterally, drawing relationships among seemingly unrelated factors rather than focusing exclusively, in linear fashion, on the plan at hand.

Directors of a medium-sized commodity distribution concern, for instance, helped avert a confrontation with an industry giant. Managers were intent on plans to build a new processing plant to produce raw materials for use in manufacturing. In a presentation to the board, they mentioned that the small amount of the plant's production not needed internally would be sold on the open market.

But directors spotted an unforeseen risk: No matter how insignificant the sales of excess product might seem to the company, moving it onto the open market could spark broader retaliation by the giant competitor that dominated that market. Instead of inviting a pricing war, the directors suggested, why not negotiate to sell the excess directly to the big company?

As the directors pointed out the risk, "I pictured two bulls with their heads down, with the other guy being the bigger bull," recalls the CEO. "It was a very, very good suggestion, a win-win proposition."

Reasoning by analogy is another important technique. A well-chosen board will probably include people from businesses in some way analogous to the CEO's — in markets, distribution techniques, industry structure, and so on. The board of a funeral home chain, for instance, might include the head of another business that syndicates new retail outlets, such as a restaurant chain. A baked goods concern developing new branded lines might have as a director the head of a specialty gifts concern with a similar sensitivity to changing consumer tastes (see Chapter Five).

As each director listens to the problems and questions facing the company, he or she filters them through personal experience. "How would I face this in my business? What would it be like if I were in their shoes?" The result can be invaluable input into the decision-making process.

Mr. Mathile of the IAMS Company recalls a plan he once developed to set up an in-house university for all the company's distributors. But when his outside directors, who had experience with three different distribution systems in various industries, heard the idea, they suggested training only those who needed it. His directors' advice also prompted Mr. Mathile to sell IAMS's company-owned distribution centers, freeing $1 million in working capital.

Valuable Corporate Relations. Many business owners intent on improving planning and decision making at their companies discover that their outside boards have an unforeseen benefit: better corporate relations with constituents ranging from employees, suppliers, and customers to lenders and the community at large.

The business owner's willingness to account to a board of respected peers carries great weight with employees, customers, and others. It is an emblem of the owner's dedication to the business and awareness of his or her personal fallibility. "The fact that the business owner has succumbed to some scrutiny from the outside gives the employees comfort," one CEO says. "They tend to respect you more." All of these factors can help in recruiting top job candidates and retaining valued employees.

An outside board can raise employee morale and confidence in the future. On board-meeting days at IAMS headquarters, "people dress up — even if they don't see the directors. It's an important event around here. People take real pride in the fact the board is coming," Mr. Mathile says.

A respected board can lend prestige. One CEO found that on a recent trip to Tokyo, prospective business contacts sought him out because they had heard that he had a prominent scientist on his board. Adds Mr. Hudetz of Solar Press: "We are so proud that we share with a lot of customers and prospects that we have this blue-chip board — that we're not just a bunch of brothers out here. It has become a valuable marketing tool."

Perhaps most important, the existence of a respected board conveys the message to anyone with a stake in the company's future that the owners are interested in continuity and stability. It also lends major decisions credibility among employees and shareholders. When directors have approved a new policy or tough initiative, everyone knows it is not just a random thought by the CEO. "It's important to have some sort of ceremonial process to go through in making policy," says Shirley Brinsfield, an experienced entrepreneur, executive, and corporate director. "It legitimizes it in the eyes of other people, who know that the board is where the buck stops."

A Social Argument

Private businesses labor under many public stereotypes and misperceptions. Many people — and consequently, many regulators and politicians — regard private companies with suspicion. They assume closely held businesses take advantage of their independence by evading taxes, exploiting employees, and committing other kinds of corporate and personal misdeeds.

An active outside board can send a clear signal to all of a company's constituencies that the owners share certain American core values of *review, accountability,* and *disclosure.* The mere existence of the board suggests business owners are open-minded, unafraid to expose their operations, and interested in the long-term success and perpetuation of the business rather than in short-term profit.

In a larger sense, the existence of an outside board is a symbol of the owners' awareness that ownership is both a privilege and a responsibility. It signals the owners' consciousness of the need for accountability — not only to themselves, but to the community. Often, outside directors can play an important role in helping the business owner weigh his or her diverse and often conflicting responsibilities, not only to individuals but to society at large.

"If you believe in private capital and the free enterprise system, you have an obligation to the country, to your customers, your employees, your outside advisers, your bankers, to be responsible as a manager," Mr. Mathile says. "If private enterprise is going to survive, it will be because it was good for society and for the people who work in it."

Summary

An active board of outside directors is one of the richest resources available to private companies today. A variety of fears and misconceptions contribute to the fact that fewer than 5 percent of private companies across the United States involve active outsiders on their boards. But those prejudices often vanish in the light of experience with effective directors.

Many business owners credit their outside boards with improving the decision-making and planning processes at their companies and providing a sounding board and confidential ally for the CEO. Outside directors can be of help to almost any company with more than fifty employees. Smaller firms may benefit from a less formal panel of experienced advisers.

2

Outside Directors and the Family-Owned Business

Charles Hoch ran his successful specialty baked goods concern for twenty-five years without any help from outside advisers or directors. Like his entrepreneurial father before him, he had made his own choices in life and started his own business, and he counseled his two sons to do the same.

But when both boys began showing an interest in making careers in the company, Mr. Hoch faced new issues that were both strange to him and complex. Pointing proudly to a portrait of the two handsome youths on his office wall, he says, "All of a sudden, you've got a whole new set of issues."

Today, Mr. Hoch's outside advisers are helping him lay plans to perpetuate family ownership and position the company for the future. And both he and his wife take comfort in knowing that if he should die suddenly or become disabled, she will have trusted aides to guide her through the ensuing transition.

Family business ownership creates a special set of privileges and challenges. Family business owners face many of them alone every day: balancing the interests of the family against those of the business; grappling with the CEO's divergent roles as parent, manager, and shareholder; and planning for the future of both the business and the family. Any of these challenges, if poorly met, can sink a family business.

"Most family businesses fail precisely because they can't reconcile the imperatives of sound management with family and emotions," says Nan-b de Gaspé Beaubien, vice-chairman of Telemedia, a large family-owned media concern based in Montreal. "It is very hard to combine entrepreneurship and operating skills, on one hand, with the values and aspirations of the family on the other. That's why 88 percent of family businesses don't make it through the third generation."

An active outside board is uniquely able to help smooth the way. The objective, confidential, and caring counsel of an effective board can help the family business owner sustain wise and competent leadership. A board is also crucial in spurring the adoption and integration of the multiple long-range plans needed in the family business: the estate plan, the succession plan, the strategic plan, and the family plan (all of which will be discussed later in this chapter).

A recent survey of eighty family businesses in their third generation or later showed that the existence of an active outside board had been the single most critical element in their success and survival (Ward, 1986). Let us take a look at some special benefits.

Planning for Orderly Management Succession

For some entrepreneurs, relinquishing the reins of the family business is one of the hardest things in life. The prospect can raise thorny issues that no manager relishes, from choosing among one's children to planning a diminished role for oneself. No wonder so many family business owners delay or avoid succession planning, often with devastating consequences. A 1989 study in one major midwestern city showed that owners of more than one-third of the family businesses with CEOs over fifty-five had failed to groom successors, leaving most of the companies on the brink of failure or liquidation (Goozner, 1989).

The outside board can be invaluable to the succession process in several ways: raising the issue at the right time, helping the business owner examine his or her options, preparing the successor, and helping plan for and complete the process.

No other resource is as rich in helping achieve continuity and objectivity as a business passes from generation to generation.

The Board as Insurance Policy. A crucial role for the family business board is as an insurance policy for the business owner's spouse and family in the event of a succession crisis—the death or disability of the owner-manager, with no well-prepared successor. Such crises often breed hasty and sometimes disastrous reactions, such as an untimely sale of the business or the ascent of a person ill qualified to be CEO. At the very least, the spouse will be deluged with advice—from lawyers, accountants, family friends, and anyone else with an opinion or a vested interest. Whom can he or she trust?

Only an outside board is equipped with a knowledge of the family's goals, values, and philosophy, coupled with an absence of any vested interest in selling the business or grabbing power. Thus outside directors are uniquely able to play a guardian's or facilitator's role, evaluating the alternatives and counseling the spouse and other family members. For this reason, spouses should become well acquainted with directors, attending board meetings at least occasionally (see Chapter Seven).

"If something were to happen to me today, at least my wife has some people who are astute and could give her some advice as to what to do," Mr. Hoch says. "I think it would be helpful to her to know that she was not alone."

Aid in Timely Succession Planning. A board can be instrumental in raising the succession issue at the proper time. Typically, that is several years before the CEO's planned retirement, and often before he or she even recognizes the need. Some business owners ask their directors up front, as part of their mission statement, to help them identify the appropriate time for them to step down (see Chapter Five).

For others, the issue is much more difficult to face. This is how one such entrepreneur's oldest son, who is now president of the 125-employee family business, describes the role of an outside board in his succession: "I wouldn't be in this office right now if it weren't for the board. Dad had to overcome some gigantic barriers to decide to finally name a successor to the presidency, to let go and step back.

"The board was very instrumental. It was obvious to me that we needed an objective perspective, a getting beyond the old tapes — how I behaved when I was thirteen years old affecting how he sees my performance now, that sort of thing.

"The board helped define the issues in getting to the point where dad could make a decision. 'What does my dad see as the problems with me? All the things I did when I was fifteen years old? Gee, dad, I'm 45, cut me some slack. I've been out in the world. I went off and did my own thing, and I did very well. Give me some credit.'

"I think the board was constantly pushing my dad too: 'So there are a couple of things you don't like about him. But who else is going to take over? So what if he does this or that? It's not going to undo the company.'"

Today, this successful family business is running well, and the outside board is continuing to smooth the succession process, defusing tensions between father and son and helping each prepare for the future.

Helping the Business Owner Examine the Options. For some business owners, weighing the leadership alternatives for the next generation can raise some major and confusing questions. Should this company stay a family business? What strengths are needed in my successor, based on the business's future strategic challenges? Who is available to succeed me? Are my children capable of taking over? Should I want them to? If so, how can I select among them?

In the privacy of the board room, the business owner can examine such questions honestly, without fear of alarming or hurting other family members or employees. The board can also help the CEO analyze the business's future leadership needs and weigh candidates' qualifications in light of those conclusions.

Often, directors can provide the necessary missing link — a vote of confidence, a new idea, affirmation of the business owner's judgments or instincts — that he or she needs to proceed. Other times, the board can relieve the business owner by suggesting alternatives that might have been too difficult to promote alone.

Help in Setting the Succession Process. A smooth management transition does not happen overnight. "Succession is not an event. It's a process," says one CEO. "Ours started ten years ago and will take three more years." Ths process requires careful planning and preparation.

Many CEOs wonder, What method should I use to choose a successor? Should I groom a designated person? Hire a consultant? Let a few top candidates "self-select" by competing within the business? Or split up the business? Half of all private company management successions involve more than one offspring, increasing manyfold the complexity of the task (Ward, 1986).

Directors can be of great help in selecting the process for choosing a successor; in moderating the process to keep it healthy, deliberate, and open; and in providing support to both the CEO and the successor candidates.

"I saw an outside board as an opportunity to get help with the selection of the next CEO," says Al Hoffman, owner of a locksmith supply distribution concern with three children working in the business. "It's very difficult to separate your roles as father and boss. I didn't really feel capable of making a decision purely on a business basis. I felt my wife, although her judgment is very good, would get involved emotionally.

"And if I went to my children and asked, 'Who should run this company?' I'd have no volunteers. None of them really wants to say yet, 'Dad, I'll take your place.' Again, it's my being the father that gets in the way."

Finally, directors can lend credibility and authority to the process by ratifying the owner's choice. The half-owner of one family business says the board helped the family select a son-in-law over his and his brother's two sons as the heir apparent — a decision they knew was right but was still extremely difficult. "It was a bitter pill," the CEO recalls, but the board's approval helped make it palatable for everyone concerned.

Help in Preparing the Successor. Once a decision is made, outside directors can be invaluable in helping prepare the successor for the top job.

The board can keep an objective eye on the learning opportunities afforded a successor. Often, directors discover that successors are not being challenged enough — that they need to be thrown in over their heads to develop skills and discover the depths of their capabilities. The board can help suggest new challenges and tests.

Interaction with the board can help the successor develop professionalism and a sense of accountability. He or she can be asked to give reports to the board, for instance, and hear directors' feedback. When the successor is still in his or her mid to late thirties and several years from succession, it is usually best not to make him or her a board member; there still may be issues the CEO needs to discuss without the successor present.

But as the CEO approaches retirement, the board can provide a formal vehicle for the succession process. First, the successor can be integrated gradually into board meetings, eventually as a member and finally as CEO, with the previous CEO advancing to chairman of the board. At this point, of course, the successor begins managing the board and preparing the agenda.

This process provides many opportunities for grooming and encouraging the successor. A director of one large industrial services concern recalls that when the founder's daughter first joined the board as the heir apparent, she was timid and overwhelmed at the impending responsibility. The directors saw that she was also extremely capable, however, and they encouraged her to ask questions and develop self-confidence. Today, her self-esteem has blossomed to the point where she is eager to take the reins at the appropriate time.

Some business owners ask directors to act as mentors, instructing successors on reading financial statements or other basic skills, or spending time with them away from the company. They may visit the director's business, learning about management systems, human resources, training, and other aspects of professional management. Often, successors who have little tolerance for hearing their parents reflect on the good old days are more receptive to learning from the experiences of respected nonfamily directors.

Other directors meet informally with successors on the job, offering advice and guidance. One director of a family-held foods concern stops at the company on his way home from work periodically to talk to the owner's sons "about a particular problem they may have, in sales or marketing or operations," says the owner. "When my oldest son wanted to start retail units within department stores, we had no idea how a department store works. But this director did. He was able to give him pro forma financials and helped him organize the unit."

The board can also be an excellent vehicle to provide peers from the successor's age group as role models. Many family business successors lack helpful peers because they tend to assume positions of influence and responsibility far earlier than their peers from school or the community; they also tend to be better off financially.

By selecting directors who are contemporaries of the successor and who may be entrepreneurs or family business successors themselves, the business owner can provide highly influential role models for achievement, initiative, and responsibility. These esteemed contemporaries are often particularly compelling because they have much more in common with the successor than his or her natural peer groups. They can help allay the common worry among business owners that the next generation of management will not be as entrepreneurial as the previous generation.

Directors also can provide a network of business leaders and other successors to provide role models for leadership development. In meeting and getting to know these people, the successor can learn about the many important dimensions of family business leadership that are not taught in textbooks — not only good management skills but leadership in the family and community and social, civic, and philanthropic obligations.

Finally, directors can help decide when a successor is ready to take over. "Quite honestly, I'm anxious to get out of my spot," says the head of one family-held foods concern. "I'd like to let someone else be CEO. But I talked about this with the board about a year and a half ago, and they didn't feel my oldest son was ready then. We will take it up again in another year or so."

Monitoring the Final Stages. The final stages of succession can be the most difficult. Many business owners have a hard time letting go. Yet it is almost impossible for a successor to say, "You're getting too involved. You're second-guessing me too much," or, "You should be working through me, dad, instead of going around me all the time."

Sometimes, outside directors can help the founder step back. During an informal annual weekend retreat, one CEO says his outside directors helped him make the decision to step aside to the chairmanship from the presidency of his business, clearing the way for younger successors. Board members helped him see the need, he says, and to recognize his own desire to pursue other interests as well.

Directors can greatly increase the effectiveness of the new CEO during this period. Sometimes, the board can be a release valve for airing tensions. Other times, it can provide a much-needed sense of professionalism and credibility to the new generation of management. "Without these directors," says the third-generation head of an industrial products concern. "I would still be the son reporting back to the parents."

Often, directors can keep family tensions from blocking important management decisions. One second-generation CEO, who just took over the family business from his father, says, "I'm convinced that my dad will never say to me, 'You've arrived!' That's just the way he is. He's never quite satisfied.

"But the board has helped me in a lot of ways. We have an old plant in Cleveland that we've outgrown. But if I walked into dad's office and said, 'Dad, we've got to do something about Cleveland,' the first thing he'd ask me is, 'How much is it going to cost? We can't look at that kind of spending.'

"But when I introduced that issue at a board meeting, we could bring it out in the open and discuss it logically. My dad asked the board, 'Do you realize how much this is going to cost?'

"And one of the directors said, 'But Jack, this is your business you're talking about. You can't look only at cost. You've got to grow your business.' The board agreed that it made sense, so we're going ahead in Cleveland.

"When our directors walk in through the door," the CEO concludes, "they bring an objective world with them."

Help with Organizational Succession. An aspect of succession that is often neglected is *organizational* succession: the changes that new leadership will bring throughout the company. As a business owner contemplates management succession, broader questions arise: What organizational changes lie ahead? How will the new CEO change the nature of the organization? What does this change mean for the development and promotion of other family members in the company and for key non-family managers? How can we provide for a continuing evolution of leadership? How do we reassure employees that the strengths of our culture will be preserved?

Outside directors can help business owners plan for organizational succession, attending to the company's future as well as to the needs of all its stakeholders. The existence of an active outside board can also send a message to all constituencies, from employees to the community at large, that the future of the organization is an important and valued dimension of the family's stewardship.

Help with Other Family Business Issues

Financial Matters. Even the closest-knit family can fray under the financial pressures raised by business ownership. Compensation of family members working in the business, dividend policy, valuation of the firm, benefits and perks for family members — all are issues that can fragment a family.

Consider the case of this loving family, for whom shared decision making was nothing new:

Even when the ten children were very small, the family held weekly meetings on issues of common concern. "We would sit around the kitchen table, with the littlest one still sucking his thumb," recalls one of those former children, who is now the CEO of the family's highly successful business.

"My mother would read the minutes of the last kitchen table meeting, and we'd approve them. Then, there would be suggestions — things like, 'I don't want to wash the dishes anymore,' or, 'I think we should only have to wash them once a week.' We have always been pretty close and able to overcome our differences."

But as the siblings grew up and assumed joint ownership of the fast-growing company their father had founded, some unprecedented tensions arose. Although management bonuses had long been based on a percentage of profit, some brothers and sisters not working in the company began to resent what they viewed as windfall compensation of their three siblings in management.

"We had brothers and sisters running to the library to research the typical pay for somebody in this industry," the CEO says. Another brother who decided to seek his fortune elsewhere wanted to sell all his stock, placing heavy financial demands on the company. "Emotions were starting to run high, and feelings were getting hurt at some of our family meetings," the CEO recalls.

For this family, naming experienced outside directors was the answer. The board helped restructure management compensation, cutting salaries and capping bonuses but adding long-term stock options and certain perquisites for managers. Directors also helped lay out a stock buyback plan. Family members were relieved to have help with these issues, the CEO says. "The board has freed us from the burden" of battling through the issues within the family.

A board can provide support, guidance, and objective counsel to a CEO grappling with a wide range of sensitive financial matters. In some cases, directors can offer information about what certain kinds of jobs are worth, what perks and incentives are typical, and so on. In other cases, the board will recommend and help review the findings of a reputable outside consultant.

In either case, directors can bring objectivity to potentially explosive issues. In cases where owners' interests clearly diverge, directors can be particularly valuable. One business owner recalls acquiring a family-held company that had been doing well under the leadership of the second-generation owner-manager. But the CEO's mother and sister, the other two holders, were dissatisfied with their returns from the business, so they sold out. "He was living well, but they got tired of getting nothing out of the business," the owner recalls.

"If I were a passive holder, I would feel more comfortable having an outside board," the CEO says. Directors "can be responsive to a mix of outsiders and insiders and ensure adequate returns to holders."

Nonfinancial Issues. The family business CEO might justifiably feel sometimes that he or she is playing the entire cast of a Broadway play—alone. The roles range from parent to shareholder, from president and chief manager to community leader, from employer to entrepreneur.

Nowhere outside the board room can the business owner be as effectively reminded that he or she wears multiple hats. Outside directors are uniquely able to help the business owner manage this complex balancing act and to point out conflicts. The board may say, "You're sounding like a father on this question, and it's a management issue," or, "It's great to plow every cent back into the business, Hank, but you need to start thinking about your own retirement, too."

One CEO, for instance, found it easy to neglect returns to the business's shareholders (himself and his wife). But his paternal instincts led him year after year to pay enormous salaries and bonuses to family members and others in the business. While his employees were overjoyed and he felt gratified, he was threatening the long-term viability of the business.

Another business owner plowed so much capital into a son's new business unit that he deprived the company's other operations. He was "so enamored of this project that his child has embarked on, that he was risking the goose that laid the golden egg," says an outside director, who raised questions about the allocation of resources.

Often, all a business owner needs is to be reminded of his divergent responsibilities and made aware when interests clash.

Successor and Sibling Evaluation. Evaluating the successor or other family members in the business can raise all kinds of conflicts for the family business owner. In some cases, business owners may struggle endlessly with important personnel decisions because of problems in assessing family members' abilities objectively. These family members also may suffer from a lack of thorough, objective feedback on their performance.

Outside directors can provide valuable input and support to a CEO in this process and lend credibility to the evaluations as well. Many CEOs even ask the board to evaluate their own performance each year, measuring them against the goals and objectives they have identified for themselves.

Help with the Special Family Business Plan

The family business at its best is a tapestry of entrepreneurship, industry, and enterprise interwoven with the family's heritage, values, and dreams. To keep those close-knit patterns in harmony requires a unique blend of long-range plans (Ward, 1987). Four distinct plans are the foundation of family business planning: the *strategic plan,* to ensure the business's future health; the *succession plan,* to assure orderly leadership change; the *estate* or *personal financial plan,* to provide for the business owner's future security; and the *family plan,* an overarching statement of the family's philosophy or mission that weaves together elements of all of the other plans.

The mere existence of an outside board will be a catalyst to preparing these plans. An effective board will soon raise questions about all these aspects of the family business's future. Directors will be reluctant to address major issues without knowing how they relate to the owners' overall mission and objectives. Once the plans are in place, the effective director will continually rely on the information and insights therein to weigh issues that come before the board.

The Strategic Plan. As mentioned in Chapter One, planning a business's future strategy and goals is a function of management, not the board. But directors can help get the process under way by raising the questions such a plan should answer. They also can bring invaluable experience and perspective to the process and help avoid certain pitfalls.

If the plan is a product of the top-management group planning process that is popular at the moment, for instance, the business owner risks getting a plan based on what employees think he or she wants to hear. Another pitfall is that the document is so diluted in making it acceptable to everyone that it lacks excitement for anyone. Board review is an excellent antidote for these problems, and directors can be helpful in monitoring implementation as well.

The Succession Plan. As discussed earlier in this chapter, the succession plan answers the highly sensitive and confidential questions, "Who is eligible to succeed me?" and "What happens to me in that event?" These two issues must be decided in concert, and a board is uniquely able to address both without bias. Until a succession plan is developed, directors are likely to raise the issue frequently: How is the organization developing? How are leaders developing? What would happen if you got hit by a truck?

The Estate Plan. Every business owner needs to provide for his or her financial future and that of the family. Directors also need some knowledge of a business owner's financial resources and future cash needs to anticipate capital demands on the business. Thus a good board will raise questions about the owner's estate plan and often provide valuable help as well in reviewing options for retirement, transfer of stock or other assets, and long-term personal security.

One owner asked his directors, for instance, "What basic philosophies of personal asset management should I consider? How much income should I shelter from taxes? How much insurance do I need?"

The Family Plan. This fourth plan brings the other three plans together. As a statement of the family's mission, philosophy, vision, and goals for the business, it maps out the family's role in the business, identifies the goals of individual family members, and formalizes the family's commitment to the company's future. It affords the family an opportunity to discuss family goals and business opportunities and to formulate a family philosophy. Once complete, the family plan can guide both the family and the board in helping to shape the future of the company.

With these four plans in place, a family business has done

as perfect a job as possible of planning for successful perpetuation of the business.

While directors often serve as a catalyst to begin forming these distinct plans, they also can be helpful in weighing the tradeoffs implicit in the plans. The process is certain to give rise to some competition for resources. Estate planning may necessitate drawing funds from the business to ensure the owners' future financial security. Succession planning overlaps here as well, because family members not employed in the business may be treated differently in the estate plan.

Strategic planning may interact with succession planning because some family members may be better equipped to oversee certain strategies for business development than others. The board is uniquely able to act as a sounding board on these issues.

Help with the Special Strategic
Pitfalls of Family Businesses

While most private companies tend to undershoot their potential, family businesses are especially likely to do so. Many entrepreneurs, after gaining some success at last, become reluctant over time to stretch themselves and the company in ways that involve greater risk and loss of control. Their companies have grown a bit; they have something to lose. Thus they begin to enjoy a sense of control and an absence of monetary risk.

These entrepreneurial managers still like challenge and fun — dimensions they are beginning to miss in their bigger, better-established businesses. But mounting new ventures at this more advanced stage raises some formidable hurdles, such as abandoning reliance on internal cash to borrow from the bank or venture capitalists, or perhaps even to go public. That would mean giving up some control and taking more risk — a sacrifice that may loom increasingly large. Thus many entrepreneurs stagnate well short of their firm's potential.

Family businesses face the same obstacle, plus several more. Many owners hold themselves back from aggressive new ventures because of nagging uncertainties in several areas. Some may lack confidence in available successors. Others know they lack the ability to give up the CEO's position and step back, and they fear that inaugurating new ventures will make retirement even harder. Still others are not sure their personal financial plan is adequate, making the prospect of assuming more risk untenable. The result is a leader who is chronically hesitant and a business that is often underleveraged, timid, or never developed to its full potential.

These afflictions can best be aired and understood in the board room. Many family business owners are not only aware of a vague sense of holding back; they cannot put a finger on the reasons. Others find their reservations too sensitive to review with family or employees.

Only under caring questioning by experienced peers can they identify and face their concerns. Often, directors can help remove obstacles by taking steps to improve succession or estate planning. Other times, they can suggest strategies that involve acceptable degrees of risk. Sometimes, all that is needed is a frank, empathic discussion to help the business owner realize how he or she has shackled entrepreneurial instincts. Such matters are fundamental to the role of the board, says Jerome Stone: "It's the encouragement of the family to spread their wings, to get into these uncharted areas, and, by the experience of others, to find an easier way or to discover other options."

A Resource to the Family

An outside board can have a stabilizing influence on the family business, playing a role Mr. Stone likens to "a balance wheel" in times of high emotion or conflict. Family members often feel foolish airing petty squabbles before esteemed directors. "We have these respected and accomplished people on our board, and we're sitting here arguing about whether the company car should be a Buick or a Cadillac?" a family member might wonder.

Putting a contested issue on the board's agenda can defuse arguments. After one family business board had discussed such a matter, one of the shareholders present said, "You don't realize how many problems you solved for us by merely letting us hear you all talk about it!" While the directors had not been aware that family members were deeply divided, their debate lent new perspective that was helpful to family members.

One business owner grappling with estate planning found his board an invaluable resource: "The board could certainly be a wonderful arbitrator if the family were in a life-and-death battle. But I find the mere existence of the board keeps things from coming to that — to the right-or-wrong, win-lose, Charlie-versus-Julie" kind of showdown.

Directors can serve the same lightning rod function for family members who need to air their goals, ambitions, frustrations, or concerns privately, without consulting each other or their parents. The board can also act as a wedge to break deadlocks between family members.

One business owner recalls invaluable help from an outside director during a dispute between himself and his father. The director "took me out to lunch and said, 'Hey, you've got a problem with your father that's partly a problem with you, too, and it needs to be resolved.' So I had a couple of discussions with my father and we started to make progress.

"Then, bam! at the next board meeting, the thing hit again. The director turned to my father and said, 'Hey, you've got a problem you need to resolve,' and he booked a luncheon to discuss it with dad and me. It's great, because both of us are going to learn through this third party."

Another business owner in uneasy partnership with his brother says outside directors enabled the contentious siblings to work together in relative peace for years. Whenever a conflict arose, the brothers laid position papers before the board and agreed to abide by its decision. Without the help of directors, "we might have shot each other," the owner says.

While the board might mediate or conciliate a family dispute occasionally, this should generally be avoided (see Chapter Nine). Ideally, a director's role stops short of forging alliances. He or she can discreetly urge resolution of the conflict, for instance, or point out sticking points that might be missed by the combatants. But taking sides in such a battle typically marks the end of the director's effectiveness. "That would be like trying to dive into a marriage," says one CEO.

Family Education

Outside directors' educational role reaches beyond the CEO and his or her successor. Directors can provide a role model for the entire family as a forum for shared decision making — a skill crucial to healthy family interaction. Learning how a mutually respectful group tries to build consensus can be critical to the future functioning of the business, too, if a large number of family members become involved in management.

The board can provide a conduit of information from the business to the family. Reading board agendas, observing meetings, and attending social gatherings with directors all provide unique opportunities for the family to learn about the business. The board room can be a tremendous educational environment for family members unschooled in strategic and organizational issues.

The Board as a Symbol of Continuity and Dedication

The common stereotypes about privately held companies mentioned in Chapter One — that they take advantage of their independence by evading taxes and committing other kinds of corporate misdeeds — are applied with even more critical force to the family business. Judging by examples highlighted in the media and popular literature, one would assume that most family businesses are torn apart by sibling battles or plundered and abandoned by negligent, self-obsessed owners.

The existence of a board of respected outsiders can allay those suspicions. It reassures all concerned that the family is attending to the long-term best interests of the business. It sends a message to suppliers, customers, and the community that the family intends to make succession an orderly event rather than a dramatic accident or postscript. It also conveys a signal that the owners are accountable, open, vulnerable, and aware of their own fallibility.

For many business owners, these are values well worth conveying to the next generation. "Hopefully, this idea of accountability is ingrained in my kids now," says one business owner with an active outside board. "They have seen me do it for five years now."

Al Hoffman, second-generation owner of the locksmith supply concern, asks his three children to sit in on meetings of his outside board for the same reason. "I have lived a very satisfactory life, growing mentally and financially with the company and getting a lot of happiness out of it. I'd like to convey this to them and make it possible for them to hand it on to someone else later on," he says.

"I hope this will be an educational process for my kids. I hope they come out with a vision — to decide what would be best for the company."

Summary

The active outside board holds special benefits for the family business. It can help with all aspects of management succession: planning the process, making the selection, preparing the successor, and monitoring the final stages of the transition. Directors can also act as a valuable insurance policy for a spouse, offering objective and well-informed counsel in the event of the business owner's sudden death or disability.

The outside board can offer objective advice on such potentially sensitive issues as family compensation, dividend policy, and benefits. It can help the business owner manage and distinguish among his or her many roles. Often, the mere existence of the board also serves as a catalyst for important planning efforts, including the strategic, succession, estate, and family plans.

Finally, an effective board can be an invaluable resource to the family, helping elevate the debate, educate family members, and resolve conflicts. It can provide a role model for skills and values, such as shared decision making and professional management, that can greatly help the family's efforts to perpetuate the business.

3

The Role of the Board
in a Private Company

Nowhere are directors freer to serve the best and highest possible purposes than in the private company environment. Just as management of the private company often has greater latitude — to have a bad quarter now and then in pursuit of longer-term objectives, to rest easy amid a wave of hostile takeovers, and so on — private company directors are often freer to play a uniquely helpful role as a special resource to the CEO. This is particularly true when the CEO is also the dominant shareholder.

In such intimate situations, the role of the private company board can go beyond typical board room conventions to explore broad questions of policy, philosophy, and planning, such as:

- Examining and helping express the company's mission and philosophy.
- Assessing the organization's culture and determining its impact on the company's effort to achieve selected objectives.
- Formulating a meaningful human resource plan that will attract and keep highly qualified employees and ensure continuity of management.
- Improving the quality of strategy. This means much more than strategic planning and evaluating strategic choice. It is all that has to do with strategic thinking — assuring the long-term survival, development, and prosperity of the firm.

Many owners of small and medium-sized businesses voice similar goals. Many business owners make such ambitious objectives explicit in formal mission statements for their boards (see Chapter Five). In a nationwide survey of private business owners by the National Association of Corporate Directors, most ranked "helping the CEO be effective" — including offering expertise, insisting on planning, acting as a confidant to the CEO, and other functions — as the main reason to have an active board (see Table 1).

Table 1: Why a Board of Directors?

Reasons for establishing an active board of directors
(Ranked in order of importance)

	Private Business Owners[a]	SEC[b]
Help the CEO be effective	1	—
Establish objectives and policies	2	—
Help management make decisions	3	—
Represent shareholders	4	—
Protect employee pensions	5	3
Protect shareholders	6	1
Perform board duties	7	—
Act in crisis to ensure company survival	8	2
Select the CEO	9	4
Lend credibility and enhance company image	10	—
Promote the company	11	—
Act as arbitrator	12	—
Report to shareholders	13	—
Necessary nuisance	14	—

[a]From informal surveys of private business owners
[b]From rules and regulations of the Securities and Exchange Commission

This does *not* mean that private company directors are free to tinker with operations. Operating the company is management's role. One unusually blunt but experienced director sometimes enforces that axiom by interrupting the CEO during his or her presentation: "Excuse me, but that's an operating matter. It doesn't belong before the board."

Nor should the board try to replace technical or management consultants or in-house experts. By one rule of thumb, directors should never become involved in operations to the point that they feel they have made the decision.

Nevertheless, many business owners believe the relative freedom of the private company environment enhances their board relationships. "With a public company board, directors have fiduciary responsibilities to so many stockholders, and so on, that they have to be very careful about what they say and do," says one business owner who also serves on several boards. In contrast, he says, "my directors can express their true feelings and opinions about what I ought to do."

The Legal Role of the Board

Private company boards must fulfill the legal duties of corporate directors, of course. These legal mandates lay a firm foundation for the special opportunities discussed in greater detail later in this chapter. Most of the board's duties are set forth in general terms by the Model Business Corporations Act. This legislation has been adopted in more than twenty-five states and reflects principles that also exist in most other state laws.

The fundamental responsibility of directors is "to represent the interests of the shareholders as a group, as the owners of the enterprise, in directing the business and affairs of the corporation within the law" (Committee on Corporate Laws, American Bar Association, 1978). Directors are also required to adopt or change corporate bylaws; approve amendments to the articles of incorporation; approve mergers, acquisitions, and changes in capital structure; declare dividends; and elect corporate officers.

Individual directors also have important legal obligations regarding the quality of their service, including attention to the duties of care, loyalty, and attention. (These concepts will be discussed at length in Chapter Four.)

Beyond that, the law sets forth relatively few specific functions that must be performed by the board. Instead, directors are assigned broad responsibility for protecting the assets of the corporation, reviewing corporate objectives and policies, monitoring corporate performance, and ensuring competent management.

From those mandates has evolved an array of common board practices and duties. Table 2 provides a listing of func-

Table 2. Directors' Duties.

	Legally Required	Strongly Advised	Good Practice
Corporate Objectives and Policies			
Review corporate objectives	x		
Monitor performance of the enterprise	x		
Adopt or change bylaws	x		
Approve amendments to the articles of incorporation[a]	x		
Approve acquisitions	x		
Review major corporate policies		x	
Approve strategic plan		x	
Approve operating budget		x	
Approve major price changes		x	
Approve building programs or real estate transactions		x	
Request periodic audits of compliance with corporate policy		x	
Approve entry or exit from major lines of business		x	
Management Performance and Continuity			
Elect corporate officers	x		
Select competent senior executives	x		
Assure continuation of competent management	x		
Review performance of senior managers	x		
Approve top-management compensation		x	
Approve policy relating to basic management development		x	
Approve selection of outside legal counsel		x	
Be informed of the legal and ethical conduct of business, including pending litigation		x	
Ratify selection of outside auditor[a]		x	
Review audit report		x	
Review firm's compliance with applicable laws		x	
Authorize officers to sign written instruments or take financial action		x	
Inquire into causes of major deficiencies in performance		x	
Approve major corporate contracts and leases		x	
Approve major settlements of litigation		x	
Review major changes in corporate organization		x	
Serve as advisers to the CEO and, with his or her approval, to others in the company			x
Approve duties and limits of authority of the CEO			x

Table 2. Directors' Duties, Cont'd.

	Legally Required	Strongly Advised	Good Practice
Identify roadblocks to company performance			x

Capital Structure

	Legally Required	Strongly Advised	Good Practice
Cancel reacquired shares[a]	x		
Change registered office or agent	x		
Approve any plan of merger or consolidation[a]	x		
Recommend dissolution	x		
Approve dividend actions	x		
Allocate to capital surplus consideration received for shares without par value	x		
Approve capital budget and major changes therein		x	
Review capital expenditures of major significance		x	
Periodically review borrowings		x	
Approve changes in capital structure or debt policy		x	
Approve long-term loans		x	
Approve limits on short-term debt		x	
Review transactions involving major assets		x	
Review firm's program for protection of assets, including insurance arrangements and cost		x	
Monitor formations or dissolutions of subsidiary corporations		x	
Approve policy relating to effective tax planning			x

Management of Board

	Legally Required	Strongly Advised	Good Practice
Select board chairman and secretary	x		
Assure adequate information flow to directors		x	
Approve board meeting schedules		x	
Appoint, abolish, and define the powers of board committees		x	
Nominate directors		x	
Periodically review committee provisions in corporate bylaws			x
Periodically review board mission statement			x
Set policy regarding employment of board members as consultants			x
Receive reports of payments to board members for nonboard functions			x
Review at least every two years the board mission statement			x

Table 2. Directors' Duties, Cont'd.

	Legally Required	Strongly Advised	Good Practice
Relations with Shareholders and Various Constituencies			
Set record date for annual meeting	x		
Call special shareholder meetings	x		
Assure accuracy of public disclosures		x	
Approve reports to stockholders		x	
Approve employee compensation, benefit, profit-sharing, and retirement plans		x	
Approve trustee for pension or profit-sharing plan		x	
Approve major exceptions to established benefit plan		x	
Monitor the performance of profit-sharing programs		x	
Review accountability to employees, customers, suppliers, and the community		x	
Review philanthropic policy			x
Approve annually a blanket contributions budget			x
Be advised by the CEO of any position or decision likely to lead to a strike			x

ªSubject to shareholder approval

tions that must be performed by directors in accordance with the Model Business Corporations Act, as well as a thorough sampling of common board practices that are either strongly advised or widely viewed as good practice.

While fulfilling these legal responsibilities is a fundamental duty of directors, the well-chosen board is far too valuable to be used only for its custodial and fiduciary purposes. Let us take a closer look at some of the special roles a board can play in helping the private company achieve its potential.

Reviewing Business Policies

The life which is unexamined is not worth living.

—Plato

Few things can freshen a business owner's perspective on the distinctive strengths of the company and its culture more than the involvement of an experienced board. By observing and pointing out some of these special attributes, directors often act as a catalyst to the important process of weighing and articulating the company's mission, philosophy, and organizational culture.

Balancing Stakeholder Interests. Continuously, often without realizing it, the business owner makes Solomonlike decisions — complex choices about how to allocate the company's resources among the multitude of constituents it serves.

The wise director can help the CEO weigh the importance to the company of all stakeholders — not only the shareholders, but also the company's employees, customers, suppliers, and community. Each plays an important role in the company's fortunes. And the interests of each need to be measured against those of the shareholders and the company itself — a difficult balancing act. If any one constituency is exploited to benefit another, the entire company is weakened, and all stakeholders — including shareholders — will pay the price.

If the customer is not satisfied, the growth of the business will slow and employees, suppliers, and shareholders will suffer. If employees are not satisfied and productive, the resulting personnel and product-quality problems can badly impair corporate performance. And if shareholders are not content, they may flee for greener pastures and higher returns — raising the company's cost of capital.

One can even argue that each constituency is in competition with all others. Lowering a price to customers may reduce net returns to shareholders. If we compensate by squeezing suppliers, how will that affect those crucial long-term relationships? If we increase employees' pay to reduce turnover, will we be forced to raise prices to maintain cash flow?

More often than many CEOs realize, such stakeholder issues surface in practical ways. The board can help the CEO be aware of stakeholder conflicts, examine the tradeoffs he or she is making, and determine whether they are the right ones. "What's your preference? What's your philosophy?" directors may ask. "If you have to break a tie, which way will you go?"

A difficult tradeoff arose for the CEO of one private company when he realized that he needed to raise salaries to attract and retain professional managers. With the help of his outside board, he weighed the problem and decided to hold down S-chapter dividends for a few years to free cash. While he sometimes asked himself whether it was foolish to reduce his own income, he saw the reduced dividends as a reasonable tradeoff for the sake of an improved management climate.

Other stakeholder tradeoffs are more risky. The owner of an industrial controls concern badly wanted to provide more cash for an aggressive new-product design and engineering program. After discussing the risks with his board, he decided to accomplish that by holding employee pay well below the industry average.

To continue to attract and retain competent, motivated employees, he made another unusual choice: He decided to create an above-average learning environment for his employees. He invested in management development programs and encouraged employees to attend training seminars. He held frequent in-house meetings on new management ideas and even opened many board meetings to employees. The result was an open, stimulating environment that he felt offered employees an extraordinary opportunity for personal growth.

In this business owner's view, the savings on wages and salaries were a fair return on his investment in employees' personal growth. With the help of periodic board discussion and review, he sees the policy as a reasonable tradeoff that does not hinder him in attracting ambitious, highly motivated managers.

Balancing these divergent interests, of course, is a nearly impossible theoretical challenge. No CEO can keep all corporate stakeholders happy all the time. But with the help of an active, effective board, his or her chances of maintaining a healthy balance rise significantly.

The Corporate Mission Statement. The corporate mission statement defines the company's business and expresses management's view of its goals, competitive strengths, and growth strategy. It may specify target customers and markets; identify principal products, services, or core technologies; express commitments; articulate sources of corporate identity, or describe the firm's desired public image. Mission statements can take a variety of forms. They might express such goals as becoming a household word, achieving a target market share, serving a specific market, or capitalizing on competitive advantages.

One company, Solar Press of Naperville, Illinois, stated its mission in a paragraph: "Solar Press is a worldwide leader in specialized printing, packaging, and other related products and services for the direct marketing and publishing industries. Our mission through 1991 is to significantly expand new markets while maintaining leading positions in established markets. This must be accomplished without compromising the product quality, personalized service, and financial stability that have characterized Solar Press" (Solar Press, 1988, p. 1).

At one point in its history, Parco Foods of Blue Island, Illinois, stated its mission in a sentence: "Parco Foods will aggressively fill consumer needs for premium quality specialty bakery products, concentrating on establishing a larger presence in the branded retail and food service market segments" (Parco Foods, 1987, p. 1).

Other mission statements continue for a page or more, defining the business and outlining major strengths, areas of emphasis, commitments, and goals.

An effective board can serve several purposes in preparing a mission statement. First, directors often highlight the need for one by raising fundamental questions. "We're here to help you," directors may tell the business owner. "Now what do you want to do? What businesses, markets, and goals are important to you?" Any major corporate move—an acquisition, the startup of a new product line, a personnel reorganization—can raise questions about its consistency with the company's mission.

The board can offer examples and counsel that can help the business owner tackle this sometimes strange and intimidating task. "How did you come up with a mission statement in your companies?" the business owner may ask. Directors can suggest a variety of methods: The CEO might organize a shareholder retreat specifically for that purpose. He or she might hire a consultant to interview key employees for ideas.

The board is uniquely able to help the CEO avoid some pitfalls at this stage. Some business owners try so hard to involve everyone in the process of writing a mission statement, for instance, that the end product is too diluted by political compromise to convey much meaning.

Directors can help with the substance of the document, too, pushing management to crystallize thoughts and ideas, focusing management energy, and firming up execution plans. Often, board discussions of the corporate mission statement occupy more time than any other single topic.

Finally, the board can help the business owner have patience with the process. Any mission statement evolves over time, and it is designed to be reviewed periodically to continually sharpen the focus of the business.

The Corporate Philosophy Statement. The corporate philosophy statement is a distinctive expression of management guiding values. It differs from the mission statement in that it expresses the beliefs and principles that guide the company, not its business directions or financial goals. The philosophy statement should also be a relatively personal document that reflects the character and style of the owner or owners.

As a company grows and evolves, the philosophy statement can help convey to all constituencies a sense of identity and shared values. As with the mission statement, the process of articulating the corporate philosophy can help the owner weigh priorities and proceed with a greater sense of identity and resolve.

One company's philosophy statement might stress its pride in retaining employees and attracting their friends and children. Another might emphasize the commitment of shareholders to perpetuating the company as a private business. Yet another might underscore the importance of the owner's "partnership" with suppliers, customers, and community.

One company expresses its philosophy as "to remain a healthy growth business." In a one-page summary, the company, Cardinal Meat Specialists of Mississauga, Ontario, goes on to outline its major goals: "serving the needs of its customers; striving to maintain an environment which will attract, retain and motivate the best people possible; promoting teamwork."

The statement concludes, "Honesty and integrity will be the cornerstones of all our dealings with customers, employees, suppliers, and the public. By doing these things in a professional, planned manner, we expect to generate a fair profit and to remain a healthy growth company" (Cardinal Meat Specialists, 1986).

The philosophy statement for another company emphasizes its belief in its employees as "the fundamental vitality and strength of our company." In addition, this company stresses "being a responsible leader within the free market economy . . . [and] contributing to the well-being of the countries and communities where we conduct business."

Directors, with their unique insights into the business owner, can often encourage him or her to make the philosophy statement a distinctive and meaningful document. Directors can also offer constructive and confidential reactions to drafts of the document.

Assessing the Organizational Culture. "Corporate culture," a buzzword of the early 1980s, has taken on new meaning as managers gain greater understanding of its relevance to corporate performance. In fact, corporate culture—the shared values and expectations of the organization—can profoundly affect the company's ability to accomplish goals, implement strategies, and fulfill objectives.

An effective board can observe and articulate special aspects of the corporate culture that may have gone unnoticed by the business's owners. Directors can offer suggestions on emphasizing and preserving aspects of the culture that hold potential business or personal value. The board can also spot areas of cultural dysfunction, or contradictions in the culture.

One business owner, for instance, was guiding his company through the transition from entrepreneurial to professional management. Like most entrepreneurs, he had long run the company by the force of his personality and authority as owner. For years, his relatively closed, paternalistic management style had been part of the corporate culture.

As the company grew, the business owner began to see, with the help of his board, the potential contribution of first-class professional managers. But even as he began recruiting a few top people for key positions, he unconsciously resisted a crucial related step: creating a sense of greater openness, sharing of information, and participation in the corporate culture — all necessary aspects of professionalization of management.

The idea of sharing financial information was anathema to him. Like many business owners, he had always thought it an unwarranted violation of his personal privacy. With the help of directors, he was able to see this cultural contradiction, discuss it confidentially, and gradually overcome it.

But even as the board eased the evolution of the corporate culture, the same directors also became champions of preserving certain aspects of it. The company's tradition of integrity and loyalty to its employees, as well as the character, history, and flavor of the business — all were important cultural aspects worth highlighting, directors said. The board urged the business owner to take greater advantage of those strengths, articulating them in speeches and newsletters to employees and drawing on examples from the company's history to recognize achievements by current employees.

The culture of the small to medium-sized private company, of course, is often a very personal matter. In some cases, the culture is intense and unique, reflecting the owners' personalities, family history, and heritage. These qualities pose special opportunities to create among employees and other constituencies a sense of identity and importance.

The often unique intensity of the private company culture can also make transition during major corporate changes such as management succession especially difficult. An effective board can help ease such changes, pointing out areas of inflexibility and supporting new managers through the transition.

Assessing the organizational culture yields continual benefits once the CEO is aware of the culture. A trusted board can help a CEO examine how his or her personal style can affect the corporate culture, and the CEO can learn to make adjustments when appropriate.

A business owner's decision-making style, for instance, can have a profound effect on a company's morale and momentum. Some executives are collegial decision makers who seek consensus on most issues. These managers would be inclined to draw workers together from several areas and talk problems out. While this approach can foster a strong sense of teamwork, it can be too cumbersome in situations that demand quick decisions.

Others are rational decision makers, who delegate most questions or decisions to the in-house expert. If it is an engineering question, it goes to the vice-president of engineering. Personnel problems wind up with the head of human resources. While this approach is orderly and efficient, it sometimes discourages creativity and new ideas. It also can silence the voices of significant minorities who may have strongly felt, important opinions.

Some executives prefer a competitive decision-making style. These CEOs may ask several managers for recommendations and invite them to argue their points. Indirectly, they set up an internal competition to produce the "best" idea, with the CEO's approval as a reward. Ths style is widely used in advertising agencies, where in-house teams compete to produce the campaign the client likes best. While it can foster creativity, it can also engender unease and poor morale among the losers.

With the help of trusted directors, the CEO can often employ these styles selectively, depending on the demands of the situation. Like many other elements of organizational culture, a decision-making style can become a valuable tool for achieving strategic goals.

The Human Resource Plan. Most business owners are acutely aware that competent, motivated people are crucial to any plans they make. But many unconsciously neglect the need to develop this resource systematically. As one company interviewed for this book discovered, the lack of effective human resources planning can foil the best-laid strategy. While its owners aspired to growth through acquisition, they sometimes had to pass up prospects because of an internal shortage of qualified managers.

An effective board can be invaluable in ensuring sys-

tematic and effective human resources planning. This entails
planning for succession to all positions, not just to top management. It includes policies on compensation and incentives, training and development, promotion opportunities and minimum
hiring requirements. It raises questions about the company's
ability to attract top people, the company's posture on relocat-
ing employees, and a variety of other issues.

Many business owners find their boards help them continually review management depth and quality in a way that
no other adviser could. By tracking the progress of employees
confidentially over time and helping plan incentives, the board
can help build a management development system that yields
a manager-in-waiting every time a new opportunity opens up.

In other cases, directors can help avert a wide range of
other problems, from rapid employee turnover to sagging morale.

Improving the Quality of Strategy

Strategy is, more than anything, a way of thinking about the
business. An effective board is uniquely able to contribute to
this process by raising crucial questions that could affect the business's future strategic health. "More than anything," says one
business owner, "I want my board to help me think about strategies for survival and growth of the organization. That is the
number one concern I have for the company."

Directors can play several roles. They can help ensure
a high-quality strategic plan. They can provide needed support
and discipline to the CEO trying to implement the plan consistently. And they can encourage the business owner to make a
habit of thinking strategically — to pay sustained attention to all
the factors that really create the future.

"My primary responsibility as a director is to ensure that
the business has a future," says John R. "Ted" Kennedy, retired president of Federal Industries Consumer Group (a unit
of Federal Industries in Toronto) and a director of several companies. "The first thing I look for is a viable strategy that will
ensure the successful continuity of the business."

Evaluating the Strategic Plan. When presented with a strategic plan, the effective director will likely ask him or herself one overriding question: How good is it? Every strategic plan should identify the company's business objectives, its product and market scope, and its requirements for success. That, of course, is management's job.

Beyond that, the effective director will work with the CEO to examine the assumptions and the process that underlie the plan. Together, they can examine the plan's internal consistency and its likely effect on employees and other constituencies. They can evaluate the quality of information that went into the plan. And they can determine whether the plan is consistent with the business's overall mission and philosophy.

If a CEO unveils a strategy to devote most of the company's available resources to expand into Germany, for instance, the effective board member may begin the discussion by saying, "I don't know whether you should go to Germany with your business or not." The same director might then raise helpful questions about whether the idea is consistent with the company's principal thrust toward establishing itself as the dominant low-cost producer in the industry.

The director might also be able to share valuable related experience. In one instance, the owner of a manufacturing concern laid out a plan to localize customer service by purchasing new mainframe computers for branch facilities. When one director heard the proposal, he said, "That may work fine in your company, George. But I want you to know that when we tried to decentralize data processing in our company, we created a monster. Every EDP [electronic data processing] center turned into a fiefdom at war with every other one, and we ended up selling the stand-alone computers in favor of a larger, centralized system." In this case, the director's sharing of experience saved the CEO from a potentially costly mistake.

Is the Plan Internally Consistent? Internal consistency is another quality that effective directors will look for. Does the plan harbor any strategic contradictions? If positioning the company as a top-quality, high-priced producer is a major goal, for instance, selling surplus production through a high-volume discount outlet does not make good sense. Directors might not only spot such inconsistencies but also help come up with a more consistent (but equally efficient) idea for disposing of surplus products.

Inconsistencies can crop up in almost every area. If part of a company's strategy is to develop teamwork among salespeople, for instance, it makes little sense to base their compensation and incentive plan solely on individual performance. While such inconsistencies may seem obvious, they can be difficult to spot amid the day-to-day pressures of running a business.

How Will It Play in the Ranks? Creating a strategic plan provides an opportunity to build consensus and support within the organization. Directors can help assess a strategic plan's chances of accomplishing this and anticipate its effect on all constituents.

Will it help motivate employees and gain their commitment? Is the plan itself exciting? Does it convey a sense of momentum and clarity? Without these qualities, a strategic plan may fall far short of its potential to energize a company and sustain its progress.

Garbage In, Garbage Out? Another major issue is the quality of the information used in preparing the strategic plan. No matter how much inspiration and clever thinking goes into a plan, the final result is no better than the quality of the authors' information about the marketplace.

Effective directors will raise several questions:

"Do we have good information about market share?" Charting a future course requires a sound understanding of where the company stands now. Concrete market-share data is crucial, not only in making realistic forecasts but in anticipating competitors' behavior. If the company is not gaining market share, for instance, managers should not deceive themselves into believing they have a clear and powerful competitive advantage.

And if the business leads its industry, strategists would be foolish not to anticipate competitors nipping at its heels.

"How strong is our competitive advantage?" Many companies believe they hold a firm competitive advantage in the marketplace—that customers perceive the relative quality of their products or services as significantly better than competitors'. "Customers think our product and service are pretty good," managers may say, without gauging specific areas of strength and weakness. In fact, going beyond broad assumptions to measure perceived advantage or quality relative to one's competitors is crucial to effective planning. Understanding one's weakness in the marketplace can produce more realistic goals. And knowledge of one's strengths can help the company focus on making the most of them.

"How well do we know the competition?" Too often, strategic plans read as though the subject company were alone in the marketplace. In fact, any good strategic plan should acknowledge the role of competitors—their relative strength, their apparent strategy, their likely next move. Many CEOs find it helpful to divide the competition into *strategic groups*—subcategories of competitors that have major characteristics in common. A company with seven major competitors, for instance, may face only two that compete cross the board in all its markets, in all its products. The remaining five may fall into two other subgroups: niche players, who compete indirectly in a specialized area; and competitors who sell, say, only through distributors. Members of these subgroups are more likely to behave like each other than like members of other subgroups. A thorough understanding of these subgroups will help the company focus its strategic planning on staying ahead of target competitors and avoiding wasted effort.

"How productive is our company?" A company's actual financial performance can be obscured in many ways. Inflation, price increases, raw-material price swings, and a variety of other factors can mask real results. Many CEOs are not fully aware of the message conveyed by their financial statements, and their

strategic planning is blurred as a result. If sales are up 7 percent after an 8 percent price increase, the business owner should hardly be complacent about the company's prospects. A board can help spot these aberrations and help the CEO see what is really happening to financial performance.

"Are we capitalizing on the economies of scale in our business?" Most companies make most of their money in a few areas of operations. For one, the biggest profit may come on the output of a particularly efficient plant. Others make money by distributing products more efficiently than competitors. Still others may have the best computerized customer service system in the industry. Directors can help the business owner identify areas of greatest efficiency and ensure peak operations in those areas, or suggest future strategies to exploit those particular strengths.

Should we go to three shifts at the manufacturing plant to make the most of our economies of scale there? directors might ask. Shall we concentrate on making sure our delivery trucks are filled to capacity, to maximize profits there? Or is it more important to get our sales force selling more products, because they're the best in the business? Questions like these often are not obvious in the press of day-to-day operations, and directors can help make sure that they are not missed altogether in strategic planning.

"Can we allocate resources to get all this done?" Many strategic plans look great on paper and never progress much farther than that. Once the business owner has performed the Herculean task of completing a strategic plan, the board can help him or her translate it into action. Have you figured out who will implement the plan? directors may ask. How will you hold them accountable for implementation? What money can you make available to accomplish it? And what's a reasonable schedule to implement this plan? All are crucial issues in preventing the strategic plan from gathering dust in the corporate files.

How Good Was the Planning Process? It is easy for a business owner intent on preparing a strategic plan to lose sight of the quality of the process. Yet the process can have a profound effect on the plan.

As objective outsiders with special insight into the CEO, directors can evaluate the dynamics of the process by raising some important questions. Was the process "top-down" or "bottom-up"? directors might ask. Did you ask for input from your top operations or financial people? What questions did you ask, and how did you present them? What kinds of responses did you receive?

A CEO who tries to accommodate everyone in a group planning effort may end up with a document so diluted that it is meaningless. On the other hand, a particularly strong-willed and powerful CEO may be unaware of the chilling effect of his or her personality on debate and questioning by managers. The result may be an incomplete or ill-founded document.

To the first CEO, directors might urge restoring some of his or her personal vision and drive to the document. To the second, they might suggest neutral and unthreatening ways to gather important information from subordinates.

Directors can also suggest new processes, new formats, and new techniques to keep the planning process fresh. Without such measures, strategic planning can grow routine and stale after the first two or three years.

Encouraging Strategic Thinking

Strategic thinking goes beyond putting a plan on paper. While a sound plan is an invaluable basis for progress, strategic thinking is much more: It is a mind set, a way of thinking about the business to constantly prepare the company for the future. Directors can provide invaluable support and discipline in this effort by raising crucial strategic issues like the following.

Performance Versus Potential: How to Close the Gap? Many closely held businesses are undermined by a common strategic weakness: a tendency to undershoot their potential. As discussed briefly in Chapter Two, many entrepreneurs become reluctant to assume greater risk or to jeopardize any personal control when their companies grow established and successful. Once these hard-working CEOs have something to lose, they begin to enjoy a new sense of security. They may resist mounting new ventures that require increased borrowing or selling stock to the public. Such snowballing conservatism can lock a promising young company in a strategic straitjacket, leaving it timid, underleveraged, and stagnant.

The board room is the ideal place to dissect these fears and reservations, examine their merit, and explore alternative routes to growth. Often, directors can suggest creative solutions to apparent strategic dilemmas. Other times, they can bolster the business owner's confidence in his or her own instincts, encouraging bold new initiatives.

"I get a real kick out of the entrepreneurial zing you see in these companies," says Federal Industries' Mr. Kennedy, an experienced director. "I want to foster that at all times — to challenge the imagination of the management team, to stimulate a fresh new way of looking at things."

This process of unlocking a company's potential can take many forms. But almost always it involves resolving a dilemma inherent to private company ownership.

Recent research on the strategies of forty medium-sized private companies showed that the vast majority were pursuing more conservative strategies than their planning and personal opinions and assumptions suggested (Ward, 1987). After assessing their industry and market environment, plus their relative competitive strength, they concluded that they should be pursuing more aggressive or ambitious strategies (see Figure 1).

Many business owners privately lack confidence in their leadership succession plans. But the most frequent barrier to achieving full strategic potential is fear of risking more capital or taking on more debt, the research shows (see Figure 2).

One of the most common and creative discussions a board can undertake is aimed at resolving this fear. Directors may be able, for example, to help the business owner tap his or her reputation and talents to raise more capital from others.

The experience of one funeral home chain provides an example. In three generations of family ownership, the company had built a strong regional reputation and presence. But a powerful, publicly held chain had mounted a national expansion drive, snapping up funeral homes all over the country.

Figure 1. Perception Versus Reality: How Most
Private Companies Undershoot Their Potential.

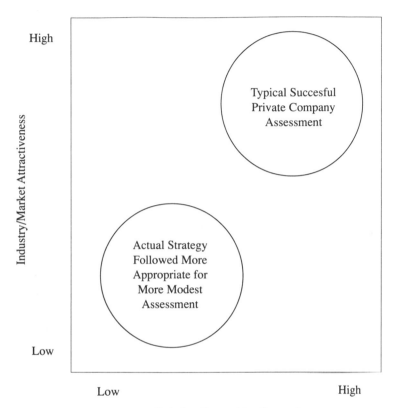

Through brand-name advertising, direct mail, and new service offerings, the national chain was creating intense pressure on competitors to do the same. At the same time, real-estate prices were soaring, raising the ante significantly for any smaller player seeking to expand.

"How can we compete as a small, self-financed firm?" wondered the owners. "Our territory is too small to justify a promotional campaign as broad and intense as theirs. And we can't afford to expand by building or buying up new homes."

The regional chain's outside directors provided the an-

Figure 2. How Strategy Can Affect the Business Owner's Attitude.

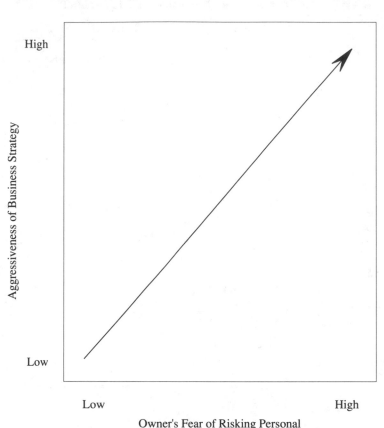

Owner's Fear of Risking Personal
Equity and Loss of Personal Control

swer. The chain's owners had been accustomed to viewing new funeral home acquisitions as a capital expenditure. Why not view acquisitions more as a real-estate deal instead, directors urged, suggesting that 75–80 percent outside financing is appropriate for real estate, even if it sounds high by business standards.

To raise money, directors also suggested putting together groups of investors interested in real estate. These private syndicates could act as investment partners in various funeral home locations, while leaving the funeral home company free to operate the business on each site. The idea opened a new way of thinking for the owners, helping them see how to raise capital without selling stock. The discovery shored up their confidence in the future of the business and helped reduce their fears of taking on new debt.

For another private company intent on fielding unproven, capital-intensive new products in an increasingly competitive environment, the board helped identify several sources of new capital that entailed no risk of security: a joint-venture project with a foreign partner; syndication of a particular project to investment partners; and shared funding by a direct marketing firm for a percentage of the royalties from the product.

Are We Looking for Growth? Or a Good Return? The wave of leveraged buyouts in the 1980s forced participants to put a greater premium than ever on short-term profit. Many companies must stress quarterly returns merely to service debt and satisfy lenders. For most companies, however, the issue of short-term profit versus longer-term growth is still a real one. Many wrestle repeatedly with the question: Should we harvest our core business or reinvest in new opportunities?

"My directors ask me questions like, 'Are you committed to growth or profit? When push comes to shove, is it market share or is it raising prices?'" one business owner says. At this point, he has decided that "investing in the market is good business. The market is growing." But if circumstances change, he says, his perspective might shift as well.

Directors can be of enormous help to the CEO weighing these alternatives. The second-generation head of one industrial concern relies heavily on his board for support in this area. First, directors affirmed the CEO's difficult decision to reduce profitability in order to open new branches, invest in better equipment, and raise professional salaries. Then, the board supported the CEO when he met resistance from the company's profit-oriented founder. To the older man, any slackening of profit reflected a loosening of management discipline. Before long, the founder was blaming every earnings swing and operating problem on the new CEO's growth strategy.

The board helped defuse the tension, monitoring the exact

impact of the new CEO's investments and moderating the debate. When the founder complained that profits were hurt by the opening of a new branch, directors pointed out that the new-plant cost was only partly responsible for the profit drop. When the founder objected to a small inventory buildup as a sign of the sloppy management that was hurting profits, directors pointed out that the inventory increase was in fact tiny in comparison with sales growth.

The new CEO was able to sustain his growth strategy as a result, significantly improving the company's long-term outlook.

Slack Resources: Creativity Versus Productivity. Few CEOs consciously weigh the idea of deliberately allowing slack resources — spare time for employees, discretionary budget expenditures, and so on. But building in slack resources for employees to devote to new initiatives or creative pursuits can make a big difference — in current productivity on the one hand, and in the company's future capacity for innovation on the other.

By allowing some of its technical people to spend up to 15 percent of their time on pet projects, Minnesota Mining & Manufacturing Company has spawned such products as Scotch tape, Post-It notes, and Scotchguard fabric coating. "We're able to fly a little bit, and that little bit means an awful lot," said one employee (Minnesota Mining & Manufacturing Company, 1977, p. 118). For other companies, such a strategy would be inappropriate. A commodity processor intent on peeling razor-thin margins from high-volume operations would probably be intensely selective in parceling out slack resources.

In either case, the CEO should have a philosophy in mind. "This is going to be a lean and mean operation," one business owner may decide, and adjust staffing, incentives, employee communications, and the corporate mission statement accordingly.

Another CEO may conclude, "I want to make sure I'm staffed at a level that permits everyone some time for developing new ideas." If the competitive climate permits, this CEO may build as much as 20 percent slack into key employees' schedules to permit new initiatives and undertakings.

To stimulate new product and marketing ideas, the owner of an industrial controls firm assigns all of his managers one of the company's markets to oversee. A plant manager, for instance, might be in charge of the office building market, and he might be expected to attend industry conventions, read trade publications, and stay abreast of participants' concerns. The result, the CEO hopes, will be an increased market sensitivity throughout the company, as well as a better internal capability for new-product development and review.

Assuring Earnings Predictability. What are we doing to assure that we have the most predictable earnings in the industry? This may not be the first question on the CEO's mind as he or she reaches the office each morning. But it can be extremely important — not only to shareholders' short-term interests but to the long-term cost of operating the business and, ultimately, to the value of the company.

The CEO who can demonstrate a consistent earnings performance — that is, by achieving his or her forecast and meeting expectations — has a significant chance of lowering the company's cost of capital. If a company poses little earnings risk, shareholders, lenders, and prospective partners may reasonably expect that it also poses little investment risk. And the returns required by these prospective sources of cash, in the form of interest or dividend yields, should decline accordingly.

Some business owners strive for consistency of earnings specifically to hold down the cost of capital. One company delayed write-offs on a couple of questionable projects because the CEO knew the company would soon need to raise significant amounts of capital for a long-planned new venture. While the decision cost the company some immediate tax benefits, it increased its appeal to prospective lenders and investors.

The owner-managers of another company found that a consistent earnings performance was among the best ways to shore up a fragile truce among several shareholders who did not work in the company. The owner-managers reasoned that the nonmanagement shareholders would have more confidence in management — and thus less tendency to question its decisions—if presented with a predictable earnings performance each quarter. Indeed, the shareholder group has remained mostly peaceful and intact, thanks largely to the control and confidence demonstrated by the managers.

What Is Our Cost of Capital? The owner-manager of a private business has an inherent conflict of interest on this question. As chief executive, his or her goal should be to seek the lowest possible cost of capital. This demands, in part, holding down dividends to shareholders to free cash for growth opportunities. But as an owner of the company, the owner-manager's goal should be to maximize the return to shareholders. The shareholders' level of interest in long-term growth and their enthusiasm for owning a private company can affect their view of a fair return, of course. But if shareholders press for increased quarterly dividends, the CEO can lose a significant degree of flexibility.

The board can help the CEO probe his or her position on this issue and examine the potential consequences of alternative positions. If shareholders are denied attractive returns for a long time, they may cause an upheaval by selling out. On the other hand, the opposite policy may leave shareholders fat and happy and the company stagnant and drifting. Whatever the balance, the issue is a real one.

What Is the Value of the Firm? Many business owners view this question as a first step toward selling the company. In fact, it should be a constant and central yardstick for management performance. Management should continually be concerned about whether it is performing well enough to increase shareholder value significantly over the long term.

In many small and medium-sized firms, the board can help ascertain the approximate shareholder value of the business. Unlike other measures such as the current stock price or dividend yield, shareholder value reflects the present value of future cash flows. Essentially, it measures the value today of the future earnings of the business, when discounted to reflect the company's cost of capital.

The power of this financial measure lies in its focus on

future earnings and investments and on the continuing return on the company's current investments. Thus monitoring shareholder value automatically imposes a valuable management discipline: It forces a continual reappraisal of the performance of various investments. It requires management to do more than talk about making investments for the future; it requires a demonstration that they are paying off.

Directors can be invaluable in helping enforce this discipline. Jerome Stone, co-founder and chairman emeritus of Stone Container Corporation and an experienced director, says he always asks the CEO to document expected returns from major capital investments. "If management comes forward with a recommendation, I want them to document for me what they expect to save or gain. Then three years down the road, I want to look at it again. I ask for that discipline."

Monitoring shareholder value is also a lesson in the importance of the cost of capital. Even a half-percentage point change in a company's cost of capital can make a vast difference in shareholder value, as reflected by the current value of future earnings over a period of years. A good board can be of enormous help in monitoring these important financial measures.

Directors can also help tackle some related strategic questions. How can we increase shareholder value? Would another owner be able to realize added synergies? If the business would be worth more in the hands of a different owner, why? What is it about that change that would make the firm more valuable? A lower cost of capital? Greater operating synergies? How can we acquire some of those advantages for ourselves? By acquiring the other business? By entering its areas of business? Or does it mean we simply can't compete in the marketplace? Is that a signal that we should exit the business?

By answering these questions, the business owner also can learn much about what product, market, customer, and technological alliances have the highest strategic value in the industry.

Business Cycle Vulnerability. Any company needs to be aware of its boom-and-bust tendencies to engage in effective planning. If a business is highly cyclical, no amount of careful management and forethought is going to insulate it from the next downturn in the business cycle.

The board can help examine the company's vulnerability and decide how to manage for it — by taking conscious steps to prepare the organization for the consequences. A company in a capital-goods business, for instance, might fortify its balance sheet in preparation for the inevitable slumps and help employees brace for the periodic bad quarters or years. At the same time, it might remind employees during the inevitable boom years that the market will not go up forever.

On the other hand, a company in a relatively stable business, such as consumer foods, should educate employees to expect and manage for stable returns. The culture of such a company would likely encourage seeking ways to moderate raw-material price fluctuations and other variables. It also would probably discourage such extreme risks as broad-scale commodity speculation.

Setting Learning Goals for the Company. Many entrepreneurs do not think about setting learning goals as part of their jobs as managers. In fact, identifying learning goals for the company can be an important part of preparing for the future. Just as reallocating capital can change a company's strategic direction, changing an organization's learning goals can alter the flow of the company's *human* capital — the direction of the talents and energies of its people. In another sense, learning goals are a means of setting priorities for the organization that are easily understood by everyone.

One company, for instance, had long assumed that it could easily stay a step ahead of competitors. But within a short period, it was twice surprised — once by the emergence of a new competitor, and a second time by another rival's clever new marketing strategy. With the help of the board, managers soon admitted that the climate had changed. They set "anticipating competitors better" as their top learning goal.

In another case, a company saw a rich business opportunity in Europe. But none of its managers had experience there, and questions were flying: Should we buy or build a plant or enter a joint venture? Do we send our own marketing staff or hire Europeans? What will be the impact of planned changes in trade regulations? With the help of the board, the CEO set "learning how to do business in Europe" as the company's top goal, and began tackling the questions with a variety of resources.

Sometimes, directors can raise seemingly simple questions that spark important corporate learning efforts. Clayton Mathile, president of the IAMS Company, a fast-growing pet food manufacturer, recalls one "pearl" from his board. Several years ago, when the company's primary emphasis was dog food, a director said, "Clay, you're in the *pet food* business. You've got to start thinking more about cats." He added, "If cats ran the world, what would they want?"

The idea piqued Mr. Mathile's interest. IAMS intensified research into the cat food market and increased promotion of its cat foods, and the products took off. "Today, 25 percent of our sales are cat food," Mr. Mathile says.

Directors can raise other issues as well. What is our highest learning priority? How should we articulate it? How do we encourage learning? How do we monitor our learning potential? These are all questions that will arise as management continually reevaluates its learning goals.

Assessing the Risk-Taking Propensity of the Organization. Every entrepreneur is born with a personal propensity for risk-taking. In the early stages of his or her business, there is usually little need to analyze it; the entrepreneur leads the organization by a combination of guts and instinct, seizing opportunities as they present themselves.

But as the company and its work force grows, so does its employees' need to understand its risk-taking posture and philosophy. Although the entrepreneur may still not even be conscious of his or her propensity to risk, that personal trait colors almost every major decision — acquisitions, the hiring of a top officer, the treatment of a new-product idea. It becomes a major aspect of the corporate culture and can have a profound effect on strategy and its implementation.

An active board can help the business owner address this

issue consciously, usually through probing questions. "What new risks are we taking?" directors may ask. "How much risk do we want to take? What is your attitude toward risk-taking? How do you monitor it within the corporation? How should the company's risk-taking posture be communicated to the organization? How should we prepare the organization for the kinds of risks the company will be taking?"

The role of the board is not to influence the CEO but to help him or her identify a desirable risk-taking posture and make it explicit throughout the organization. This can help management chart a steady course that encourages employees to fall into line.

A company that encourages risk-taking, for instance, might expect employees to float new ideas. In contrast, when the whole organization understands that management places a higher premium on stability and security than on risk-taking, no one will be shaken or demoralized when a high-flying project proposal is grounded. This knowledge can help the organization manage itself. It can also be helpful in explaining apparent contradictions to employees — when one part of the business is high-risk, for instance, compared to another unit that is treated more like a cash cow.

Contingency Planning. Every effective corporate strategist harbors a bevy of contingency plans — answers to questions about the "what if" events that can throw a company seriously off course.

What if our assessment of the market's interest in our new product is wrong? What if there's a strike? What if interest rates skyrocket? What if our competitors retaliate after we enter this new market?

Worrisome issues indeed, and the kind that business owners may easily neglect in the heat of inaugurating projects, opening new markets, or just growing the business.

The board's role in raising these questions can be invaluable in preventing surprises — something almost no business owner likes. One business owner dabbling in national advertising-media markets for the first time recalls helpful advice from one of his directors: "Always make the assumption that your advertising mix is wrong, and that you're going to have to fix it. You never want to get married to one program." The suggestion, he says, prepared him for some of the high-stakes advertising decisions that followed.

Directors also can encourage a measure of forethought and preparation that will prevent the business owner from being caught completely off guard by a negative turn of events. Either function can be crucial to the success, and even the survival, of the company.

Summary

Private company boards, free from some of the pressures and obligations that burden public company directors, are able to fulfill some special opportunities to help improve corporate performance and decision making.

Directors can encourage and help produce a statement of the company's mission and philosophy. They can help assess the organization's culture and its impact on performance. And they can help formulate a meaningful human resources plan to attract and retain good employees and ensure continuity of management.

In perhaps the most potentially creative frontier, the board can also help improve the quality of strategy. This encompasses all aspects of strategic thinking—from overseeing strategic planning and implementation to gauging shareholder value, setting learning goals, and ensuring sound contingency planning.

4

Liability and the Private Company Director

Irving L. Blackman, principal of a successful Chicago accounting firm, is well aware of the epidemic of liability fears that has swept corporate board rooms nationwide. Yet in years of experience as a director and adviser to many companies, Mr. Blackman has never been the target of a liability action. He is selective in accepting invitations to serve, of course, weighing the capability and integrity of management, the financial stability of the company, and other potential areas of risk. But on the whole, he finds that the personal rewards of serving on an effective board vastly outweigh the risks.

"It's like flying, or swimming in the ocean. You forget about the risk, go do it, and enjoy it," he says. "Serving as a director is challenging. It gives me an opportunity to help people. And I always learn something myself in the process."

Fears of director liability among many business owners are greatly overblown. While small and medium-sized private companies often cite potential liability claims as the main obstacle to inviting outside directors into their business, the conscientious director in such an environment typically faces negligible risk. Based on the most comprehensive survey data available, the Wyatt Company, a Chicago-based risk management consultant, found that companies with less than $50 million in assets and under

78

500 shareholders had only a 1 percent chance of facing a director and officer (D&O) liability claim in the entire nine-year period from 1980 through 1988 (Wyatt Company, 1990b).

Clearly, these companies' size, ownership status, and mode of operation sharply reduced their liability risk in comparison with big, publicly held companies, which are as much as forty times more susceptible to claims. At the same time, the *rate* of claims filed against small and medium-sized companies is actually flat or falling, compared with an overall annual increase for large companies of 5–15 percent, Wyatt found. Moreover, more than half of all claims are settled without any payment to the claimant (Wyatt Company, 1990a).

Thus for the small and medium-sized private company, this specter haunting the modern board room — the fear of director liability — is little more than that: a phantom that fades on close inspection. For directors of privately held companies who make a conscientious effort to perform their duties responsibly, "the risk of being held personally liable is fairly low," says John C. Coffee, Jr., a Columbia University law school professor.

This chapter is designed as a guide for owners and directors of small and medium-sized private companies in assessing, understanding, and managing their actual liability risk. It describes directors' legal obligations in some detail. It discusses various lines of defense, including corporate indemnification and directors and officers insurance. Finally, it helps directors and business owners know what to expect in the unlikely event that a claim is filed.

But the chapter's comprehensiveness is not intended to deter business owners from involving outside directors. Rather, the author hopes a clear look at this widely misunderstood issue will encourage most business owners to move ahead with confidence that the rewards of involvement with an effective board will vastly outweigh the risks.

Taking Stock

Several factors help insulate the small and medium-sized private company from the daunting, highly publicized risks faced by big, publicly held concerns.

    The most thorough and authoritative available data on
director and officer liability, an annual survey performed by the
Wyatt Company, shows that the rate of D&O liability claims
is closely correlated with the size of the company. A company
with $25–$100 million in assets was less than one-third as likely
to be sued as a company with $400 million to $1 billion in assets,
according to Wyatt's 1989 survey of 1,537 companies and organizations (Wyatt Company, 1990a, p. 12). For companies
with under $25 million in assets, the likelihood was less than
one-eleventh as great (see Table 3). For closely held companies
the likelihood is even less. For example, for firms with under
$25 million in assets and with fewer than 500 shareholders, the
chance is less than one-twentieth as great—less than 0.1% per
year. Companies with less than 500 shareholders were hit by

Table 3. Likelihood of D&O Liability Claims by Size of Company.

Company Size (Assets)	Susceptibility[a]	
	1979–87	1980–88
Under $25 million	4%	2%
$25–$100 million	11%	6%
$100–$400 million	15%	14%
$400 million–$1 billion	22%	23%
$1–$2 billion	31%	34%
$2 billion or more	43%	43%

[a]Susceptibility is the likelihood of a company having one or more claims
made against it in the nine-year experience period.
Source: Wyatt Company, 1990a, p. 12.

claims about one-third as often as more broadly held companies,
the survey showed. This is not surprising when one considers
that shareholders were the leading source of claims.
    Private companies' relative safety from the merger-and-
acquisition wars fortifies their resistance. A ten-year study by
Marsh and McLennan showed a strong correlation between
merger-and-acquisition activity and D&O claims (Weber, 1986).
Merger, acquisition, and divestiture activity is "the single largest
issue for shareholder claims," more than doubling the average
rate of D&O actions against a company, says Kenneth Wollner, a risk management consultant for Wyatt.

Smaller companies are typically less vulnerable to employee and product liability suits because of their smaller numbers of employees and products. Generally, the liability exposure of these corporations under securities laws is reduced as well, since most do not seek public financing (Schipani and Siedel, 1988).

All of these factors help explain why serious liability problems in the small to medium-sized private company are not the crippling threat portrayed in the press. Indeed, only two of the 169 companies in Wyatt's 1989 survey with under $50 million in assets and fewer than 500 shareholders experienced D&O claims in the nine years between 1980 and 1988. Of these, one claim was brought by an employee alleging wrongful termination, and the other by a shareholder over an alleged conflict of interest (Wyatt Company, 1990b).

Caught in the Updraft

Nevertheless, the winds of fear have buffeted small and medium-sized private companies, often unfairly, in the form of increasing D&O insurance rates.

Closely held firms do face some special risks. Feuds among shareholders in family-held companies, for instance, can be bitter indeed. Without firm buy-sell agreements to allow disenchanted minority owners a fair route of escape, shareholders can turn upon each other like caged animals. (Buy-sell agreements are discussed in greater detail later in this chapter.) The absence of a family council to foster consensus and smooth decision making can worsen such clashes (see Chapter Ten).

None of these obstacles should be sufficient, however, to deter most companies from naming outside directors or, at least, from forming a council of advisers, as is discussed in more detail later in this chapter. Let us now take a close look at the first line of defense against liability: appropriate conduct by directors.

A Behavioral Prescription

William May, the retired chairman of American Can Company and an experienced director, once recalled a time early in his career when board meetings were casual, low-key affairs. "We'd combine meetings with lunch and a glass of sherry, or maybe something stronger," he told the *Wall Street Journal*. "The chairman would describe what had happened, give some numbers and a projection, and we'd all go home" (Bennett, 1986).

Those days are past, notes Jerome Stone, chairman emeritus of Stone Container Corporation and an experienced director. "The old-boy days of just going to a meeting, having a couple of drinks, having lunch and saying, 'Well, if that's what the chairman wants, that's fine,' are gone forever."

Clearly, directors today must display and document close attention to their duties, as well as loyalty and honesty. Applying these personal disciplines is the best way for directors to decrease the likelihood of litigation and the risk of personal liability. "Do your homework, show up, and speak up. And if you disagree, make sure your dissent is recorded in the minutes," is potent advice for any director.

While these prescriptions sound like common sense, they have solid underpinnings in corporate law. Most states have taken steps in recent years to reduce directors' and officers' liability exposure, but certain fundamental principles of director conduct remain intact. Briefly, here is a sampling of activities the prudent director should avoid:

Actions that damage the company
Antitrust violations
Bankruptcy
Breaches of trust
Bribes
Conflicts of interest
Dishonesty
Violations of employee rights
Exceeding authority of charter or bylaws
Excessive borrowing
Excessive compensation
Excessive use of company funds in a proxy fight
Failure to attend meetings
Failure to call stockholder meetings

Failure to disclose material information
Failure to discover and prevent antitrust violations
Failure to exercise due diligence
Failure to exercise good faith
Failure to police a fellow director
Failure to stop actions that damage the company
Misleading forecasts of corporate performance
Foreign payoffs
Fraud
Improper press releases
Improper relations with financial analysts
Imprudent investments
Imprudent loans
Incurring losses
Incurring penalties
Insider trading
Kickbacks
Laundering information
Misleading statements
Mismanagement
Misrepresentations
Misstatement of financial position
Negligence
Pension fund irregularities
Questionable political contributions
Pollution
Poor business judgment
Price fixing
Shortcomings in product quality or safety
Illegal or unethical securities purchases
Self-dealing
Short-swing profits
Unethical behavior
Unwarranted dividend payments
Watering stock

Let us take a closer look at the legal definition of sound, defensible conduct by directors. (The descriptions that follow arise mostly from the Model Business Corporation Act, as interpreted by the American Bar Association.)

The Duty of Care. This principle requires the director to "perform his duties . . . in good faith, in a manner he reasonably believes to be in the best interests of the corporation, and with such care as an ordinarily prudent person in a like position would use under similar circumstances," according to the Model Business Corporation Act. This measure has been interpreted to mean that a director operates in an honest manner; it implies that the director must avoid negligence, either active or passive. The director must not rely on information he or she knows to be untrue and must seek to be objective.

While the standard of good faith is subject to interpretation by the courts, it is generally interpreted as what directors believe to be in the best interests of the corporation and its shareholders. Directors acting in bad faith, for instance, might take steps aimed solely at maintaining their own control of the company, such as issuing stock to a friendly third party in the face of a takeover attempt.

"An ordinarily prudent person," under the law, is viewed as someone with common sense, practical wisdom, and informed judgment. The person does not necessarily have to have specialized training or experience in the field of business, finance, or environmental law but can be a generalist with basic intelligence appropriate to the task.

The principle also implies that the director must devote to corporate matters the attention they deserve. The nature of the director's role depends on such factors as the size, complexity, and circumstances of the corporation at the time. The issues facing directors of a huge company facing a hostile takeover attempt, for instance, demand greater attention than those facing directors of a small, single-owner business that is running smoothly and quietly.

The Duty of Attention. This principle entails the responsibility of directors to participate actively in overseeing the corporation's activities. It requires regular attendance at board meetings. It assumes directors will review adequate information about the company and will request that information if it is not made available. It also assumes that the director will make sure he or she is given adequate time to make informed judgments about corporate issues.

Neglect of this duty can result in personal liability. In a New Jersey case, a director was found liable for the fraudulent acts of others even though he was unaware of them. The reason: He had not even read financial statements disclosing misappropriation of trust funds (Schipani and Siedel, 1988).

The Duty of Loyalty. This principle requires the director to avoid using his or her corporate position to make a personal profit or gain. It involves the potential conflict of interest in directors' dealings as individuals with the corporation.

Under this tenet of board-room law, the director must disclose to the board any material personal interest in a contract or transaction with the corporation, and he or she should abstain from voting on the matter. Directors may be held liable unless the director's conflict is known to the board or to shareholders and the transaction is approved anyway by a majority of disinterested directors or by shareholders. The transaction also must be judged fair to the corporation; among other things, the terms must be at least as favorable to the corporation as would be a similar transaction with an independent third party.

The principle also underlies the concept of fiduciary duty to shareholders. To that end, the director may not disclose inside information or use it for personal gain. While the corporation itself might suffer no direct harm if a director knowingly buys its stock ahead of a large self-tender, for instance, such a transaction would be viewed as a breach of the duty of loyalty. Any profit the director made would likely be viewed as the property of the corporation.

In the case of a closely held company, a majority shareholder could be held liable for damages to other shareholders if he or she bought their shares without disclosing to them first a plan to sell the company at a higher price.

Reliance. This principle is one of the most significant tools a director has in insulating him or herself from liability. Under it, directors are entitled to be protected by and to rely upon the books and records of the corporation. This includes reports, opinions, financial data, and other information supplied by officers, board committees, or independent experts, assuming directors have no reason to be suspicious of the information.

For instance, directors may rely on the opinion of an independent investment banker in evaluating the price of a tender offer, or on the advice of an attorney in deciding whether to take legal action. If directors act on such matters *without* the advice of professional experts, however, they open themselves to liability.

The Business Judgment Rule. This principle assumes that directors are entitled to exercise reasonable judgment without interference by the courts. When applied, it assumes that directors' decisions were made in good faith and with reasonable business purpose. The court presumes that directors acted in an informed and honest fashion. This tenet also means that the party who challenges a business decision bears the burden of proof.

Business judgment requires attentiveness; directors must be able to prove they have paid attention to a particular issue, informed themselves, and reviewed all the material facts surrounding it.

Adequate Documentation. As an added safeguard against liability, the director should ensure that his or her role is well documented. A director who disagrees with a board decision should make sure his or her dissent and the reasons for it are recorded in the minutes. Otherwise, silence or abstaining from a vote can be construed as agreement. The minutes should also clearly reflect directors' participation in meetings and discussions. In all cases, documentation demonstrating the board's good-faith efforts to comply with the law and with individual directors' legal duties should be sufficient to withstand a challenge in court.

This principle is just as important in entrepreneurial or

family businesses as in larger corporations. Typically, "the corporate veil" protects business owners from personal liability. But if owners fail to treat the company as a separate entity and document its compliance with corporate law, the courts might be more inclined to pierce that veil and hold individual owners, directors, or employees liable.

Thus all corporations should document legal functions in a businesslike way, filing required reports with regulators, maintaining accurate board minutes, keeping corporate and personal assets separate, and so on. A professional mode of operation can be a big help in protecting the company and its owners and directors from liability (Schipani and Siedel, 1988).

Mounting a Defense

Business owners can construct several additional lines of defense to protect members of their boards or advisory panels from liability. Most fundamental of all is the requirement to provide directors with all the appropriate data and reports they need to make informed judgments about the business. At a minimum, directors should have:

- The charter and bylaws of the company
- Quarterly profit and loss statements
- Corporate books
- All reports and proposals submitted to shareholders
- Policies governing all financial operations of the company
- The corporate mission statement
- Annual operating and capital budgets
- Letters between the CEO and general counsel
- Top-management performance reviews and ratings
- Top-management salary information
- Biographical data on all directors, officers, and key managers
- Board minutes
- Management incentive plans
- Summary of employee benefit and bonus plans
- Board meeting agenda and summary of pertinent board issues in advance

- At least two days' advance notice, in most states, of special board meetings
- Access to general counsel
- Access to auditor
- Minutes of board committee meetings
- Conversations with key top executives
- Access to other professional advisers
- Press releases
- Status of material litigation

A related, and implicit, obligation is to conduct the company's affairs in a way that inspires director confidence in the honesty and capability of the CEO. "An open relationship with a management that manifests integrity should make a director much more comfortable about liability risk," says Bernard Hale, a vice-president of Bergen Brunswig Corporation in Orange, California, and an experienced director.

Beyond that, several mechanisms exist that can significantly reduce liability risk to the board.

Corporate Indemnification. Corporate indemnification is by far the most common line of defense. It is a promise, contained in the corporate charter, bylaws, or individual contracts, to protect directors from personal liability and legal costs, barring criminal liability or negligence.

Many states, including Delaware, have recently broadened the right of corporations to indemnify directors from personal liability. Historically, most claims against directors and officers can be covered by the corporation (Wyatt Company, 1990a).

If a company fails or goes bankrupt, of course, such promises are worthless. Corporate indemnification runs only as deep as the financial resources of the company. Some businesses post surety bonds to protect directors in the event of corporate insolvency or bankruptcy.

Shareholder Indemnification. This line of defense, although far less common than corporate indemnification, is especially effective. It entails a promise by shareholders to indemnify directors against personal liability. Presumably, this deepens the financial resources available to defend the director and shields him or her from shareholder actions as well.

In a recent survey of 147 private companies in the Midwest, only 20–25 percent of the firms had shareholder indemnification (Ward and Handy, 1988). For family businesses with several shareholders, this is a useful tool that might be considered more often.

Directors and Officers Insurance. Most directors of small and medium-sized private companies are willing to serve without D&O insurance. And most companies of this kind choose not to carry D&O coverage. The Wyatt Company found that only 40 percent of smaller firms with less than 500 shareholders carry the coverage, with many saying they saw no need for it (Wyatt Company, 1990b). In the midwestern survey, only about one-third of the privately controlled companies polled had D&O insurance (Ward and Handy, 1988).

Nevertheless, D&O insurance does protect assets when directors are exposed to personal liability. Most policies complement corporate indemnification in two ways. First, they protect the personal assets of directors and officers by insuring against liability for which the corporation does not provide indemnification. Second, these policies also protect the company's assets by reimbursing it for payments made to indemnify officers and directors.

The average annual cost of D&O insurance for firms with 100–499 employees was about $20,000, the 1988 midwestern survey showed. The average cost for firms with more than 499 workers was higher, ranging from $35,000 to $100,000 a year. The higher premiums reflect, at least in part, the fact that many of those larger privately controlled firms were publicly traded.

D&O insurance has several important limitations. Deductibles have risen sharply in the past decade. Insurers are writing an increasing number of exclusions into their policies, including fraud, takeover battles, public offerings, environmental changes, punitive damages, and lawsuits filed by one director against another or by a company against its directors (Verespej,

1987). Directors typically remain liable for violations of federal securities and antitrust laws, racketeering violations, and misuse of inside information.

Nevertheless, D&O insurance is widely available again following the crisis of the late 1980s, and it can serve to protect corporate and personal assets and to reassure some candidates who may be hesitant to join a board.

Product and Environmental Liability Insurance. These thorny areas warrant careful attention by business owners and directors. All should be aware of areas of potential liability, make sure adequate standards of corporate performance are in place, and ensure sufficient insurance coverage. Most D&O insurance policies do not cover environmental liability, and many insurers resist paying claims for punitive damages relating to product liability litigation.

A company's exposure in these areas should be among the things a director candidate assesses in deciding whether to serve on a board. A major environmental or product liability claim can raise criminal liability issues, as well as threaten a company's financial stability.

The Council of Advisers. Some business owners may be especially nervous about director liability. They may find themselves in an unusually risky environment, perhaps facing potential shareholder disputes or serious environmental claims. For these CEOs, a council of advisers can be an attractive alternative to asking outsiders to serve on a legal board. This alternative, when properly managed, can diminish liability exposure.

These smaller, less formal advisory councils can serve many of the same helpful functions as an outside board — providing a confidential ally for the CEO, improving the quality of strategy, monitoring the planning process, and so on. But without the legal status of a board of directors, the advisory council can be insulated from most of the official responsibility associated with the threat of liability claims.

Advisory panels have some drawbacks. Some employees, shareholders, and other constituents might take advisers less seriously than directors, diminishing their potency in helping to resolve problems. Part of directors' clout comes from the aura of officialness that surrounds the corporate board. Also, a position on an advisory council might be perceived by some director candidates as less appealing and prestigious than a seat on a board of directors. That perception could in some cases hurt the business owner's ability to attract top-flight people.

Other candidates, however, will respond favorably to the advisory council concept. It can be an effective antidote to liability risk and a way of eliminating the need for D&O insurance. Capable businesspeople who refuse to serve on corporate boards often will agree to positions on advisory councils.

The council must be structured carefully to avoid the risk that potential litigants will view it as a board of directors operating under a different name. The key to minimizing risk is to keep the council separate from the board. Advisers should not also hold seats on the board, for instance. And if management consistently follows the advice of the advisory panel, it might be viewed as a "shadow board" with the same legal responsibilities (Verespej, 1987).

Here are some concrete suggestions for structuring an advisory group to minimize liability risk (Tillman, 1988):

- Keep the advisory group separate from the board and permit it to function only on an advisory basis.
- Do not permit membership to overlap except where necessary, such as in the case of the chief executive officer.
- Make sure the board actively performs its legal functions.
- Organize the advisory board as an advisory *panel* or *council,* not as an advisory *board.*
- Be prepared to provide documented evidence of the separation between the advisory panel and the board.
- Confirm in all documents involving the advisory group, including statements of purpose and even invitations to join it, that it is advisory in nature and that the board is the proper entity for decision making.
- Make clear that the company cannot implement the council's recommendations unless they have been considered and adopted by the board.

- Keep clear and complete records of the advisory group's
  meetings, including notes that recommendations and requests have been sent on to the board of directors.
- Document the board's exercise of its legal responsibilities
  in the minutes. Make its independence clear by ensuring
  that it explicitly accepts, rejects, or tables the advisory panel's
  recommendations.
- Keep file memoranda on suggestions of the advisory panel
  that are not brought before the board — again, to document
  the panel's independence and separation from the board.

The Buy-Sell Agreement

Many attorneys are fond of warning business owners that private companies are deeply vulnerable to bitter court battles. Indeed, emotions among even a handful of controlling shareholders
can erupt into destructive clashes that can disrupt strategic planning, tie management up in court for years, and drain corporate
assets. The Dorrances of Campbell Soup Company, the Halases
of Chicago Bears fame, and other well-known business families
are cases in point.

The best antidote to director liability in such situations
is good-faith, businesslike conduct, as described earlier in this
chapter. No matter how friendly shareholders may seem to each
other or to the board, it is a mistake for directors to assume
that they can conduct the company's business casually and without concern for its legal responsibilities.

Business owners and directors can also help avert shareholder warfare by creating buy-sell agreements. These contracts
promise that holders will tender their shares to the company
according to a preestablished price or formula before selling to
an outsider. They guarantee restless or embittered shareholders
an out — a liquid market for their stock.

Pricing these agreements is a sensitive issue. The owner
of a young company should avoid setting the price so high as
to jeopardize the business. But as the company grows and ownership becomes more widely dispersed among members of successive generations, the price should move closer to the stock's

full market value, as determined by qualified professional advisers.

Who Is Most Likely to Sue?

Shareholders are the most common source of D&O liability claims by far, accounting for nearly half of the total (Wyatt Company, 1990a). Another 20 percent is attributable to employees, and only slightly less (17 percent) to customers. The remainder is more or less evenly split between competitors, government, and other sources (Wyatt Company, 1990a).

Conflicts usually associated with public ownership give rise to most shareholder complaints. More than 57 percent of the shareholder claims in the survey arose from such issues as financial reporting, mergers and acquisitions, and stock offerings. Among the remaining causes of claims, conflict of interest, spinoffs or divestitures, contractual obligations, and loan or investment decisions were most common.

According to the survey, employees were most likely to sue for wrongful termination or breach of their employee contract. Customers, clients, and consumer groups most commonly cited (1) extension of credit or loans or (2) the quality or availability of products and services as causes for complaint. In criminal prosecutions, mail or wire fraud, pollution or antitrust activity, tax fraud or evasion, conspiracy (such as price fixing), securities fraud, and perjury are common areas of complaint against individual directors and officers.

What Can We Expect If We Are Sued?

For most directors and officers facing liability claims, the main hurdle is the cost of defending themselves.

Less than one-half of one percent of all directors who are sued are actually found guilty in court, estimates John Nash, president of the National Association of Corporate Directors. (This statistic excludes directors of financial institutions, whom the courts tend to hold to a higher duty of responsibility.) The Wyatt survey shows that about 60 percent of all claims, including those filed against financial institutions, are closed without any payment to the claimant (Wyatt Company, 1990a).

But cases usually take about six years to resolve, and the average cost of defending against a complaint is $470,000, Mr. Nash estimates. Most claims are settled out of court, largely because corporations want to avoid the cost and aggravation of a trial. In those that do go to trial, directors and officers seldom achieve a clear victory. Juries usually tend to find directors and officers liable on at least some of the numerous theories of liability presented by the plaintiffs' lawyers (Greenberg, 1989, p. 3).

Nevertheless, the most highly publicized and alarming cases of director liability usually involve instances where directors' actions were clearly questionable. In the 1985 Trans Union case in Delaware, *Smith* vs. *Van Gorkum,* for instance, where directors were found personally liable for millions of dollars in damages, board members had approved a surprise 1980 buyout proposal without getting advice from an independent attorney or investment banker. They did not even take detailed minutes.

On the evening of the same day, the chairman signed the agreement at a party celebrating the opening of the new opera season in Chicago. Whether or not the price was fair, shareholders believed it was too low, and Trans Union officers and directors were not able to persuade the court otherwise.

In most situations, directors can avoid such risks by making responsible, conscientious service their highest priority and documenting their actions and attention. "You must educate yourself about the company and participate in discussions and decision making. Those are critical elements," says Ronald Taylor, president of DeVry Institute in Evanston, Illinois, and an experienced director.

"The real protection you have as a director," he adds, "is to do your job. Sometimes that's uncomfortable. It's most likely to be uncomfortable at the time that it's most important."

Summary

The liability fears that have swept corporate board rooms across the country in recent years have infected many private business owners as well. In fact, the risk faced by directors of small and medium-sized private companies is significantly less than many business owners fear.

The liability issue should not deter formation of an active board, provided that the business owner takes steps to understand and manage the risk. Corporate or shareholder indemnification of directors, D&O insurance, and sound buy-sell agreements with shareholders can help avoid problems. A carefully structured panel of advisers can help reduce the liability risk while serving many of the same purposes as a legal board.

Perhaps most important, directors can help shield themselves by making sure they understand their obligations under the law and performing their duties accordingly.

Part Two

SETTING UP
AND MANAGING
THE BOARD

5

Structuring the Board

When Kenneth Nowak, president of Variety Vending and Food Service Company, a family business in Warren, Michigan, decided to form an outside board, his first step was a thorough analysis of his own company. "We drew up a board profile based on the question, 'What is distinctive about our business that someone else might not understand or be familiar with?'" Mr. Nowak says.

The self-study helped him narrow his search for directors by eliminating people who did not match his business needs — including a vice-president of a Big Three auto maker. "I wanted people with some entrepreneurial spirit," he says.

The profile also told him that he needed directors familiar with custom contracting with industrial customers, among other things. As a vending service company with a variety of unique clients, "We didn't want somebody who made widgets, where every salesman had a book, and everything was priced uniformly," he says.

For Mr. Nowak, whose case will be explored in more detail in Chapter Six, structuring the board correctly "was a crucial process." It not only contributed to his board's success but also lent new insight into the challenges his business would face in the future.

For many business owners, the benefits of building an active outside board begin even before they contact the first director candidate. Structuring a board requires the business owner to articulate the reasons for having one—and thus to focus more intensely than ever before on the most pressing issues facing the business.

This chapter is the first of three offering detailed guidance on the actual process of setting up and managing a board. In this chapter, the reader will find help with the preliminary planning phase, including preparation of a board prospectus, or statement of purpose and practices. Chapter Six will provide information on identifying, approaching, and screening outside candidates for the board. And Chapter Seven will address the tasks associated with preparing for and running meetings.

For the business owner with personal board experience or help from a consultant, the first step of the process—structuring the board—may be completed in a couple of days or so. The second and third steps—selecting directors and attending to board organization—are likely to take an additional three to six months.

Where to Begin

To begin planning for an outside board, the business owner should set time aside, apart from the daily routine and ringing telephone, to reflect on the most important issues facing the company. As discussed earlier, these often arise from a handful of common and compelling concerns: "We really need to put together a succession plan!" the business owner may conclude. Or, "We need an 'insurance policy' for the family, so that someone is here to fill the void if anything happens to me."

Some business owners seek greater accountability and self-discipline. Others wrestle with new strategic issues: "How can I get back on top of this changing industry?" "What factors should I consider in deciding whether to acquire another company?"

Still others face new hurdles in professionalization of management: "This place just isn't humming anymore," they may worry. "How can I get my arms around this growing organization and make sure I have good people pulling their weight?"

To the surprise of many CEOs, the board-structuring process often brings new insight as well into their own capabilities and needs as a chief executive. As many business owners consider goals for an active board, they begin to realize, "I really haven't been setting the right objectives for *myself*. I could use a little extra discipline in my own role in this company."

That new sense of accountability can bring a renewed commitment to defining the chief executive's job and striving for better ways to perform it. Often, the CEO also gains greater awareness of the responsibilities that are uniquely his or her own.

The Board Prospectus

Preparing a board prospectus is the first step in organizing an effective board. This one-to-three page document, which may take only a few days to prepare, becomes useful almost immediately. It can be a helpful tool in recruiting director candidates, and it can assist the business owner in networking with lenders, advisers, and others who might know attractive director prospects.

The statement also can be useful in explaining to others the purpose of forming an active board. It can be of great help in allaying doubts among key people who are unfamiliar with the board's role or suspicious about involving outsiders.

The board prospectus should describe clearly the purpose and goals of the board. It should convey the qualities and capabilities the business owner is seeking in directors. And it should describe the anticipated board structure, director compensation, and time demands on members.

Like the statement of corporate philosophy, the board prospectus should be a unique and distinctive document illuminating the personality and values of the owners, as well as the philosophy and culture of the company. (An example of how an effective prospectus might look is contained in Appendix A.)

Let us take a closer look at the components of this important document. (Exhibit 1 outlines these components, including the most commonly cited purposes for the board.)

Exhibit 1. Contents of the Board Prospectus.

 I.   Overview of the Company
       • Industry
       • Most important products and types of customers
       • Size
       • Nature of ownership (two brothers as founding partners, third-generation family business with fifteen shareholders?)
 II. Board Profile
       A.   Character of business
             • Stage of life cycle (rapidly growing, mature, no longer growing?)
             • Relative strengths or weaknesses (highest-quality producer in the region, need to develop more cost-consciousness?)
             • Strategic thrust (developing an international presence, seeking to grow by acquisition, committed to increasing market share?)
       B.   Purpose(s) of the board
            Most common examples:
             • Brainstorm and examine alternative strategic directions in an industry facing maturity and intensifying competition.
             • Stimulate continued professionalization of management and organizational development.
             • Aid in developing the succession process.
             • Serve as counsel to spouse and/or successors in case of death of CEO.
             • Encourage increased self-discipline and accountability for president and organization.
             • Provide counsel and support to successor(s).
             • Develop board strength to support future financing needs or public offering.
       C.   Personal criteria
             • Desired background, personal characteristics, and experience of board candidates
 III. Structure of the Board
       • Number of outsiders and owners on board
       • Number of meetings
       • Time commitment
       • Participation in committees or family business activities
       • Honorarium or compensation: amount and form of payment (per meeting or per quarter? in cash, stock, or deferred compensation?)
       • Director liability provisions
       • Term of office

Why Do I Want a Board?

The first section, which introduces the company and describes the business owner's reasons for setting up an active board, should communicate a comprehensive sense of purpose to directors.

This introductory section usually gives a concise overview of the company, including its size in terms of sales and employees, its relative strengths and weaknesses, and its major strategic goals or challenges. It should convey a sense of the company's industry, competition, customers, and market. And while the prospectus need not reveal a great deal of financial information, it should offer director candidates a clear sense of the business context.

"Although our industry's traditionally high profit margins are declining, we continue to grow at a rate of 10–15 percent a year," one business owner might write. Another might say, "We are the third-largest company of our kind in the nation, but we are losing ground in new-product development." Yet another might write, "This is a turnaround situation, aided by a sharp improvement in market conditions and the recent demise of a major competitor."

The prospectus should summarize the major corporate issues the CEO may want the board to address. Some business owners describe their need for help in dealing with changes in consumer attitudes or federal regulation. Others need to explore new sources of capital or to prepare for management succession. One business owner stressed his need for directors with marketing and sales expertise so he could keep pace with changes in his industry.

What Expertise Am I Seeking in Directors?

The second component of the prospectus—the board profile—is often the most challenging and stimulating to prepare. In this section, the business owner describes the desired criteria for board members, in terms of experience, skill, and understanding.

To reach that point, most CEOs find it useful to ask several preliminary questions. While these may seem simple at first, most executives find that trying to answer them lends new insights that can be of great help in building a board.

What Is Your Industry Profile? The first step is to thoroughly examine the driving forces in your industry. What is the nature of the competition? Is it fragmented, oligopolistic, or undergoing fundamental change? At what stage of development are the industry's principal markets—are they new, maturing, or expanding internationally? What is the nature of your customers and their buying decisions? Do they make frequent impulse purchases, or is yours a high-priced product or service that requires forethought?

How powerful a role do suppliers play in your industry? What are important characteristics of the regulatory environment? Of your competitors? What changes are under way in the competitive environment? And what is the state of technology in the industry?

What Is Your Strategic Profile? This step requires a look at the company's current stance and direction in relation to its industry. What is its market-share position? Where is its competitive advantage—in differentiating its product or service from others, or in operating at a lower cost? You should consider the labor and capital demands of the business, as well as the role of marketing, research and development, and customer service.

What Are the Keys to Success? The industry and strategic profiles flow naturally into an analysis of the keys to success for the business. Based on the company's current position in a changing industry, what types of tasks, decisions, people, and systems are needed to ensure its success? Does prosperity depend on securing more shelf space from powerful distributors? Does the business require a more highly motivated, fully utilized sales force? Is raising private capital to expand the company's retail branch outlets crucial?

What Will Be the Main Sources of Future Growth? This analysis of future challenges is a logical extension of the previous three steps. Here, the CEO identifies the most promising new markets or new products, as well as the most important threats to success, including competitive and environmental issues. An analysis of the resources that will likely be needed to secure the future is needed to build a really useful board profile.

How Will the Company's Ownership Profile Affect Its Future Direction? Many business owners seek directors with some understanding of the special ownership and management issues faced by the private business. To that end, it can be helpful to build an ownership profile, describing the relationships among owners, future ownership plans, and so on. How important to us is maintaining private ownership? is a nearly universal question. How should we address the needs of the growing number of family members who are not working in the business? is another common issue. Basic to this step is an examination of how ownership of the company is likely to evolve in the years to come. Many business owners also include a description of their management style, culture, and personality.

Once the business owner has answered these questions, several critical steps in building a board become simpler. It becomes easier to identify other businesses that demand analogous skills of their executives; easier to reach across industry lines for directors; easier to identify candidates who have already reached the goals that are still only objectives for your business. And the business owner gains confidence in screening directors for the qualities and experience that can make the board a success.

Sometimes, this process yields revelations for even the experienced business owner. Some realize, for instance, that they are not as capital-intensive as they thought, in comparison with other industries — a discovery that can change the business owner's expectations of lenders, among others.

Others discover startling likenesses with other businesses — the funeral chain owner, for instance, who realized he had a lot in common with producers of rock concerts. Both are in event-planning businesses where orchestrating details to please gatherings of people is crucial!

Let us take a look at some examples of how this kind of strategic analysis can help identify director candidates.

The Funeral Home Chain. This privately held firm has a dominant share of its market. It offers a relatively high-priced, high-quality service to buyers who only require it infrequently. The business is both capital- and labor-intensive, maintaining a wide variety of sites and employing people at a broad range of salary levels.

The keys to success for this company include dealing effectively with a wide range of employees and customers, for one. The firm also needs to be able to coordinate countless details of complex events and to respond quickly to customers' changing priorities. The ability to manage many locations simultaneously and to maintain a good word-of-mouth reputation with people who make only infrequent, expensive purchases is crucial as well.

In working on their strategic profile, the business owners identified several challenges. Tough new competition was emerging from lower-priced competitors as well as from a giant, publicly held chain, and the company needed new sources of private capital to compete. Rising real-estate prices and the growing popularity of such burial alternatives as cremation were also forcing the company to redefine its industry and identify new sources of growth.

The owners' analysis yielded several interesting analogies in other industries:

Hospital executives face the same intense capital and labor demands.

Festival, meeting, and concert planners face the same pressures to orchestrate complex events in a timely fashion to please a diverse and fickle public.

Hotel and airline operators have similar capital, labor, and service requirements.

Restaurant chains, auto dealers, fine-arts vendors, and computer store chains face similar site- and capital-management challenges.

This exercise left the funeral home chain owners at a good starting point to begin screening candidates for their board. Eventually, they developed a list of twenty-five candidates with expertise in analogous areas, weeded the list down to ten, met with six, and finally invited three outside directors into their business.

The Specialty Bakery. One of the challenges in this business is to create and exploit demand for holiday-related products—Christmas cookies, baseball cookies, and other impulse items. Among other places, this business owner looked for potential directors in the greeting card business—another industry aimed at "inventing holidays" and otherwise capitalizing on consumer whims. Both businesses require flexible work forces, able to redouble their efforts before holidays; both require nimble and creative new-product development and the ability to work with powerful retail outlets.

At the same time, product development at the specialty bakery concern demands a talent for inventing, licensing, and marketing fanciful consumer products. The CEO found analogous skills in an executive of a successful firm marketing collectibles.

Another director was the head of a food-service concern with its own line of branded perishables for the supermarket deli case. This entrepreneur brought expertise in management of perishable products, new-product development, and distribution, as well as broad food industry knowledge.

The Hardware Chain. This retail business requires many locations and constantly faces new forms of competition, ranging from Sears Roebuck to Builders Square. Yet its structure enables it to realize some economies of scale—through centralized buying, pricing, accounting, billing, and data-processing services. In structuring his board, this business owner looked for analogous expertise among owners of furniture store chains, flower shops, and other similarly structured businesses.

The Training Firm. The entrepreneurial owner of this consulting business found analogous expertise in the founder of a large association-management concern. Each organization provides management services for a wide range of clients. Each business employs a highly paid, mostly female work force to complete custom projects, including publication of training materials for clients. The result: a variety of experiences in common, ranging from personnel management to new-product development.

The training consultant also considered as director can-

didates the chief operating officer of a direct mail firm, the head
of an architectural firm, and a partner in an employee-benefits
consulting firm.

The Publisher. This firm's success rests on producing high-
quality, capital- and labor-intensive projects that can take two
to three years to complete. Yet finishing on time is essential in
order to meet customers' purchasing deadlines. Interestingly,
this company found analogous skills in the head of a major con-
struction firm, for whom finishing high-stakes, capital-intensive,
custom projects on time, and to customers' specifications, is
crucial.

Another characteristic of the business is that it sells ideas
or intangibles, in the form of books, to educational institutions
concerned primarily with quality and user support. The business owner found an executive with relevant knowledge in the
co-founder of a proprietary business school, who coincidentally
served on a public school board as well.

Other possible business analogies identified by this business owner: software producers, producers of training programs,
publishers in noncompetitive markets, pharmaceutical businesses, and professional service firms.

The Industrial Water Supplier. This sales and service business provides purified water to hospitals, laboratories, high-tech
manufacturers, and other industrial settings. The CEO found
analogous skills in the head of a vending-machine concern: Both
install and maintain equipment in customers' plants. Both supply customers on a regular basis and maintain extensive net-
works of truck routes and service representatives who sell to and
service their industrial clients. Moreover, pricing depends heavily on the reliability of service.

This business owner also considered CEOs in the heat-
ing, ventilation, and air-conditioning business. In addition to
the parallels cited above, executives in this industry face yet
another analogous challenge: They engineer, construct, and install equipment for industrial clients. The business owner was
especially excited about the prospect of involving an outside

director with expertise in this area because his company was expanding rapidly in engineering and building pure-water systems from scratch.

Beyond the strategic profile, the business owner may also be looking for peers with experience in general management, ownership, or succession issues. One might seek a CEO who has demonstrated skill in managing third-generation shareholder issues. Another might look for a CEO who has successfully selected and groomed a successor from among several siblings. Still another might seek an entrepreneur who has installed professional management systems in his or her fast-growing company.

What Personal Qualities Do I Want in My Directors?

Once the strategic profile is complete, the business owner will also want to identify some personal criteria for directors. While some desirable qualities may seem obvious, they nevertheless bear some thought before the business owner begins the screening process. Such simple criteria as integrity and courage of conviction can be crucial to a board's success. A desire to learn is an especially appealing trait in directors, and so is a strong team-player instinct. Confidentiality, discretion, and tact often show up on this list as well.

Other dimensions, such as entrepreneurial initiative, may be inherent traits that have been enriched by experience. "A person who has spent his whole career at a company like Ford Motor Company usually has no sense of what it means to be running a $3 million firm," says William Nance, a former Vlasic Foods executive and an experienced director.

The CEO might also seek people who have shown they can sustain a successful family business or people who have thrived in business partnerships. Others might look for directors who are active in political, civic, and social affairs or who have accumulated significant personal wealth. Experience with wealth can yield valuable lessons as well as comfort for the business owner seeking candidates with a similar outlook on life.

Still others may seek a broad age distribution among directors, perhaps to provide young successors with highly successful peers and role models. Others may strive for a balance between people who are primarily rational and analytical and those who are strongly creative and intuitive.

CEOs who have never experienced an effective board might also want to look for people who have served as directors at other successful companies.

At this point, the business owner is ready to state clearly in the board prospectus the qualities he or she is seeking in directors. One CEO cited "development and administration of both direct and indirect sales and marketing forces" and "appreciation for a publishing type business—producing and marketing inventoried product or software from ideas created by authors," among other things, as desired criteria. "Experience as a director" and "active in the community of ideas, leadership, and service" were high on this CEO's list as well.

A test of the success of this document is whether it makes clear to a prospective director why he or she is a candidate. "I know why they thought of me," the candidate should respond. "This isn't just a cold call. I'm a logical person for them to talk to!"

How Will the Board Be Structured?

The third section of the board prospectus should describe the CEO's plans for managing and structuring the board in enough detail that candidates will know what will be expected of them if they make a commitment. This section should outline the structure of the board (or council of advisers), members' compensation, expected time demands, insurance issues, and so on.

What follows is a discussion of the factors affecting board size, terms, composition, and compensation, as well as the frequency, scheduling, length, and structure of board meetings. (D&O insurance and the council of advisers as an alternative to the legal board are discussed in detail in Chapter Four.)

How Many Members?

For many business owners, the first step in structuring an effective board is to shrink it. Ideally, the active board should be kept relatively small, with no more than seven members. In a 1988 survey of 147 private midwestern companies, 11 percent of the respondents urged keeping boards even smaller, with several recommending seven members as the maximum (Ward and Handy, 1988). That echoes sociological research showing that seven is the peak size of most effective groups in order to maximize group dynamics and allow each member to express him or herself. It also helps the CEO reduce the time required simply to manage the board.

At the same time, a board must have a critical mass of at least three outside members, in addition to the chairman or other big shareholders, to be effective. Keeping board size in the four-to-seven member range affords enough flexibility to involve a critical mass of outside directors, in addition to any stockholders who may have to be included.

Many companies find that four members plus the chairman is an ideal board size. Restricting the size to four outsiders at the outset allows the CEO flexibility to add another outside director, should he or she encounter an attractive candidate, without expanding the board too much. Also, if one director should resign or become unable to serve for some reason, the board would still have the critical minimum of three members. Natural attrition — retirement, a move, and other personal events — tends to claim at least one board member every three to four years.

Terms of Service

While most private company boards tend to be structured informally, many experienced CEOs recommend setting formal terms of service for outside directors.

In the midwestern survey, nearly two-thirds of the 147 participants did not set terms for directors. But 7 percent of the CEOs with outside boards urged setting up formal terms, likely in the belief that terms would help in promoting some rotation or change of membership (Ward and Handy, 1988).

The CEO's goal in structuring board terms should be to maintain both freshness and stability. The business owner needs on the one hand to be able to keep the board vital, relevant, and responsive to the changing needs of the company. But he or she also needs to afford directors an opportunity to gain a long-term perspective on the business and a deep acquaintance with its owners and their values, temperament, and goals.

Setting up formal terms of two to three years is useful. This allows directors to become acquainted enough to develop a chemistry, or group dynamic, that can improve the quality of decision making. Directors who have worked together long enough develop a sense of each other's strengths, enabling them to tap each other's expertise efficiently. Effective directors often serve several successive terms.

On the other hand, terms of office induce the CEO to review director performance periodically. They also afford an opportunity to make changes.

The structure of director terms should be made clear to director candidates in the board prospectus. Neither reelection nor rotation should be automatic at the end of the term. Candidates should understand that the needs of the business may change and that the owners may eventually need to bring in new members to reflect changing strategy, business issues, or ownership goals or characteristics.

At the same time, new directors should be asked to serve a minimum of two years. The business owner might explain that while shareholders can obviously replace a director at any time, he or she expects it to take at least two years to get things rolling. The CEO should also make clear that he or she is not comfortable committing to a longer term of four to six years before the board is well established.

The owner should also set a retirement age for directors, probably between 62 and 65 years of age. This gives the business owner yet another opportunity to make a change gracefully. But again, this should not be a rigid requirement that could force premature resignation by an effective director. Instead, it should be a tool for the business owner to use at his or her discretion, to freshen the board or open a slot for a promising newcomer.

Makeup of the Board

The Shareholder as Director. The ideal board consists of only outside directors, plus the CEO as chairman. One or two insiders may supplant the outsiders, but only if they are substantial equity partners. Such a board allows the CEO the maximum possible access to the expertise and support of esteemed peers, as well as a high degree of confidentiality in discussing matters relating to personnel or ownership issues. As discussed earlier, insiders — members of management, shareholders, or even paid advisers — may have an ax to grind, and they are presumably already available to the CEO anyway. The board should offer a new and unique opportunity to gain outside counsel and expertise.

Anyone who is a major stockholder, or who represents a branch of a family with major stockholdings, of course has a right to a seat on the board. These partners in the business cannot be excluded. If ownership is dispersed among several branches of a family represented by four different directors, then outside directorships will probably have to be limited to three or four, in order to keep the board at a manageable size. (Even that number of effective outsiders can have a big influence on the quality of decision making.)

If branches of the family each have substantial shareholdings, voting trusts can be established with designated trustees representing each branch on the board. This can help unify shareholders and avoid politicking and maverick activity by dissatisfied or restless individuals with small holdings.

If ownership is even more fragmented among third- or fourth-generation shareholders, a family council or organization can serve as a mouthpiece for various ownership branches. Another alternative is to make the legal board the vehicle for family members (a structure sometimes called an "asset board"), while organizing a separate council of advisers composed only of independent outsiders to serve the CEO and the business.

Some family businesses have family members as trainees on the board — observers who serve one-year terms as nonvoting board members, with the intent that they will eventually serve as a voting representative of the family on the board. Others create a nonvoting observer slot as a vehicle for one family member to keep the rest of the family informed about board operations. Both of these techniques can serve the dual purpose of building family members' trust and enthusiasm for the role of outside directors, as well as their understanding of the business and its strategy. (All of these issues are addressed in greater detail in Chapter Ten.)

Top-Management Directors. The widespread practice of reaching into top-management ranks for directors has significant drawbacks for the CEO intent on making the most of the board.

First, the presence of senior managers can inhibit board discussion of such confidential matters as succession, management compensation, organizational development, and so on. The presence of management directors also can reduce opportunities for the business owner to be truly candid—to doff his or her "employer" hat and unveil deep-seated doubts, fears, and questions. If the CEO has to resume the role of boss to one of the directors the next day, he or she is likely to want to appear consistently confident, unruffled, and in charge. That deprives the business owner of the chance to luxuriate in the confidentiality and intimacy afforded by the all-outsider board. Instead, the CEO has to make private appointments with outside directors to discuss truly sensitive issues.

While this kind of confidentiality may not seem important to the business owner just setting up an active board, it almost inevitably will become important at some point. Effective directors raise a variety of questions that touch on confidential issues. Discussions of strategy, mission, and commitment raise questions about the business owner's motivation, personal goals, life-style, and vision. The more spontaneous and candid these discussions, the better—for both the business owner and the future of the business.

Moreover, the business owner cannot foresee all the sensitive matters that might arise in his or her personal future. One CEO, for instance, raised with trusted outside directors the issue of his impending divorce as a financial issue. A planned multimillion-dollar settlement to his wife included some stock, raising major questions about the potential cash drain on the company. Discussions of the matter included such creative potential solutions as restructuring the board and the company itself— matters that never could have been addressed if a corporate vice-president had been sitting at the table.

This does not mean that insiders should be excluded from board meetings. The controller or other top executives may be included in most, or even all, board sessions. But management insiders should always be present by invitation; that preserves the CEO's right to ask insiders to excuse themselves when sensitive issues arise. It is invaluable that for at least part of each meeting, no one but directors be present.

What About a Transitional Period?

Some companies prefer to add outside directors to their boards gradually, over a transition period of two to three years. This is particularly helpful in cases where shareholders currently serve as directors. Retaining shareholders' trust and confidence in directors is crucial during the establishment of an active outside board, to avoid creating the perception that they have been forced out or shunted aside. Often, a gradual phase-in process that permits shareholders to interact with and gain confidence in outside directors can make the difference between success and failure.

As a first step, for instance, one company with a large board composed entirely of family shareholders named one trusted outsider to sit in on family meetings. "We decided, 'OK, we want an active board. But we're not sure how it's going to feel to get undressed in front of strangers,'" the CEO says. "'Why don't we tiptoe into this?'" The experiment worked so well that within five years the company had added four outsiders to its board and reduced the number of family directors to three from twelve.

If the presence of management directors is at issue, the solution may be different. If the inside director is near retirement age, the business owner might choose to let him or her remain on the board until that time.

In other cases, though, it is better to tackle the issue directly. Often, the business owner can simply explain to key employees that he or she has decided to change the character of the board, "We want you to be part of this process and to attend many of the meetings, and we want you to become well acquainted with our outside directors," the CEO might explain. "But we have decided to limit board membership to outsiders."

Scheduling Meetings

How Many Meetings? Most private companies find that holding four board meetings a year meets their needs (Ward and Handy, 1988). Issues seem to arise often enough that quarterly meetings are practical. At the same time, the three-month gap gives the CEO a break from board preparation and management without permitting board issues to lapse into inertia.

As a rule, the business owner should not plan more than six meetings a year. Beyond that, directors' discussions tend to overreach into operating matters, which are management's turf. At the opposite extreme, holding fewer than three meetings allows board matters to drift too long.

Many companies have an average of one additional, unscheduled meeting each year (Ward and Handy, 1988). Acquisition opportunities and other major business questions that arise without warning may warrant special meetings. Business owners should be cautious about calling too many unscheduled sessions, however. More than one special meeting a year is a signal that the CEO may be depending too much on the board in everyday decision making.

Many business owners also like to schedule a once-a-year social gathering for the board with shareholders, key employees, and advisers (see Chapter Ten).

Business owners should remember in planning the board calendar that additional events such as plant dedications, employee picnics, lunches, and other gatherings can add to the demands on a director's time during the year. Effective directors typically spend about a half-day preparing for each meeting from materials provided by the CEO and often are on call informally for another half-day each quarter. That adds up to an average of one and one-half to two days of time required each quarter, or an average of about six days a year. Any committees the board forms will further increase the time requirements. All these factors weigh in favor of holding down the number of regularly scheduled board meetings.

How Should Meetings Be Structured? Board meetings typically should run about three to five hours. Most boards cannot accomplish all they need to in less than three hours. At the same time, most groups grow less effective in meetings of more than five hours.

The morning time slot—from 8:30 A.M. until 12:30 P.M., for instance—is usually best for directors, who typically are "morning people" who function best before noon. Many companies serve a light buffet lunch afterward. Managers or family shareholders are often invited to join in these informal meals, a gesture that helps build trust and rapport with directors.

Another important courtesy is to set a departure time and stick to it. If you promise that directors will be free to leave by 1 P.M., they should be able to count on that.

If committees are organized, some companies leave open an hour or so before the full board meeting for their sessions. (Usually, the bulk of the committee work needs to be done at separate, longer sessions.)

Compensating Directors

The amount of the planned honorarium, or compensation, for directors should be included in the board prospectus. That enables prospective directors to know, even before the first meeting with the business owner, exactly what remuneration will be involved in any invitation to serve.

The business owner setting director compensation for the first time should begin with the assumption that he or she cannot pay qualified directors what they are worth. Often, directors come from bigger companies and have already achieved the goals the CEO is still hoping to attain. Most are busy people with abundant other demands on their time.

The CEO should try simply to set a fee that honors the director (thus the term *honorarium*). The fee should roughly reflect the time the director is expected to devote to the company, at a rate similar to what the CEO pays him or herself in salary for comparable time. In other words, board work totaling six days a year would warrant an honorarium equaling about 2–3 percent of the CEO's annual pay.

The honorarium should be high enough that it reflects a significant commitment to the board on the part of the business owner — an investment in the company's future. It also should be generous enough that the business owner will not feel guilty making occasional extra demands on the director's time — to attend a plant opening or strategic planning meeting, for instance.

The fee per meeting, depending on the company and industry, usually ranges from $500 to $2,000 per meeting. Most private companies with outside boards pay directors about $1,000 per meeting, according to the midwestern survey (Ward and Handy, 1988). Assuming a five-member board that meets four times a year, then, total director fees would be $20,000 a year. (For companies with 100 to 1,000 employees, a higher per-meeting payment of $1,500 to $2,000 is probably most appropriate.)

For the medium-sized private company, board costs, including rough estimates of travel, meal, and materials expenses, might be expected to total $25,000–$35,000 without D&O insurance and $50,000–$60,000 with insurance. On the basis of the midwestern survey, the total cost of having a board was $20–$25 per employee per year — probably much less than 0.1 percent of the company's total payroll expense.

While that seems expensive to many business owners, it is less daunting when viewed in light of the $20,000 to $25,000 a major consulting firm would charge for a *single project* — such as a compensation study or an organizational or strategic assessment. With an active board of capable, concerned outside directors, the business owner can reap continuing benefits in all of those areas, and more.

While honoraria can be structured on either a retainer or per-meeting basis, a quarterly retainer usually works best. Presenting a check directly to board members at the end of each meeting, with a handshake and personal thanks, is a gesture that can make many directors feel appreciated. Few are so rich or successful that they do not value receiving an envelope with a $1,500 check inside, a grateful handshake, and a sincere "thank you." Directors should also be reimbursed promptly for any board-related expenses.

Directors should be paid even if they miss a meeting. While some business owners think directors need a financial incentive to come to meetings, that is typically the farthest thing from the mind of the capable board member. Rather, the business owner should try to underscore the directors' role as a consistent resource to the company. This attitude will usually yield rich rewards, encouraging directors to take a sustained interest in the company and to make themselves available to help in a variety of ways.

If directors spend a lot of time in committee sessions, the business owner might consider an additional fee. Most board committees in the small or medium-sized private business meet infrequently. But if a committee begins to assume a disproportionate amount of work, the CEO should respond with fair compensation, perhaps on a per diem basis.

In the midwestern survey, pay for committee work varied widely. The average fee paid per committee meeting was $250, although one-third of the participants paid no committee fee. Larger companies with 500 employees and up typically paid $500 per committee meeting (Ward and Handy, 1988). (Board committees will be discussed in greater detail in Chapter Seven.)

Most small and medium-sized private companies handle directors' honoraria as ordinary income to them for tax purposes. Some, however, set up for directors a deferred-compensation plan enabling them to receive their fees at a specified future date. Often, this enables directors to defer income until after retirement.

Larger companies often augment director compensation with various benefits. Typically, this occurs in firms with more than 500–1,000 employees.

If the company's stock is relatively widely held and liquid, some business owners offer directors the option of taking their compensation in stock or participating in a stock plan for employees. This can offer tax and investment advantages over a direct cash payment.

However, business owners should be aware in presenting such an offer that it can entail some disadvantages for directors. Once offered the opportunity, some directors may feel obligated to take their payment in stock, even though they would rather have cash.

Summary

For many business owners, the benefits of building an active outside board begin even before they contact the first director candidate. Structuring a board requires the business owner to focus more intensely than ever on the most important questions and issues facing the company.

Preparing a board prospectus is the first step in organizing an effective board. This document becomes useful almost immediately in recruiting directors and explaining to shareholders and others your purposes in forming a board.

The introductory section of the prospectus gives a concise overview of the company, including its size in terms of sales and employees, its relative strengths and weaknesses in comparison with its industry, and its major strategic goals or challenges. The second section is the board profile, describing both the personal and professional criteria desired in board members. The third section gives a nuts-and-bolts description of the board structure, time demands, and compensation for directors — all crucial information in the candidate's decision whether to serve. Once this planning process is complete, the business owner is well equipped to begin recruiting and screening prospective directors.

6

Finding and
Selecting Directors

Finding and selecting outside directors is one of the most challenging and rewarding dimensions of building an active board, many business owners say. This chapter is designed for the business owner who has reached that stage. He or she has completed a board prospectus. As discussed in Chapter Five, that means envisioning the board's role in the company, developing a list of criteria for directors, and planning the board's structure and meeting schedule. This CEO is ready to seek out candidates for the board, meet with them, and answer any questions they may have about serving. The ultimate goal: to assemble a group with a wellspring of experience relevant to the business owner's needs.

The process is much like hiring an important employee. "The whole key is getting what you need, just as if you were a manager filling the weak spots in your division with quality people," says John Honkamp, president and owner of Hydrite Chemical Company, a Milwaukee-based chemical concern. The major difference is in the way you might *reject* a candidate, as discussed below.

This chapter will offer guidance on whom to consider for the board. It will describe some subtleties of the search, including mapping a desirable age or gender distribution among directors and dealing with fears of rejection or error. It will discuss

121

how to approach candidates and make selections. Finally, the chapter will offer a closer look at how one business owner, mentioned briefly in Chapter Five, assembled his board, and what results he yielded.

Beginning Your Search

"Whom do I leave off?" is the first question many business owners ask in establishing an active outside board. "How can I possibly include on my board all the deserving candidates — my customers, my suppliers, my old friends, my banker, my accountant, my lawyer, my family, my vice-president for sales . . . ?"

The answer: Leave them all off.

Politics, bolstering egos, repaying debts, conveying thanks, rewarding performance, satisfying interest groups — ideally, none of these factors should play a role in selecting directors. Instead, the CEO should design the board with one purpose in mind: to meet the needs of the company, as well as the needs of the CEO as the leader of the business.

Let us look at the strengths and weaknesses of various kinds of outside board candidates:

Competitors. Competitors or potential competitors should *never* be directors, because of their obvious conflict of interest. Directors of competitors should be ruled out, too; the law prohibits "interlocking directorates," wherein the same people serve on the boards of competing companies.

Another risk of seeking directors within the industry is that the CEO reduces his or her chances of breaking out of traditional industry thinking — something the CEO already knows well. The business owner should seek fresh perspective and new insight from directors, not an affirmation of what he or she already knows. As discussed in Chapter Five, the best place to find such insight is often in different industries facing analogous challenges and problems.

Consultants. Paid advisers are not usually good candidates, either. The services of these professionals are already available to the business owner, and they bring to the board room an inherent conflict of interest.

"These people work for you. They're not the right people to challenge you," says Richard Kent, an entrepreneur and experienced director. The CEO can always invite trusted advisers to attend board sessions and treat them with as much respect and appreciation as they deserve. But it is usually not necessary to make them directors to reap the benefits of their knowledge.

Some business owners find it pays to make exceptions for advisers who have broad exposure to top executives of a wide range of businesses. These professionals often develop executive skills and can be a valuable resource, even if they lack experience starting or running a company. Paid advisers should not dominate the board, though.

Friends. Trusted friends usually are not good choices as directors, either. Friends are harder to find than directors, and their advice and counsel is usually freely available anyway. Why jeopardize a good friendship by subjecting it to the stresses of the board room?

"One reason I stalled in creating my board was that I couldn't decide who among my friends I would ask to be on it," says Alfred McDougal, chairman of McDougal, Littell and Company, a publishing concern in Evanston, Illinois. "Finally, I decided not to ask any of my friends, and I think that was a good decision. I can see that leading to tension."

Another business owner faced a dilemma after naming a longtime family friend to his board. When the business owner asked the director to step down after several years to permit him to bring some fresh perspective to the board, the director called him the next day.

"Henry, I couldn't sleep last night. I was hurt," the director told him. "I've been with the family all these years. Do you mind if I sit in the back of the room at the board meetings and just listen?" This awkward and painful situation led the CEO, against his better judgment, to retain the director.

Charles A. Hoch, president of Parco Foods, a Blue Island,

Illinois, foods concern, recommends "a board of strangers. You shouldn't pick people just because you golf with them and they're successful."

Retirees. Another common temptation among business owners is to focus on retirees as candidates. After all, many retirees are highly visible and available and have abundant experience. But while retirees can be excellent directors, the CEO should be cautious in overusing them. One risk, of course, is that many retirees eventually lose touch with the mainstream of business.

Another is that directorships can become too important to the retiree. If holding seats on corporate boards is a major source of ego support and stimulation, the retiree can become so fearful of losing the directorships that he or she grows too timid and too eager to please. This compromises the independent contribution the retiree might otherwise make and amounts essentially to a conflict of interest.

Academics. The CEO shold be equally cautious about packing the board with representatives of nonprofit institutions. In some cases, people from universities, schools, charities, think tanks, or other organizations can be excellent directors. Arguably, they also tend to be more available than corporate CEOs. Nevertheless, the performance-driven business owner runs a risk in enlisting someone without experience in a profit-making organization.

People Who Hold Other Directorships. Candidates who already serve on several boards are risky recruits. First, the business owner may find him or herself in a position of having to compete for that person in the marketplace of director fees. Most owners of small and medium-sized private businesses are not eager to enter that competition.

Second, the appeal of the learning opportunities afforded by board membership dims for the person who already serves on several boards. This also increases the chances of rejection.

Other CEOs, Entrepreneurs, and Business Owners. As discussed earlier in this book, "risk-taking peers," in the words of

Léon Danco, a leading family business consultant, often make the best directors. People from larger private companies who have weathered the crises or surmounted the hurdles that still lie ahead for you are the best candidates of all.

These candidates bring to the board room none of the conflicts of interest or weaknesses associated with other kinds of candidates. More important, they offer unparalleled experience, perspective, and empathy for the business owner.

However, the business owner should avoid any CEO on whose board he or she serves and any CEO who holds a directorship that overlaps with their own on another board. Overlapping directorships risk compromising the director's independence and creating an incestuous situation. If a director has in the back of his or her mind the relationship with the CEO as a director on his or her own (or another) company's board, that director may temper his decisions and comments to protect that other relationship.

Division Heads. Heads of divisions or subsidiaries of big public companies can be good directors. But as a rule, the business owner should avoid functional vice-presidents, such as heads of marketing or research. If marketing expertise is a criterion for directors, for example, then find the CEO of a marketing-driven company!

Aim High

Above all, the business owner should set high standards in the search for directors, seeking out the very best people he or she can find. The CEO should think of the ideal board as a panel tailored to his or her needs.

Solar Press, a Naperville, Illinois, printing and direct mail concern, named as a director Jerome Stone, co-founder and chairman emeritus of Stone Container Corporation, the $6 billion packaging concern, among others. "We wanted people who had wisdom from years spent at companies much bigger than ours, who had gone through things they could share with us to prevent us from making some serious mistakes," says Frank Hudetz, president of Solar Press.

The CEO of one company with a generous employee stock-purchase plan did not feel he was reaping the potential benefits associated with employee ownership, so he sought out as a director another CEO with a long and successful track record with such plans.

Another business owner contemplating the eventual sale of his company named two directors who had already started, then sold, their companies. The CEO of a high-tech chemicals manufacturer recruited as a director the foremost scientist in his company's field.

Another CEO wanted to explore joint ventures and acquisitions. For help, he sought out as a director an entrepreneur who had sold his family commodity-foods business for $100 million and reinvested in several successful new ventures with stronger growth prospects. Now the director is helping the CEO identify targets for investment or acquisition.

How Do I Find Candidates?

One of the best ways to begin networking for board candidates is to ask for suggestions from all those people you *left off* the board.

Customers, suppliers, friends, bankers, lawyers, accountants, and consultants can all be valuable sources of referrals. A letter with the prospectus enclosed is a good way to ask for help.

Members of professional associations, including the Young Presidents Association, chapters of the Executive Committee, and other CEOs' groups can be helpful as well. The National Association of Corporate Directors in Washington, D.C., maintains a list of director candidates.

Other CEOs scan regional listings of the 50–100 largest public and private corporations and consider CEOs of those organizations. Most metropolitan or regional business publications and newspapers carry such listings from time to time.

The business announcement section of the local newspaper can be helpful as well, particularly reports of changes at the board and executive level of corporations in your area.

Perhaps most important, the business owner should not be discouraged if appealing candidates do not surface easily. Finding directors who are at once trustworthy, unbiased, and highly qualified is "a tough job for a private business owner," says Clayton Mathile, president of the IAMS Company, a Dayton, Ohio, pet food manufacturer.

Using a Search Firm. Search firms can be helpful, and a few conduct director searches regularly. The CEO should be prepared to pay the equivalent of one year's director's fees for the service.

Some business owners value search firms because they can act as third-party recruiters, making it less awkward for both a candidate and the business owner to break off discussions if one party is not interested.

In practice, search firms are rarely used to find directors. A 1988 survey of privately controlled midwestern companies showed that of seventy firms with outside directors, only 9 percent used search firms to identify director candidates. Executives at 77 percent of the companies selected directors who were personally known to them, while 14 percent made contacts through other business owners or professionals (Ward and Handy, 1988).

The Nominating Committee. For many CEOs, making the first round of board picks is a once-in-a-lifetime experience. Once a board is established, a nominating committee of directors can handle future candidate searches. While some companies include the CEO or, if ownership is dispersed, a representative shareholder, on the nominating committee, others restrict membership to outside directors. (The committee's makeup and functions are discussed in more detail in Chapter Seven.)

Subtleties of the Search

No matter how carefully the business owner may have considered the criteria for directors listed in the board mission statement, some additional and more subtle criteria may warrant some thought at this stage.

The Age Factor. Some CEOs seek a particular age distribution on the board. Many CEOs who have chosen a successor like to have as a director at least one person in that person's
age group, to provide a role model or peer. A balanced age distribution, including directors in their forties through sixties, can
also lend freshness, perspective, and continuity to a board.

Al Hoffman, owner of H. Hoffman Company, a Chicago
locksmith supply business, constructed his board as a bridge
over "the generation gap" between himself and the next generation of managers in his family business — his son and two daughters who are working in the company. Among his three outside
directors, one is a male about Mr. Hoffman's age with accounting, marketing, and family business expertise. Another is the
young female chief financial officer of a family business. The
third is the CEO of a larger, family-owned wholesale distribution firm in another industry, who is between Mr. Hoffman and
his children in age. His children were deeply involved in selecting
directors and had veto power over his choices.

The board members also provide a philosophical bridge,
as Mr. Hoffman sees it. He intentionally selected directors he
believes will be more progressive than he is. He thinks their
philosophies will harmonize better with his children's. "This
board really is the kids' board," he says.

Gender and Cultural Representation. Some business owners seek directors who mirror the gender and cultural patterns
of their shareholders or employees. This serves to represent
different perspectives on the board. It also makes a statement
about corporate identity and values, sending a signal that the
company values diversity and will give power to socially less
enfranchised groups.

A service firm with a large number of professional female
employees might seek women directors with similar backgrounds,
for instance. A company with ownership concentrated in the
hands of family members might seek directors with an understanding of family business. But CEOs should be aware of the
risk of unwittingly creating a constituency board, in which individual directors feel an overriding loyalty to certain shareholders, employee groups, or other constituents.

If the head of a family business places an experienced family business owner on the board, for instance, there is a risk that family members will seek out that person as their special representative. In such cases, the director should be perceptive and strong-minded enough to stress his or her attentiveness to the interests of all stockholders, and to the company as a whole (see Chapter Nine).

The U.S. Senate provides a useful analogy. Like senators elected at large from each of the fifty states, the directors' duty is to represent the interests of all corporate shareholders at large—not of interest groups, family branches, individuals, or other constituencies within the company.

Covering Crucial Areas of Expertise. Striking a balance among directors with various backgrounds is another subtle but important factor in building an effective board.

If the CEO has identified one or more crucial areas of expertise for directors, such as marketing or research and development, he or she should probably recruit at least two people with some expertise in that area. That provides an insurance policy that all or most aspects of the field will be covered and that some expert input will be available at every board meeting. A CEO who is taking his business overseas, for instance, might want two of the three to five outside directors to have international expertise.

The business owner should avoid overloading the board with people of similar backgrounds, however. The goal should be to assemble a group with complementary, not equivalent, experience.

"A board that functions well usually has people with complementary professional skills," says Bernard Hale, a vice-president of Bergen Brunswig Corporation of Orange, California, and an experienced director. "The directors shouldn't all be in the same profession and competing with each other to be the most brilliant person in the field."

Help for the CEO Lacking Board Experience. The CEO who lacks experience with an active, outside board might consider recruiting one person as a kind of facilitator or board manager, particularly in the first few years of the board's operation. That person may or may not be a voting director. But he or she should have broad experience with board operations, a working knowledge of board management details, and an ability to tactfully and discreetly guide both the chairman and the directors toward the common goal of a well-functioning board.

The corporate secretary or outside legal counsel, or perhaps a business partner, can sometimes serve this role. In other cases, a professional adviser or consultant is a candidate. If the facilitator is receiving a consulting fee, of course, he or she should disclose that fact at the first meeting of the board, to make clear to other directors the potential conflict of interest.

The Importance of Board Experience for Directors. People who have served on other boards, or who have outside boards of their own, are often the best director candidates. Ideally, at least two directors will have such experience, particularly in cases where the CEO has not been exposed to active boards before. As well, the business owner should also seek people with at least some experience on the boards of profit-making organizations. A background with the boards of nonprofit organizations or financial institutions is often less helpful, as discussed earlier in this book.

Dealing with Fears of Rejection or Mistakes

Any CEO approaching truly worthy board candidates is almost certain to have some qualms. "Why would these top-flight people want to serve on *my* board?" the business owner may wonder. Or, "What if I choose the wrong people?"

In practice, rejection is not very likely. As discussed earlier, many people relish the opportunities afforded by membership on an active, vital board. (This is most true of people who do not already serve on more than one board.)

Often, CEOs are willing to participate for the learning experience and enjoyment. "CEOs serve on boards for the same reasons they want other CEOs on their boards: to be part of a community sharing the same problems and looking for solutions. The information exchanged at a board meeting can be just as useful if it is someone else's board as if it is your own," wrote George Melloan, an editorial writer for the *Wall Street Journal* (Melloan, 1988).

Most business owners are flattered when another CEO approaches them and says, "Look, our business is facing these challenges over the next several years, and I know you've been successful in these areas. I think you can help me." In fact, the odds that a candidate will accept an offer of a directorship are usually better than 50-50. Contacting candidates through mutual acquaintances or friends of friends increases the odds of their accepting to around 75-25.

Here is how John R. "Ted" Kennedy, an experienced director and the retired head of a division of Federal Industries of Manitoba, Canada, explains those odds: "The reward is the thrill of participating. You get satisfaction from associating with a company and its officers, and with the other board people. There's a pride and a challenge to it. You learn something every time you handle a different situation."

Also, he says, "I've done pretty well in business, and it's nice to feel you're repaying the business community to some extent. I feel it's my responsibility to help younger managers and small companies. I feel I'm just furthering the whole free enterprise system to a degree. . . . And lastly, you can really become attached to the owner of the business. There's a great deal of personal satisfaction in helping him achieve his personal dream and vision."

The business owner who takes care in selecting his or her first outside board should not worry too much about getting a lemon, either. In practice, the likelihood of recruiting someone who fails to make a contribution is very low. The midwestern survey of privately controlled companies showed that only about 1 percent of directors were replaced each year because the CEO was dissatisfied with the board member. Over a ten-year period, the 147 companies surveyed had replaced only 68 directors — from a pool of 565 directors in all (Ward and Handy, 1988).

How to Approach Candidates

You have done the hard work of preparing to approach candidates, and you have a long list of prospects. What is the next step?

A letter of introduction is usually the best way to make the first contact. The letter should include at least a brief statement of your purpose and plans, including the fact that you are interviewing a number of people as candidates and have in mind several criteria for directors that meet the needs of your business. This lays the groundwork for a clear understanding by the recipient that he or she is a *candidate,* not the recipient of an offer.

The board prospectus (described in Chapter Five) should be enclosed with the letter. It serves as a kind of job description for the director candidate.

The letter should be followed by a phone call to arrange a meeting, typically over lunch. In either the letter or the first conversation with the candidate, the business owner should give a brief explanation of why he or she is interested in the candidate. "Our mutal friend John Smith recommended that I meet you. I know you have led your company to some tremendous successes in Europe, and that's a market we're interested in entering soon," the business owner might say.

The business owner should be careful throughout these initial contacts to use the word "candidate" rather than "director," to avoid creating a misimpression among recruits that their selection is automatic. The CEO might explain, "We're interviewing about eight people to try to find a mix of candidates whose backgrounds complement each other and serve the needs of our business. We'd like to get to know you better and give you a chance to know us. Can we have a meeting?" This approach opens a door at the outset to terminating the discussions without an offer.

A visit to the candidate's business can provide helpful insight. You might offer, during the first phone call, to meet the candidate at his or her office; if a tour is offered, accept! Meeting at your own place of business is a good alternative, to give the candidate a similar opportunity. (The candidate should visit the corporate headquarters, and perhaps another major facility, at some point during the selection process.) Least useful is meeting at a neutral location, such as a restaurant; that way you pass up a major chance to learn more about each other.

At the first meeting, either the CEO or a companion selected to help (such as a professional adviser) should take a few minutes to introduce him or herself and the company, to describe the objectives of the meeting, and, if appropriate, to explain how he or she came to contact the candidate. Candor can help the get-acquainted process along. "I'd like to share with you some of my thinking about the problems we face," the CEO might tell the candidate. After a summary of some issues, the CEO might ask, "How does this compare with your experience?" The response will speak volumes about the candidate's ability to provide helpful insights.

Asking questions about the candidate's own business can help put him or her at ease. The answers will help demonstrate the resources this person might offer as a director and allow you to gauge his or her candor.

Many CEOs also like to describe at this first meeting the expected role of the board in relation to the CEO. The business owner might make clear, for instance, that he or she does not intend to abdicate management responsibility to the board. The directors will not be held accountable or made to feel responsible for decision making, but their advice and opinions will be highly valued.

The CEO probably should not progress to a second meeting with a candidate unless he or she is fairly sure of making an offer. As discussed a little later in this chapter, the CEO should have cross-checked the candidate's appropriateness with at least one third party, and the CEO should be comfortable with the relationship. Protracted talks followed by a "no thanks" can create hard feelings. Also, by the second meeting, the business owner should feel comfortable sharing more financial data and business details, to give the candidate a clearer picture of the board issues that lie ahead.

Some CEOs wonder how hard they should try to sell an attractive candidate on a directorship. It is appropriate to do some selling, partly because most candidates want to be persuaded. Your proposal may be a foreign concept to most candidates, and you may need to help them overcome concerns about the time commitment required, their legal liability, and so on. The business owner should probably be cautious in selling the board too hard, though, lest he or she succeed in recruiting someone who truly lacks the time, interest, or commitment to do the job well. The business owner should also scrupulously avoid creating any sense among candidates that they are in competition with each other.

Consulting Other Acquaintances

Checking out candidates is a crucial part of the search process. The business owner should not rely solely on a primary referral. He or she should seek out other individuals who know the candidate well and ask for more information. Again, the more candid the CEO can be in these conversations, the better. As demonstrated by the case study below, third parties typically respond in kind.

The cross-checking process is one reason board selection can take several months or more. It requires identifying mutual acquaintances who have had personal or business association with the candidates and contacting them in an unhurried moment for a confidential talk. But it is one of the most important ways to avoid mistakes in the board selection process.

Making the Final Selections

In screening director candidates, the business owner above all should be both comfortable with and proud of his or her choices. Some of the most important qualities to consider are also the simplest. The candidate should evince integrity, above all. He or she should be able to maintain confidentiality in all dealings.

"I wouldn't want a director who might be an excellent business person but not share our business ethics," says Nan-b de Gaspé Beaubien, vice-chairman of Telemedia, a large family-owned media concern based in Montreal. "That is a very important point for us."

The chemistry must be right. No matter how appealing a candidate's background or experience, the CEO should reject people with whom he or she simply does not feel any affinity. Even if you cannot articulate your nagging feeling that a person is not quite right, trust your instincts and go with the feeling.

The candidate should show candor, an eagerness to learn, and a lively interest in the business. He or she should demonstrate a courage of conviction, a readiness to say what he or she believes. The candidate should also demonstrate the kind of personality that can be effective in a board room setting—an ability to be a team player, for instance.

"You can't have somebody on the board who is going to speak their mind in an arrogant, 'I know better' way. That will never fly" in most private companies, says Mr. Honkamp of Hydrite Chemical. "The director has to have people skills. He has to be able to get his point across, but in a tactful manner, so that everybody feels like falling into step."

Depending on the business owner's tastes, desires, and needs, other qualities may figure into the final decision as well—anything from family values or creativity to status and wealth.

The Veto Concept

The CEO should be especially cautious in this first round of director selections that all key shareholders are comfortable. Important family members or shareholders should be involved in board selection. The veto concept should apply here: If a shareholder or family member is not confident from the beginning that a candidate will be a good, trustworthy director, then the CEO should reject that candidate, without grilling the shareholder or family member on his or her reasons. The process works a little like jury selection, and it helps ensure that the new board will begin on a positive footing.

At the same time, the CEO should guard against letting the selection process deteriorate into a contest among various constituencies. This can yield a constituency board, with each director feeling a sense of responsibility to a particular shareholder group. This setup can cause major problems in the event of a shareholder dispute.

Sometimes, the business owner can designate a trusted associate or outsider—a consultant; a director; an accountant, attorney, or banker—to act as an objective facilitator for the board-selection process to ensure that everything goes smoothly.

How to Say No

Many business owners worry about how to say no to candidates they have rejected. Indeed, this dimension of building a board probably differs significantly from most things the business owner has done before.

As mentioned before, the CEO should be careful not to let the screening process go too far unless he or she is strongly interested in a candidate. It would be a mistake, for instance, to set up more than one meeting with a candidate or ask him or her to your buisness to "meet the family" unless you were fairly sure that you wanted him or her as a director.

When the time comes to say no, the best approach is to emphasize the goal you mentioned at the outset of the screening process: to select a complementary group of people with a mix of backgrounds and expertise to match the needs of your business. If the candidate does not meet the needs of the business at the moment or complement the group you have assembled, that is no reflection on his or her merit. The business owner might explain, for instance, that he or she has selected other directors because they had abilities specific to the problems the company will face in the next two to three years.

At the same time, the CEO should express appreciation for the candidate's talents and experience, enjoyment at getting acquainted, and thanks for the time the candidate has spent. If appropriate, the business owner might also mention his or her eagerness to stay in touch or to work together in some capacity in the future.

What If I Make a Bad Choice?

Despite the favorable odds mentioned above, people sometimes make mistakes in selecting directors. Errors usually do not become clear immediately. It typically takes a year or two for a business owner to conclude that a director simply is not making a contribution.

Once mistakes are discovered, most business owners act promptly. The midwestern survey showed that most CEOs replace a director when they become dissatisfied, however uncomfortable that process may be. Almost every CEO who perceived a problem reported having removed the director deemed in need of replacement (Ward and Handy, 1988).

Most CEOs find the best way to deal with mistakes is to approach the candidate directly and ask him or her to step down. Sometimes the business owner can explain to the director that the needs of the business are changing and skills and background different from his or her own are now needed on the board.

Other times, the CEO needs to say more directly, "Look, I really appreciate your contribution, but I just don't feel this is working out as we had planned. Please understand my appreciation for all that you have done."

In other cases, business owners have sought the help of professional advisers in remaking their boards, particularly if more than one director needs to be removed.

Case Study: Variety Vending

Let us take a closer look at how the business owner mentioned in Chapter Five, Kenneth Nowak, and his brother Donald, co-owner of the business, assembled an outside board.

When Mr. Nowak, the second-generation president of Variety Vending and Food Service Company, a family-owned vending concern in Warren, Michigan, began his search for outside directors, he had his objectives clearly in mind. He wanted to assure the rest of the family — including his brother and the nine third-generation Nowaks in their twenties and thirties — that management succession at the company would be handled "in an arm's length manner, with the objective input of outsiders," he says. He wanted to communicate to the company's 200 employees "that there would be opportunities in this company, whether your name was Nowak or not."

Finally, he felt he needed the discipline and accountability of a board. "I needed to step back and look at the big picture and stop getting caught up in the day-to-day problems," he says. "We've been in this business thirty years, and the skills that got us this far aren't the same skills we need to continue. I knew the discipline of an outside board would help us make the transition [to a more professional management]."

He approached the task of recruiting directors with extreme care. "It's just like hiring a key employee. If you choose the wrong one, you're going to have difficulties all the way along the line," he says.

With the help of a professional adviser and some reading on the subject, he had identified criteria for board members. First, he wanted people with entrepreneurial experience, either as CEOs of their own companies or as decision makers in family-owned businesses. "That means they've either sweated through these issues and can comfort us while we're doing it, or they've already invented the wheel so we don't need to reinvent it," Mr. Nowak says.

He knew he wanted independent outsiders who could lend perspective and objectivity to complex family business issues.

He also wanted people with some experience in contracting with individual industrial clients. "In our business, every customer contract is unique to itself. It's a little like building custom houses," he says. "One customer wants to keep prices in our vending machines low, while another wants to know how much money per square foot he can make from them. We had hoped to get somebody who was familiar with that type of thing."

He also resolved questions about structuring the board. Among other things, he considered and rejected the idea of asking outsiders to serve on a council of advisers rather than a legal board. "I originally was concerned that the quality of people I wanted might be apprehensive about liability and maybe would be more receptive to serving on a council of advisers," he says. "But I researched the legal aspect, and I became convinced that there wasn't a whole heck of a lot of difference in liability exposure. Also, I concluded that the type of person I want wouldn't be comfortable serving as an adviser. He would want to serve as a director.

"I decided I didn't want to play any games. I was looking

for a board of directors, and I didn't want to diminish those people's self-perception or their image in the eyes of anyone else in the company, either."

Then, Mr. Nowak cast his net wide to identify good candidates. "I sent letters to banks, accounting firms, insurance people, and a couple of law firms I deal with, explaining what we were doing and why, and what type of person we were looking for. I asked them if they knew somebody who might be a candidate," he says.

"I didn't get a lot of response, but I got some," he says. While he did not know any of the candidates personally, "I heard about people who were doing some fantastic things."

He begins the process of screening with a series of interviews. To prevent misunderstandings, "I intentionally used the word 'candidate'" in speaking to prospective directors, he says. "I told them, 'Your name has been suggested as someone who might be of interest to us in meeting our objectives. I'd like to sit down with you and see if this might interest you and whether I feel you'd bring to us the background we're looking for.'

"Everybody I asked," he adds, "said yes."

Throughout the screening process, he trusted his instincts. One candidate seemed a natural on paper. His business had several parallels to Variety Vending, and he was integrating into his company a new generation of family managers. "I thought, 'Boy, this is a natural fit. He's living through all the problems we face,'" Mr. Nowak says.

But when he met the candidate, the relationship did not work. "He was pleasant and willing, but I just felt something was wrong. The chemistry just wasn't right," Mr. Nowak says. He thanked the candidate graciously and eliminated him from consideration.

When he had winnowed his list to a few people, Mr. Nowak sought out third-party acquaintances. He was very open with these contacts, explaining his own needs, the family's goals for Variety Vending, and the qualities he was seeking in directors. "The information I got was unbelievable," he says. An acquaintance of one of his current directors, he recalls, was particularly gracious. "He said, 'From what you've told me, you're really going to work well with this guy,'" Mr. Nowak recalls.

The prediction has proven true. The eighteen months Mr. Nowak invested in planning, recruiting, and inaugurating his outside board was time well spent, he says. His four outside directors have expertise in managing much larger family businesses, contracting with industrial customers, operating family partnerhips with successor generations working in the company, and professionalizing management, among other things. In its two and a half years of existence, the board has made major contributions to the quality of decision making at Variety Vending and gained the respect of the next generation of Nowaks as well, he says.

"We're talking with the board now about our vision of the future and the changes we need to make to accomplish those things," he says. "Having these people as a resource gives me great emotional comfort."

Summary

Identifying and selecting directors for an active outside board can be both stimulating and challenging, and the process may take several months to complete. Most business owners find it best to eliminate from consideration many of the first candidates who occur to them — lawyers, bankers, friends, consultants, suppliers, customers, and so on. Instead, the CEO should aim to recruit risk-taking peers — fellow business owners, entrepreneurs, and CEOs, preferably from larger private companies, who have already surmounted many of the hurdles that still lie ahead for the business.

The business owner should cast a wide net in seeking candidates, networking with a wide variety of acquaintances and professional associates, consulting listings of regional businesses, or even using a search firm. While many CEOs fear rejection, the odds are surprisingly high that worthy candidates will accept an offer of a directorship. Also, the chances of making a bad choice are quite low, with only about 1 percent of outside directors replaced each year.

Candor and thoroughness throughout the selection process can greatly improve the chances of success. A cross-check of candidates' qualifications with mutual acquaintances is a must. Above all, the business owner should trust instinct, or chemistry, in the selection process and give top priority to his or her own needs and the requirements of the business.

7

Managing the Board

For John Honkamp, naming outside directors for his family-owned chemicals concern led to "a whole different mind set" in managing the board. In the past, Mr. Honkamp planned for meetings of the inside board "maybe a week in advance." Now he begins assembling the board agenda more than a month ahead of time and reviews it as often as weekly, paring it to the most important issues.

"About two months before each meeting, we have a tentative agenda, a working document," he says. "We limit it to our top priorities. We want to make sure we use these people as wisely as possible in that day and a half they're in town." A sense of the preciousness of this new resource — a board of carefully chosen, experienced outside directors — settles on many CEOs as they prepare to organize and manage their boards. This chapter is designed to help in that task.

Many business owners are surprised to learn that the CEO has significant latitude under the law to focus board attention on matters of greatest concern. Above all, the business owner should structure the board to ensure efficiency and clarity of purpose. That means managing all aspects of the board's operation, from the agenda to the meeting schedule, with an eye on the highest and best purposes possible for directors.

This chapter offers suggestions for the business owner designed to help directors do their jobs in an atmosphere of trust and confidence. It provides information on board organization, including forming and managing committees. And it offers practical advice on running the first meeting, keeping in touch with directors between meetings, and evaluating and promoting the board.

Advance Planning

Typically, business owners spend one to two hours of preparation time for every hour spent in session with the board. More important than the amount of time spent, though, is the quality of the time. If board planning becomes too routine, with sales forecasts and reports on operating performance consuming every agenda, it is a signal that the CEO is not making the most of the board.

He or she should take time to reflect on each agenda, deliberating on ways directors can be of most help to the company. It is often helpful to remember that there are few laws on board room procedures, and there is no need for the CEO to behave as though constrained by elaborate protocol. As discussed in Chapter Three, the business owner has significant latitude, particularly in the private company, to allocate the board's time to useful topics.

To that end, developing an effective agenda alone can take at least three to four hours. For some business owners, the agenda for a future board session becomes a disciplinary tool that they review as often as weekly.

The business owner should also allow time to prepare a succinct, quarterly "CEO's letter" to directors, updating them on important developments. He or she also needs to allow time to plan and review other advance meeting materials, including the chief financial officer's quarterly letter, if there is one. If topics are to be presented to the board by individual managers, the business owner should also prepare those people and review their presentation plans.

Where Should Meetings Be Held? While many CEOs' tendency is to schedule meetings at corporate headquarters, non-
company locations have some big advantages.

Holding board meetings "off campus" reduces the chances
that the chairman will be interrupted in midsession. It also
affords privacy and security, erasing the possibility that employees will overhear (and perhaps misunderstand) the board's
deliberations.

A burst of laughter from the conference room, for instance,
might lead some employees to conclude that the board is just
a social club. Or a worried look on the face of a CEO taking a
bathroom break might be construed as a harbinger of trouble.

The presence of directors at company offices and plants
does have benefits, as mentioned later in this chapter. But in
most cases, the advantages of a neutral, off-site location outweigh those benefits.

Schedules and Topics. Meetings should be scheduled well
in advance, with the next calendar year's sessions set at least
by October of the previous year. Another popular method is
to take time at each meeting to schedule the meeting twelve
months hence. This ensures a running schedule of regular meetings that is always complete at least a year in advance.

Many business owners also find it helpful to do some
agenda planning on a full-year basis. This allows efficient management of some of the formal duties and responsibilities of the
board.

One company, for instance, included as part of its yearly
board-meeting schedule a summary of plans for disposing of
several board topics. At the June meeting, the CEO scheduled
a review of regular board responsibilities, including insurance
coverage, pension plan performance, election of the general
counsel, progress on a succession plan, and so forth. Review
of the following year's operating and capital budgets and officer
compensation was set for the November meeting. The annual
audit was assigned to the March agenda.

This schedule served two purposes. First, it allowed efficient handling of most of the board's legal duties in a single meet-

ing, which was carefully planned to cover routine topics quickly. Second, it left completely free a midyear meeting, in August, for one of the most important and potentially creative functions of the board: a review of the strategic plan. (Please see Exhibit 2.)

Exhibit 2. A Sample Schedule of Yearly Board Meeting Topics.
Proposed Board Meetings and Agenda

Quarter	Date	Regular Business Topics
1	3/8	Audit Committee (total board) with accounting firm
2	6/4	Review of regular board responsibilities (pension performance, insurance, general counsel, succession, and so on)
3	8/26	Strategic plan review
4	11/28	Review of operating and capital budgets, dividends, and officer compensation

Many CEOs also find it helpful to set aside time at one meeting a year to allow directors to ask nagging questions or to suggest topics and issues that the board should address in the future. As discussed later in this chapter, the business owner can use the same technique to gather directors' opinions on how well the board itself is functioning.

Preparing the Agenda. The quality of the agenda can have a great impact on the quality of board deliberations. When properly prepared, the agenda can be not only an organizational tool to keep discussions on track and on schedule but an advance planning device to help directors come to meetings prepared. A helpful rule of thumb to keep in mind in preparing the agenda is the "80-20 rule": the tendency among most groups to spend 80 percent of their meeting time on the first 20 percent of the agenda.

Many CEOs make the mistake of putting reports and background sessions at the top of the agenda. This can allow board discussion to bog down in reviewing the latest quarter's performance or the soaring postage bill, leaving inadequate time for the critical issues at the end of the agenda. Another mistake is to organize items in a way that forces directors to sit back and listen for prolonged periods of time.

A better approach is to start the meeting with the most important issues. Then, at the end of the meeting, the CEO can schedule a half-hour to field questions on recent performance and other more routine matters. As much of this routine information as possible should be distributed to directors in writing *before* the meeting. Often, this data can be handled succinctly in the quarterly letter from the CEO or chief financial officer, as explained below. In the author's experience, reporting on past performance can be limited to 25 percent of the total meeting time, leaving about three hours at each meeting for a discussion in depth of one or two critical issues.

Many business owners also find it helpful to make the third or fourth item on the agenda an optional or slack topic. This affords the flexibility to skip it during the meeting if the earlier, more important items take more time than planned.

Exhibits 3 and 4 offer examples of imaginary good and bad agendas. In Exhibit 3, "Too Typical Company" presents a sleepy late-afternoon session loaded with routine reports and vague generalities. In Exhibit 4, "Different Company" has put together a very specific document that weights agenda items according to their importance and offers directors a lot of help in planning for the session.

As the Different Company example also shows, a good agenda includes several kinds of very specific information to help guide board discussions. First, a specific amount of time should be assigned to each major item, to let directors know in advance whether a topic is to be addressed in depth. This technique has the added advantage of allowing all board members to watch the clock and share the responsibility of keeping the meeting on schedule.

Second, the agenda requests specific responses of directors when appropriate. Sometimes, a CEO might only want directors' first impressions of a key manager after he or she makes a board presentation, to help in evaluating that employee's potential. Other times, the CEO may want a firm decision by the board on whether or how to proceed. Alternatively, the chair-

Exhibit 3. An Ineffective Board Agenda.
Too Typical Company
Board of Directors Meeting 4–6 P.M.

Agenda

1. Call to Order

2. Approval of Minutes: Board of Directors Meeting
   February 28

3. President's Report   Jim Carrier
   a. The acquisition effect on our first quarter
   b. Personnel review — salaried and hourly
   c. Profit sharing — planning update
   d. Board dates — July and October

4. Planning Report   Dick Almers
   a. Results of first quarter versus goals
   b. Update on current planning efforts

5. Sales and Marketing Report   Peter Groden
   a. Recap of first-quarter activity
   b. Review of current situation

6. Financial Report   Larry Carrington
   a. First-quarter financial results
   b. First-quarter cash flow analysis
   c. Long-range cash flow forecast

7. Annual Engineering Report   Jim Forbes
   a. Update on equipment
   b. Governmental affairs — environmental
   c. Future planning

8. Adjourn to Dinner

man may be asking for new ideas, help in deciding among existing choices, or simply a chance to inform the board. Making the goal clear on the agenda, as a subpoint under the item listing, can be very helpful to directors, who need and appreciate this kind of leadership from the chairman.

The agenda should also give information about the type of discussions directors should expect. Will the CEO be promoting "a lengthy open discussion" of the topic, or does he or she just plan "a brief informational update" with few questions expected from the board?

Major, open-ended topics should include some leading

Exhibit 4. An Effective Board Agenda.
Different Company
Board of Directors Meeting
8 A.M.–12:15 P.M.

Agenda

8 A.M.	I.	Introduction to Management Team — continuing
		A. Presentation by Bill, manager of Northside location — please review his biography
		B. Questions of Bill from board
		C. First impressions — reactions from board on Bill's presentation (Bill excused)
8:45 A.M.	II.	Owners' Brief Informational Update on Items of Interest
		A. Ongoing activities
		B. Operations performance
		C. Financial performance
9:15 A.M.	III.	Status Report on expansion into Phoenix and Southwest market — some preparation materials forthcoming
10 A.M.		Break
10:15 A.M.	IV.	Lengthy Open Discussion of Joint Venture Opportunity — some preparation materials forthcoming
		A. Brief update
		B. Board members share related experiences and opinions
		1. How do we think about form of shared business relationships?
		2. What personal financial risks and guarantees should we be willing to take?
		3. How do we live with outside business partners in shared enterprises?
11:45 A.M.	V.	Review of Quarterly Information Packet Format — any suggestions
12 P.M.	VI.	Schedule for Future Meetings — please bring calendar
12:15 P.M.	VII.	Adjourn to lunch with Charles Carroll, executive vice-president, and my daughter, Suzanne

questions as subpoints, to help guide directors' thinking before the meeting. These questions can also help directors seek out other sources of information before the meeting, if they choose.

Third, the agenda may include stage directions on when visitors to the board session will be excused. After a presentation by a manager, for instance, the agenda may note that the manager will be excused following a question-and-answer session. Again, this helps directors ask the right questions at the appropriate time.

Finally, the agenda may offer information on whether additional background materials will be made available at the meeting, or whether directors should bring with them any personal resources, such as their calendars for the coming year.

Who Should Be Invited? As a rule, only directors should expect to attend every meeting of the board, as well as any permanent secretary to the board.

The spouse of the business owner might be a frequent or even a regular guest, and top managers, lawyers, accountants, professional advisers, and other family members can be invited as often as the CEO pleases. Most private companies frequently invite nondirectors to attend meetings. The chief financial officer, sales and marketing executives, operations heads, and the outside lawyer are most commonly asked (Ward and Handy, 1988). But in most cases, the CEO should not permit any nondirector to assume that he or she will attend all board meetings. This preserves his or her latitude to take up highly sensitive or confidential matters with only directors present — a pivotal opportunity afforded by the outside board, and one that should be maintained if at all possible.

Helping Directors Prepare: The Board Background Book

Directors must depend on the business owner to help them get the information they need as efficiently as possible to do a good job. Here is a summary of the major means used by most business owners to accomplish that: the board background book.

The board background book is a comprehensive, professionally presented summary of important information about the business. While compiling the book can take some time, the business owner's investment of care and effort is usually greatly appreciated by the directors. In many ways, it reflects the CEO's eagerness to help the board get off to a running start and fulfill its promise.

The board background book should be handsomely bound

(for example, in an attractive, three-ring company binder) and organized as clearly as possible. The book should be provided to directors well before the first board meeting, to give them time to assimilate its contents. Exhibit 5 provides a comprehensive, section-by-section outline of materials recommended for inclusion in the board background book. All items might not be appropriate for all businesses, of course, and some CEOs might choose to include additional sources of information. The notebook should be roomy enough to allow directors to add their own sections — for minutes of board meetings, for example.

Exhibit 5. Outline of Board Background Book.

---

1. *Mission Statement, History, and Strategy*
   a. Preamble and Board prospectus.
   b. Brief, one-page history of business, including any good trade publication profiles or articles written recently.
   c. One- or two-page explanation of strategy, how company makes money, industry structure, and some key industry trends. (Include summaries of the economics of the industry, the value-added chain, or the product life cycle, if available.)

2. *Who's Who*
   a. Organizational chart of the company showing names, titles, ages, years with company, number of total reports. Possibly include total number of employees and any available demographics on them.
   b. Chart showing ownership of stock, amount of stock, buy-sells, value, and so on. Business valuation; any trustees and their legal role. Brief paragraph noting what happens to the stock of key owners in their estates.
   c. List of duly elected officers and their level and form of compensation.
   d. Your family tree, including in-laws, divorces, ages, employment, and educational backgrounds.
   e. List of key advisers, including lawyers, accountants, insurance agents, investment advisers, family trustees, bankers, and organizational consultants; with firms, addresses, telephone numbers, and length of service.

3. *Biographies*
   a. Key executive biographies in one or two paragraphs each, including current roles and responsibilities, past work and educational experience, ages and years with company, family situation, industry and professional associations, and personal hobbies and interests.
   b. Directors' vitae as requested and received from them.

4. *Competitors, Vendors, and Customers*
   a. List of top three to ten competitors and a brief description of their ownership, size, ways of competing, and so on.

Exhibit 5. Outline of a Board Background Book, Cont'd.

b. List of top three to ten vendors, what is bought from them, and about how much per year.

c. List of top three to ten customers, what they buy from company, and about how much per year.

d. If available, a map of the United States showing where company does business, where it is concentrated, and where it has locations, salespeople, and so on.

5. *Financial Information*

a. Very efficiently presented one-page, five-year profit-and-loss statement, especially in percentages.

b. On the same page, possibly a current-year budget and/or coming-year pro forma budget.

c. Simple balance-sheet items here or on a separate page, highlighting receivables, cash, inventories, fixed assets, payables, debt, and equity.

d. A one-page summary of financial and/or operating statistics such as return on investment, return on equity, real sales growth, number of employees; perhaps inventory turns, gross margin, sales per salesperson, product development budget, percentage of sales from new products and/or programs, and so on.

e. A one-page outline of sales per product-market category over several years, perhaps including development costs per category, gross margin, and so on.

6. *Audit and Estate Valuation*

a. Most recent year's audit.

b. Maybe employee stock ownership plan or insurance or estate valuation, especially funding formulas and redemption requirements.

7. *Budget*

a. Current year's budget.

b. Perhaps an example of most recent year's managerial financial report, showing the form the company uses.

8. *Articles, Bylaws, Indemnification*

a. Articles of incorporation and corporate by-laws.

b. Copy of director indemnification and/or legal letter and/or insurance coverage.

9. *Other Information*

a. Union status, including background on any votes, affiliations, and so on.

b. Corporate insurance coverage.

c. Result of any asset appraisals.

d. Notation of litigation pending or expected; legal letters if appropriate, specifying exposures and status.

e. Real estate or office space owned or leased, and terms and values if not clear in audit.

Exhibit 5. Outline of a Board Background Book, Cont'd.

---

    f.   Any employment contracts, stock options.
    g. Any dividend information.
    h. Pension fund information and trustees.
    i.   Any lending covenants or contingent liabilities.
    j.   Any particular corporate contributions (political, charitable, and so on).

10.   *Board Agenda*
    a. Outline of proposed dates for next four or five meetings.
    b. Perhaps a mention of key board duties at each meeting, such as audit report, capital budget, and so on.

In addition to the items listed in Exhibit 5, the business owner might consider including succinct summaries or diagrams of certain key business patterns or ratios. The goal here, again, is to orient directors as efficiently as possible to the workings of the company.

There are three types of summaries that directors might find useful. The *"economics of the industry" model* brings the industry alive in the minds of directors by describing the nature of the business through numbers. It provides a general industry profit model or financial profile, laying out average ratios and explaining what they mean. It should include such facts as the percentage of sales typically provided by each type of product, the average term of receivables, the gross margins on sales, and so on. For instance, a wholesale wallpaper distributor might report that sample books are typically 6 percent of sales and return a 2 percent profit margin. Receivables tend to run sixty days because most sales are to mom-and-pop stores, and gross margins in the industry are typically 30–35 percent.

Value-added chain traces a typical transaction in the industry from beginning to end. It describes how contacts are made, how time is spent, and how employees are utilized, all in terms of average success rates or sales. For instance, the CEO of an industrial supplier of water-purification equipment might explain that his or her salespeople typically spend two weeks making twenty calls to get one appointment. Every ten appointments might lead to an average sale of $50,000. Then it might take an average of two weeks and two person-hours to install equipment at each location, and an average of an additional ten hours of labor each month to maintain the equipment. These numbers might even be refined further into average conversion rates per dollar spent or person-hour worked. For instance, a $40,000-a-year salesperson might be expected to generate $300,000 in new sales.

The *product life-cycle picture* explains the role of new products or services in the company's overall business and describes the typical life cycle of new offerings. A business owner might report, for instance, that 30 percent of sales comes from new products in a typical year. Each product might take two years to develop at an average cost of $100,000. Its average life span might be five years, with gross margins narrowing from 33 percent to 10 percent over that period as increasing competition emerges or price-sensitive customers delay purchases.

Keeping the Board Informed

The board background book should provide directors with as much essential information as practical. This helps ensure that as little valuable meeting time as possible will be spent on disclosure of the basic information necessary to help directors do their job.

Nevertheless, the business owner should review key kinds of information, both before the first meeting and periodically, to make sure that he or she is keeping directors up to date. Exhibit 6 offers a checklist of important kinds of information that should be supplied to the board and regularly updated.

Exhibit 6. Information That Should Be Supplied to the Board.

- Articles of incorporation
- Bylaws
- Ownership of stock and stock options
- Any corporate disclosure documents
- Biographical data on all directors
- Biographical data on key executives
- Key advisers and length of service
- Corporate policies and procedures on conflict of interest and legal compliance
- Role of corporate counsel in such policies and procedures
- Current problems, prospects, critical issues

Exhibit 6. Information That Should Be Supplied to the Board, Cont'd.

- Top competitors, suppliers, and customers
- Planning documents and studies
- Relevant long-range forecasts and plans
- Information on issues involving any outside constituencies — consumer activists, community groups, regulators, legislatures — in management summary form, with any conclusions or recommendations
- Investment bank analyses and other professional reports
- Insurance coverage
- Tours and inspections of company
- Current operating and capital budgets
- Organizational charts
- Pension fund information, including trustees
- Litigation pending or expected
- Results of audit
- Number and form of legal entities associated with the corporation
- Any business valuation or asset appraisals
- Dividends
- Business owner's will
- Succession plans
- Employment contracts
- Other covenants
- Union contracts and history
- Real estate or office space owned or leased
- Lending covenants or contingent liabilities
- Major corporate contributions, either political or charitable
- Sales by product and/or line and/or market

Also, directors should visit all major company plants or facilities frequently, preferably once a year. The CEO should try to give board members a working knowledge of smaller facilities, such as minor distribution outlets, as well, perhaps with a single visit to one example. These tours help directors get a sense of the nature of the business and its work force. Plant visits can also help inform directors about environmental, morale, and employee safety issues.

A secondary benefit, of course, is the effect on workers at outlying locations. Employees often feel honored and excited by the presence of outside directors and go out of their way to present a good image.

These tours can be especially helpful if the board is weighing questions about building, expanding, or consolidating facilities. If a plant tour is relevant to a major agenda issue, it might be scheduled at the beginning of a regular board meeting. Otherwise, the tours might be scheduled right after a regular board meeting, or perhaps the afternoon before a morning meeting, with a dinner for directors afterward.

Many CEOs find it helpful to allow time over lunch or dinner for a debriefing session after the tour, to gather first impressions from directors. Often, these reactions can bring new perspectives or insight to the business owner. Directors should also be encouraged to stop by company locations if they happen to be traveling in the area.

Notifying Directors of Meetings

Regularly scheduled board meetings may be held without notice. The assumption, of course, is that they have already been approved by directors in the form of the board's meeting calendar, as discussed earlier in this chapter. Many business owners, however, find it helpful to send directors a brief, two-sentence regular-meeting reminder three weeks to one month before each session. This is an optional safeguard to protect everyone involved from oversights or scheduling errors.

The board chair and any others so empowered in the bylaws can also call special meetings. In most states, at least two days' notice of the date, time, and location is required. The notice can be written, oral, or both, although oral notice alone should be documented in the official board minute book. Special notice for regular meetings is required if certain business transactions are planned, such as changing the corporate bylaws. These conditions are specified in the corporate bylaws and state law.

Some companies require directors to let the chair know whether they will be attending the next meeting. The board secretary is the best person to handle these replies, as discussed below.

Preparing Advance Meeting Materials

Like the agenda, the preparatory board packet can greatly influence the quality of the time directors spend together at each meeting. Directors should receive the agenda and any background information, the letter from the CEO and/or chief financial officer, and quarterly financial statements about five to ten days before each meeting. These letters should include a concise update on facts and issues discussed by the board. They might update directors on the company's financial performance compared with projections, as well as on key operating ratios, market performance, and capital expenditures. Drafts of resolutions for board consideration and other material that may need board approval can also be included.

Most business owners include minutes from the latest meeting in this mailing so directors can review them and offer any corrections. Some CEOs like to send the minutes sooner after the previous meeting, however, while directors' recollections are still fresh.

Ideally, the packet should arrive before the weekend preceding the meeting; that gives directors time over one weekend to review it. It also allows time for the director to gather information on major agenda topics, if he or she so chooses. Sending preparatory materials much earlier is not very useful as most board members will typically set such materials aside for a few days if they arrive too far in advance of the meeting.

Organizing the Board

This section offers guidance on some basic organizational questions that may arise before the first meeting or during the board's early months.

The Importance of a Quorum. The absence of a quorum, or the minimum number of members required to transact business, seldom becomes a problem for the small private company board. Usually, the number required for a quorum is set by state law or the corporate charter or bylaws. It is typically one more than half the directors, or a simple majority.

Ideally, the business owner should try to arrange meetings so that everyone can attend. This is easier if boards are kept to seven members or less. If one member simply cannot be available because of a prolonged business trip or other development, most CEOs go ahead with the meeting. If more than one member of a board of four to seven directors is unavailable, the session should probably be rescheduled. On larger boards with a mix of insiders and outsiders, many CEOs simplify the scheduling process by making the presence of all outside directors the primary goal.

The Role of the Board Secretary. Ideally, a trusted and capable administrative aide or executive secretary to the CEO can serve as secretary to the board, taking minutes, preparing advance materials, and handling other organizational matters. In some companies, the board secretary also presents routine matters to the board for action.

This person can handle other record-keeping duties. This should include mailing advance meeting materials and maintaining a meeting file with a record of advance materials sent to directors, including the preliminary agenda, meeting notice, lodging arrangements, and so on. The board secretary should also keep track of which directors can attend upcoming meetings and which cannot.

The next best person to handle minute-keeping duties is the board facilitator, if there is one. As discussed in Chapter Six, this person serves either as a consultant to the board or as a director and helps manage board operations and guide board discussions in a productive way.

In the absence of such a person, one director — preferably an inside director, such as a shareholder or manager — can be assigned the task. Or, all the directors can serve in turn, preparing the minutes for a year and then handing the duty on to another director. (The one-year rotation allows each director to get used to the job.) If the general counsel is present at all meetings, that person can keep the minutes. (The general counsel typically maintains the official board minute book.) Occasionally, a business owner's spouse who attends board sessions as an observer is a willing and capable candidate for the job.

The worst choice is the CEO. He or she should remain free during each meeting to focus on the discussion and set the pace and tone of the agenda.

During the meeting, the person charged with preparing the minutes should note the following:

- The time, place, and date the meeting was called to order by the chairman and the names of all directors and other persons who were present
- The motion to approve the previous meeting's minutes, and, if appropriate, a motion to waive reading of the minutes
- Acknowledgment of the attainment of a quorum
- The times at which various people entered and left the room during the meeting
- The names of people who made reports and a summary of the reports
- Actions taken and the outcome of votes, including who voted for and against a measure and who abstained (on important issues, the reasons for dissents and abstentions should be recorded)
- Any conflicts of interest acknowledged by directors, and any abstention from discussions and votes involving any conflicts of interest
- Agreements or consensus reached during the meeting, as well as other items received or discussed
- The amount of time spent on very important issues, as well as a summary of important advice offered by professional advisers and any evidence of advance preparation by board members
- The motion to adjourn and the time of adjournment

Keeping the Minutes. Federal and state laws do not set forth any particular requirements for board minutes. Companies' minutes vary widely in form and style as a result. Some take only a skeletal record, just meeting the legal requirements for documentation of board decisions and director votes. A motivating factor here is often the fear of legal action, because official board minutes can be used as evidence in cases involving board actions. Other business owners simply want to preserve secrecy and resist any more disclosure of information about the company than is legally required. "What if competitors ever get hold of the minutes?" they worry.

Increasingly, though, many companies prefer to create a more complete, "living record" of board deliberations, including insights and unanswered questions that arose during the meeting and the pros and cons that were considered. While these business owners are aware of the worries cited above, they reason that thorough minutes of most board sessions are likely to do more to ease suspicions than inflame them. They do not include in the minutes sensitive competitive information such as secret product formulas, of course. And they assume that in the unlikely event that a clever competitor gains access to the board minutes, any financial and market goals disclosed therein probably would not surprise the competitor much anyway.

These owners tend to view each new session of board deliberations as a benchmark for the company with significant archival value. Board minutes can serve a greater purpose than simply proving that directors discharged their duties; they can also provide valuable discussion summaries that can be recalled for help in making future decisions and plans. Directors can also use them to refresh their thinking before discussions of continuing strategic issues. Such a record can have great value in maintaining strategic momentum and continuity.

Some boards find a middle ground by creating both a skeletal set of legal minutes and a complementary set of more detailed notes on the meeting, to be reviewed by the CEO (and perhaps the other directors as well).

One factor in deciding the character of the board minutes should be the audience. Board minutes can be a valuable tool in building trust and rapport between directors and shareholders or family members. If these key people receive only a skeletal set of minutes, they may wonder what is being left out! On the other hand, the minutes should be held to a reasonable length, with unnecessary detail eliminated for these readers.

On balance, many business owners lean toward creating more complete minutes as a useful communication tool. The establishment of an active outside board is often a first step toward greater openness and professionalism in management, and these CEOs believe board-meeting documentation should reflect that attitude.

Drafts of the minutes should be reviewed by the corporate counsel and the chair and presented to directors at the next meeting for corrections. Most companies also ask for board approval of the minutes. Board minutes should be kept on record permanently.

Official Resolutions. The law does not set forth guidelines for using formal resolutions. However, most boards consider them appropriate in at least the following instances:

- on matters permanently regulating management;
- on establishment of board committees and their responsibilities;
- on dividend declarations;
- on real-estate matters;
- on any amendment to the corporate charter or bylaws; and
- on any matter that requires a formal resolution according to the law, charter, or bylaws.

Forming and Managing Committees. Most boards in small to medium-sized private companies do not find it necessary to organize committees. If a matter calls for committee action, it can usually be handled by the board as a committee of the whole — especially in boards of four to seven members.

For larger boards, or boards of companies that have several hundred employees or more or are planning to go public, however, committees can be useful. The most common kinds are audit, compensation, and nominating committees. Executive, finance, strategic-planning, and human-resources committees are more rare. The board chair appoints all committees and committee chairs.

Most committees in smaller firms can do their work in one meeting a year, perhaps holding a windup meeting for an additional hour before a regularly scheduled board session. The committees then communicate with the full board both orally and through written minutes. The person assigned with preparing committee-meeting minutes should take the same notes as suggested earlier for the board secretary.

The role and authority of various board committees differ from company to company, and the law does not set specific committee requirements. Most states limit committees' authority, however; many prohibit committees from undertaking such actions as amending the bylaws, declaring dividends, authorizing the issuance of stock, or adopting an agreement of merger or consolidation.

Here is a summary of the usual role of a few of the most common kinds of board committees (American Bar Association, Committee on Corporate Laws, 1978).

The *audit committee* should be composed of independent outside directors. Its job is to recommend and review selection of the company's outside auditors and to review the auditors' report. This group should also review with the independent auditors the adequacy of internal controls, as well as any major changes in the company's accounting practices. It is useful for this committee to explore with the auditors the strengths and weaknesses of the company's financial function, as well as how the company can reduce audit fees by being better prepared for the auditors.

The *executive committee* can be empowered by state law and corporate bylaws to exercise the full powers of the board between meetings, with certain exceptions, including those mentioned above (American Society of Corporate Secretaries, 1986). The executive committee often is assigned such tasks as fixing officer compensation, authorizing long-term employment contracts, appointing the general counsel, and executing legal documents. It has special responsibility for all executive matters and can determine questions of general corporate policy. It can sometimes authorize and sign checks, notes, and contracts on behalf of the corporation, and it often designates corporate depositories and persons authorized to withdraw funds.

The *nominating committee's* job is to recommend candidates to fill vacancies on the board and sometimes to identify desirable criteria for board membership. It may also be asked to take a special interest in succession issues, recommending a successor to the CEO or other senior managers. Some nominating committees set emergency succession procedures in the event the CEO should become unable to serve. The members of this committee should be selected for their objectivity and lack of family or business ties to top management. However, some companies do permit the CEO to serve on the nominating committee.

The *compensation committee* is usually charged with ensuring that compensation is competitive and appropriate to the company's strategic and human resources objectives. Management directors should be excluded from the compensation committee, since it periodically reviews the annual salary, bonus, and other benefits for the CEO and other senior managers. This group can also be asked to review management perks and supervise pension and benefit programs.

The role of the *planning committee* varies widely from company to company. Many help conduct functions central to the entire board's mission, such as reviewing mission statements and strategies and monitoring the company's progress in light of those plans.

Running the First Meeting

The first meeting of a newly constituted board can be both an exhilarating and a nerve-wracking experience for the business owner. For many, it poses new challenges in self-expression and interpersonal relationships.

Several special measures can help ensure a good start for the board. First, it is helpful to allow an extended social session of a half hour or so before the meeting, to allow directors to meet and talk informally over coffee, juice, and rolls. The business owner's spouse, or perhaps one or two other key shareholders or family members, might be invited to this pre-meeting session as well.

The first agenda item should usually be a brief recap by the business owner of his or her purposes in setting up the board. The business owner should also introduce each director briefly, going beyond the biographical data in the board background book to explain the special expertise each person brings to the table. The CEO at this point should also express his or her pleasure at having each director on the board, conveying personal appreciation for each person's unique potential contribution.

"Jim has introduced new products at a tremendous rate at his company, and he has built an outstanding track record over the past ten years. We can't wait to learn from his experience," the CEO might say. Or, "Mary runs a highly successful company that faces many of the same consumer-marketing challenges as ours. Her professional management style is admired by smart businesspeople all over our region, and we feel fortunate to have her on our board."

At that point, the business owner might ask directors to say a little about their own backgrounds, why they are serving on the board, and what they hope to gain from the experience.

This meeting also affords a valuable opportunity to glean first impressions from knowledgeable outsiders. Some CEOs find they can learn a lot from their directors' reactions to the board background book. Their responses to the array of data presented there can highlight problems or differences that can lend new strategic-planning insights.

"I was really surprised by the fact that marketing and promotion costs in the women's apparel business have been increasing more than 10 percent a year for the past five or six years," a director might note. Or, "I didn't realize that the product life cycle in your business is shortening so dramatically; that must be putting tremendous pressure on your research and development budget."

Business owners should not hesitate to consider a variety of get-acquainted techniques at this meeting. A videotaped plant visit with employee interviews, a multidepartment presentation of the life cycle of a product, or a drive around company locations in an executive van might be enjoyable and helpful for directors. The goal should be to convey, as efficiently as possible, a flavor of the business.

Another get-acquainted item can be a discussion of a topic that is likely to get everyone involved. One approach is to ask each director to talk about how he or she sees the world and the economy changing over the next two or three years as it relates to his or her own business. This usually leads to a discussion of key issues, and it can uncover some common ground and begin building affinity among board members.

Following the meeting, the business owner might consider

inviting a larger number of key people to join the directors for lunch — perhaps as many as five to ten family members, top managers, professional advisers, and others.

Between-Meeting Communications

The quarterly information packet sent before each regular board meeting is usually the major communication between directors and the company between board meetings.

Ideally, directors should also receive some nonroutine communication from the company between meetings, although this is not always possible. Sometimes, a simple note of appreciation after a particularly successful board meeting is greatly appreciated by directors. The point of staying in touch is not only to keep the director informed but to stimulate thinking about the business, alerting him or her to prospects and ideas that might be relevant.

The business owner should also feel free to consult directors occasionally between meetings for advice and counsel, to update them on an important issue, or to invite a director to a private lunch. It is usually best to stop short of involving directors as advisers to internal management meetings, however. While a board member might sit in on an occasional meeting to observe or contribute to a brainstorming session, he or she should not be made to feel like a part of management.

Usually, major developments can be covered in the CEO's quarterly letter to directors. But any special or unusual event might prompt a call or note to directors. Three straight months of record sales or the successful recruitment of a top-flight manager might be examples. By the same token, anything that damages the long-term health of the company — such as a significant worsening of labor-management tensions or the loss of a major lawsuit — should be communicated to the board.

Employee or customer newsletters and major press releases should be sent to directors as well. Many directors also appreciate a subscription to the industry trade magazine and, if relevant, a copy of the company catalog, major advertisements, or promotional materials.

Evaluating and Changing the Board

The quality of the board's performance should be a continuing concern for the business owner. He or she can use several disciplines to stay abreast of the issue.

It is often helpful to hold informal, individual sessions with each director at least once every two years to ask, "How are we doing?" This permits the board member to offer suggestions privately, as well as any hints that the group or its individual members are not performing as well as they should. The business owner should listen carefully in these sessions for tactfully stated criticisms, such as, "Of course, Henry spends an awful lot of time talking about the need for a new computer system." This may translate into a general lack of respect for that director, a factor that can seriously hurt the whole board's functioning.

Second, as mentioned earlier, many CEOs open up an hour to an hour and a half on the board agenda once a year to discuss the quality of the board experience. "Is the board meeting your expectations?" he or she may ask. Or, "What can we do to help make this a satisfying experience for you?" While this group discussion will be less free than private conversations, it can offer valuable insight into the general direction of the board.

Third, some business owners employ consultants, either on a sustained or one-time basis, to help them evaluate their boards. This can be particularly helpful if the board seems stagnant or troubled. An industrial psychologist, organizational-development expert, or other management specialist has the advantage of being able to interview directors confidentially to glean a sense of how the board's functioning might be improved.

Although some CEOs use formal self-rating or peer-review systems, in which board members confidentially evaluate each other, many business owners do not find these techniques very helpful or even appropriate for directors.

If a director needs to be relieved of his position, the CEO probably should simply take responsibility for the decision, rather than falling back on criticism by peers as an excuse. While removing a director can be an uncomfortable process, it is also

probably best to do it the hard way — by approaching the director in as straightforward, appreciative, and empathic fashion
as possible, and delivering the message.

"Thank you for your service," the business owner might
say, "but the needs of the business are changing in such a way
that I'm looking for another director with different skills and
experience. I hope you'll understand my gratitude and appreciation for your contribution of the past two years."

Promoting the Board

The business owner can begin promoting the board even before directors have been selected.

Networking for candidates with the board prospectus is
the first step in informing important people, both inside and
outside the company, of your plan and the reasons behind it.
Lenders, lawyers, accountants, professional advisers, friends,
customers, suppliers, and others can be helpful, as discussed
in Chapter Six.

Some business owners explain their board plans at a companywide meeting, emphasizing meaningful values and goals —
such as assuring the continuity of the company, lending accountability and discipline, challenging established ways of thinking
to help the company compete more effectively, and so on.

Once directors have been chosen, employees and shareholders should be informed of their identity, backgrounds, and
board mission through internal newsletters, bulletin boards, an-
nouncements by top managers, or other means. Some companies also announce the selection of new directors through news
releases and photographs for local newspapers, trade publications, or customer newsletters.

Again, lenders, professional advisers, lawyers, accountants, employees, suppliers, and customers — almost anyone who
maintains an important relationship with the company — should
be included in any public information effort. The annual social
gathering with directors, key family members or owners, and
professional advisers can be helpful as well.

Attendance by one or more directors at company picnics

and ceremonies, such as plant dedications or anniversary celebrations, can improve the board's visibility. Some directors might also speak occasionally at management meetings if they are comfortable doing so, addressing such topics as trends in consumer markets or raising questions about organizational responsiveness to the marketplace. Such activities can aid morale by reminding employees that an esteemed, experienced group of outsiders respect and care about the company and its constituents enough to serve on its board.

Informing all of a company's constituencies about the board and its mission from the beginning, in an open and positive way, is crucial in establishing a positive long-term image for the board. That can only increase its effectiveness in enhancing corporate relations on all fronts.

Summary

Careful planning with emphasis on the most important issues facing the company is crucial to the success of the board. The board agenda, advance meeting materials, meeting schedule, and other board communications should all be designed to guide the board toward its highest and best use, including ensuring the continuity and strategic success of the company.

Few organizational requirements are set forth in the law for boards of directors, leaving the CEO considerable latitude in guiding board discussion toward the matters of greatest concern to the company and its owners. The business owner should structure the board, from the minute-taking process to committee formation, in a way that will ensure efficiency and clarity of purpose and reflect the values of the company's owners.

The CEO can take several steps to help directors do their jobs effectively, from providing needed information to encouraging positive and trusting relationships with key people in the company. Using the special talents of board members to the fullest is one of the best investments of time the CEO can make.

Part Three

HELPING THE BOARD MEET ITS POTENTIAL

8

Making the Most
of Your Board

For the head of a midwestern metals foundry, tightening government regulations were creating a real problem. Environmental
safety standards for making leaded brass kept changing so often
that it seemed he was constantly spending money on new pollution control equipment — scrubbers, filters, containment devices,
and so on. None of the spending contributed to the bottom line.
Moreover, he was wasting a lot of time worrying about the government's next move. Should he invest even more heavily now to
try to satisfy government requirements once and for all? Or should
he hold off in hopes that the cost of pollution control technology
would drop? Depressed, frustrated, and unable to see a way out
of the trap, the business owner took the problem to his board.

His directors began chipping away at the issue, and an idea
novel to the business owner emerged. Have you thought of changing raw materials, abandoning the lead that causes so many pollution problems? they asked.

"Well, we could substitute silicon for the lead," the owner
responded. Silicon brass was a higher-quality, more pleasing
product than leaded brass. But only his largest, most elite competitor used silicon; most of the industry thought of themselves
as commodity producers and stuck to traditional lead. "Silicon
is just too expensive," the owner added. He had never thought
of his own company competing in that market.

Gradually, directors stripped away some preconceptions. How did the larger firm get by? they asked. By charging more for a higher-quality, more desirable product, the owner answered. If customers of the larger firm paid more for silicon brass, wasn't there a good chance that his customers would too? Moreover, wouldn't that solve the pollution control dilemma once and for all?

The result: a higher-quality, more pleasing product for the foundry's customers, and a dramatic easing of the pollution control burden for the company.

For many CEOs, working with an active outside board is a new experience that poses unforeseen rewards — and challenges. Every board meeting can be an adventure, an exploration of the unknown. The spontaneous interaction of experienced business owners, entrepreneurs, and managers facing common questions can spark insights and ideas gratifying to all involved. The result may be breakthrough thinking — a contribution that strips away burdensome preconceptions and often transcends the capability of any individual board member.

"I've never seen a group of people get off to such a running start in my life!" Kenneth Nowak, owner of a family vending concern, says of his outside board. To his surprise, directors engaged each other in a lively debate at their very first meeting, he recalls. "There's synergy there, no doubt about it."

Yet managing this kind of peer interaction does not come easily to many business owners. For the entrepreneur accustomed to being in charge and largely unaccountable, a board room where directors ask tough questions and make novel suggestions about the business can be strange and threatening turf.

This chapter takes a close look at how a CEO can help a board function at its greatest potential. It offers insight into the new psychological and emotional challenges the business owner can expect in facing the board. It provides suggestions for sparking productive and creative board room discussions. And it describes some early warning signs that can help the CEO realize that his or her board may be underutilized or floundering.

The Value of Breakthrough Thinking

The effective outside board draws on a unique and powerful resource: a shared eagerness among members to tackle tough problems and solve them. Often directors working together can achieve creative or innovative solutions to problems that no individual member would have generated alone, proving the maxim that the whole is greater than the sum of the parts. Many CEOs, of course, strive constantly to achieve such creativity in management. What is so special about breakthrough thinking at the board level?

Consider the case of one family-owned consumer food business. The company had accomplished the difficult task of passing the CEO's job from the aging founder to his son, with the help of a succession transition team composed largely of outside directors. But coming up with a new job description for the founder was proving almost as hard. He was a charming, energetic, hands-on manager who had carved out a reputation among consumers as a producer of high-quality branded goods.

In keeping with past management practices, when the CEO's title passed from him, so did the accompanying visibility and public relations role. So far in the transition, the founder had been functioning as a sort of internal champion of quality, teaching employees the value of the company's high standards and overseeing quality control. But the transition team was not satisfied. The founder was such a potent force that his presence in an inside role was interfering with his son's freedom to run the company. His current job was not preparing the company for the inevitable — a future without him. The quality control people were not learning to work independently. Nor did the job take advantage of his value as a public symbol.

After hours of spirited and sometimes frustrating discussion, the transition team hit on a novel solution: Create a unique new outside role. Why not enhance the future value to the company of the founder and all that he stood for by building on his already powerful image in the consumer market? The founder might burnish the company's image, for instance, by sponsoring public-service and charitable campaigns on food-related issues. He might do cross-product advertising for other high-profile concerns. The company might even open a museum named after him and stuff it full of corporate lore and memorabilia from the founder's entrepreneurial adventures.

The result: a plan that delighted and energized the founder, built on the company's formidable reputation, and left the son free to operate the company!

The combined energies of this group broke through the thinking patterns that had prevailed in the food concern's management for years. Similarly, the group dynamic of the board room has unparalleled power to shatter the toughest stereotypes or prejudices, freeing management from preconceived notions that may hinder performance.

One board was so impressed with a business owner's board-room profit analysis that members persuaded him to make the same presentation to employees. To do that, the reluctant CEO had to overcome his own innate reticence, as well as a decades-old tradition of secrecy at his family-held firm. But the result was a new excitement among workers about the company's future — and a lasting commitment by the CEO to a new openness in management.

The chemistry of an effective board is a potent prescription for other ailments, including the depression that sometimes takes root in the isolation of top management.

One entrepreneur, discouraged by an industry shakeup and the untimely exodus of his son from the business, decided that his twenty-year struggle to grow the company just was not worth it any more. He told his outside board that he wanted to sell out, and his directors began helping him shore up management and organize financial data.

But the more the business owner shared his heaviness of spirit with directors, the more he recovered his own excitement and commitment. Ultimately, with the directors' encouragement, he decided to keep the company and share more of its equity with top management and an employee stock ownership plan. "What I'm doing here really has value, and it ought to work," he told his board. "And no one out there is going to appreciate it as much as we do!"

Breakthroughs like this are priceless — and often unattainable to even the most capable CEO alone, no matter how long he or she agonizes over the problem. How does one create the kind of board-room climate that encourages breakthrough thinking? Let us take a closer look at several techniques used by effective CEOs to make the most of their boards.

Monitoring Your Own Attitudes Toward the Board

The challenge to the business owner is to unleash the collective power of the directors' thinking. This can require some self-disciplines new to many CEOs.

"The chairman makes the board what he wants," says a director of one private company. The owner "throws everything out on the table, and the three of us really work at it. He just rolls . . . he's fearless. As a result, we have come up with ideas as a group that none of us would have individually."

That kind of candor, many experienced directors agree, is a powerful catalyst to effective board operations. Let us take a closer look at this and other attitudes shared by many effective board chairmen.

The Importance of Being Open. Making the most of the board demands a degree of openness unfamiliar to many business owners. It often requires bending management traditions dictating that "you just don't divulge" information about matters of concern, one owner says.

"If the business owner really thinks about it and takes an inventory of what he's worried about, those are the things he has to talk to the board about," adds Clayton Mathile, president of the IAMS Company, a Dayton, Ohio pet food manufacturer. No matter how sensitive the issue, "he's got to tell the board." Adds Mr. Nowak, the vending-concern owner: "It's paramount to let your blemishes show, so your directors can really understand you and help you."

A prerequisite for this kind of candor is mutual respect. "You're dealing with peers. They're as smart [as] or smarter than you are, so don't try to outwit them," Mr. Mathile says. "Just lay it on the table. Say, 'I've got this problem,' and toss it out there. Chances are, they'll gobble it up. These folks are aggressive and bright, and they're looking for challenges."

Many CEOs find it helpful to remember that learning was among their goals in naming outside directors in the first place. "If you have made a good selection of . . . new world-class director(s), *management* receives the orientation," one CEO told Heidrick Partners in a recent survey (Heidrick Partners, 1989, p. 18).

This may not always be comfortable. "We wanted directors who would give us feedback—and they have made me squirm!" says the CEO of a family-owned manufacturing business. "At times, it has been unpleasant. At times, I was intimidated and wished they would go away."

But a defensive reaction—falling back on routine, unimaginative agendas, jamming board meetings full of operating reports and rubber-stamp resolutions—can cripple the board.

"The chairman gets out of it what he puts into it," says one director. "If you don't share information, if you don't allow the directors to experience, touch, taste it, you're going to raise elements of distrust, and the board just won't work." To be an effective director, he adds, "you almost have to feel like one of the family."

Making the leap to candor with directors can yield unforeseen personal benefits. One business owner's three-year association with outside directors not only taught him to share financial information but also lent the self-confidence he needed to end his own long professional isolation. After a lifetime of holding high-profile, successful executives in his city at a distance, he began reaching out to others for friendships and business contacts, empowered by a new sense of self-esteem and confidence in his own abilities.

What Kinds of People Adapt Most Easily to Board Management? The chairman's role is the most demanding position in the board room. For the CEO, it means giving up control of the flow of ideas and stepping into the role of asker and listener instead. It means managing respected peers rather than subordinates. It means hearing feedback—lots of it.

This is more difficult for some business owners than others. Certain kinds of experience can be helpful. A background that includes working for others in a larger, professionally managed company, where feedback and sharing of information are common, is of great help. Membership in other peer groups such as the Executive Committee or Young Presidents Association chapters is valuable, too.

Conversely, many entrepreneurs who are self-made, self-employed people find managing a board most difficult. These enterprising individuals are used to being in control. They may never have been subject to performance review nor held accountable by others in any explicit way. Thus, they may never have experienced the learning value of probing, honest questions and feedback. They may never have had the kind of trusting, mentoring relationship that thrives on such an interchange.

Certain personal qualities are valuable in the board chair, too. Managing the board is easiest for the CEO who is open to change and takes a strong interest in management as an art. Often, this CEO understands that the company is in transition in some sense. He or she may harbor a vision of a significantly improved future. To this CEO, every idea is worth looking at, every thought is worth examining.

Conversely, the business owner who is committed to maintaining the status quo will find managing an active board difficult. Many CEOs first learn the depth of their resistance to change in early board sessions, as they tackle such issues as sharing financial information or revealing self-doubts. As discussed in Chapter Nine, an empathic director with experience in those matters can do much to ease the pain of transition for these business owners.

How Do I Deal With All the Questioning? Most business owners feel some reservations about the prospect of a rigorous, potentially critical board-room session.

"When you have your first board meeting with these outsiders, a whole lot of embarrassing things can happen," says one CEO. "My board said, essentially, 'Why are we here?' I said I needed some help in running the business, and I named several areas.

"'OK,' the board said. 'Where do you want to go?' I didn't have any idea," the CEO says. "Strategic planning was a strange term to me."

Many business owners find it helpful to remember a few rules of thumb in dealing with board input.

Rule one: Avoid overexplaining. The business owner should resist the understandable tendency during board sessions to become defensive—to overexplain the ways the business is different, or why a certain suggestion will not work. If directors note that sales are sluggish, for instance, the CEO might be tempted to leap into the discussion with an explanation of how salespeople are paid, or a rationalization on the impact of the business cycle.

Too much self-justification is a sign that the CEO is overreacting instead of just listening and posing questions. Such defensiveness can quickly choke off discussion, miring the issue firmly in the status quo. While wanting to explain one's business is natural, many CEOs find it helpful to remember that directors will ask questions about the business if they feel a need to know.

Rule two: Listen. A related demand on the CEO is to listen. Many CEOs find it helpful to remember that effective directors do not expect or even want the CEO to take all their advice. The CEO's only commitment is to listen to the ideas—not to embrace them. At the same time, while some board suggestions may seem ill-considered or unwise, it can be helpful to remember the weight of combined experience that directors bring to bear.

One CEO learned this lesson the hard way when he asked for the board's opinion on a key hire, a chief operating officer who would be the company's first number two executive. The board recommended that the CEO use an industrial psychologist to help evaluate the candidate, and two board members met separately with the candidate as well.

In a highly unusual development, the industrial psychologist strongly recommended rejecting the candidate, for reasons that seemed sound to the board. "We can't tell you whether to hire this person or not," directors told the CEO. "But when a well-regarded industrial psychologist makes such a strong recommendation, you should probably consider it. There's a chance he's wrong, but it's a chance I wouldn't take." Nevertheless, the CEO went ahead and hired the person anyway—a decision he later deeply regretted.

Rule three: Be patient. A common source of discouragement among business owners is their own unrealistic expectations. The CEO seeking a quick fix or panacea for complex business problems is certain to be disappointed. No board can act overnight to resolve problems that have been months or years in the making. Directors need time to familiarize themselves with a business and its culture, to mull problems, and to wrestle with alternative solutions.

This realization can be especially difficult for the entrepreneur seeking the bold stroke or coup de grâce that suits his or her decisive, freewheeling management style. Boards do not usually function that way.

But while boards' deliberate, interactive functioning may be alien and frustrating at first, many entrepreneurs find that patience can yield big payoffs. "Every time we meet, there's more synergy," says Charles Hoch, president of Parco Foods, a Blue Island, Illinois, food concern. The group dynamic of Parco's board, he says, "just seems to get better and better."

Rule four: Maintain a sense of humor. Few qualities are more effective in creating goodwill and cooperation than a sense of humor on the part of the board chair. An ability to share a joke and laugh at oneself is universally valued, and it can be helpful in cutting tension.

How Do I Cope with the Emotional Challenge? Despite such efforts to maintain a constructive attitude, business owners sometimes emerge from board-room sessions feeling "beat up."

"My board," admits one experienced president of a large privately held company, "can be kind of overwhelming."

Board feedback sometimes seems unfair. How do I cope with getting advice I know is inappropriate? the business owner wonders. How do I handle getting criticized in a way I know isn't entirely warranted?

Each CEO has his or her own individual style in dealing with a rigorous board session. Some find it helps to give themselves permission, both mentally and emotionally, to appear indecisive, fallible, or uncertain.

"The first time I presented something to the board that was really half-baked, I felt foolish," says one CEO. "I knew the board wouldn't meet for another three months and I wanted their input. Yet I felt kind of stupid, and it was a very unfamiliar feeling.

"Ever since I started this business nineteen years ago, I've felt like I was in control. And all of a sudden, I felt put on the spot. It's like castor oil," he adds. "I'm not sure that I like it, but it's probably good for me."

Despite such misgivings on the part of business owners, many directors like the challenge of wrestling with amorphous or unformed issues. And none expect the CEO to be perfect! Many CEOs find it helpful to remember that their directors would not have agreed to serve if they did not already respect and admire them.

Some also like to set aside time after a rough meeting for solitary reflection. Taking time to reflect on board input can help the business owner separate the wheat from the chaff. He or she can weigh criticisms and suggestions for what they are — mere opinions — and select those that are truly helpful. The rest can be relegated to history.

Many business owners find it helpful to remind themselves, too, of the board's true role. Its offerings are advice and counsel — a smorgasbord of ideas, suggestions, and feedback for the private business owner.

Monitoring the Board-Room Climate

For many business owners, one of the first steps toward creating a productive board-room atmosphere is to cast off stereotypes. A formal board-room atmosphere dominated by well-rehearsed management speeches and multimedia presentations would be stifling for most directors.

An informal board-room atmosphere usually works better today. The room should be spacious and comfortable, allowing directors to change their seating positions or pace the floor if they like. Most people appreciate having coffee-break materials at hand. The site should be arranged to eliminate interruptions and to permit directors to remain inside the room for the entire meeting. Entrances, exits, or other disruptions waste time and damage participants' sense of continuity and morale.

Thorough preparation by the CEO can help set a rigorous tone that lasts throughout the board meeting. Both advance mailed materials and conversations with directors before the meeting can create a sense of expectancy that will spark good discussions.

"I operate a little like a football coach, trying to get the players in the right frame of mind on the key issues before they even come into the room," says John Honkamp, CEO of a Milwaukee-based chemicals concern. "That way, everybody can hit the street running. We don't have to start out saying, 'Let me fill you in on everything that has happened since we last met.'"

The business owner can set a productive tone by his or her conduct toward directors. One owner, for instance, shuns excessive formality in favor of a "let's get down to business" approach, one director says. "His attitude is, 'I respect your time.' There aren't any constraints like, 'Shall we have a motion?' then something is moved and seconded and buried. All that stuff is gone." This CEO also "isn't afraid to allow the discussion to drift off the agenda and allow everybody to participate, to get the group dynamics going," the director says.

The CEO should not be upset if directors take off their jackets, lean against the wall, or pace the floor; they are probably just thinking hard. Similarly, silence is not always a sign of inertia. While a pause in the discussion can seem endless to the business owner, it can be a signal that directors are concentrating too hard to worry about sustaining the conversation. It is usually better to resist the impulse to jump in and fill the silence; you may choke off a nascent idea or distract participants from a productive train of thought!

Even something as simple as the chairman's use of coffee-break and lunch periods can influence board dynamics. Instead of lapsing into small talk about sports or the weather, many business owners underscore their respect for directors by asking questions about their own companies or industries. A simple "What's new in your business these days?" can make the director feel appreciated and yield interesting information as well.

Letting Directors Know What Is Expected

Even the most experienced directors work better if they know what is expected of them. Most appreciate decisive leadership from the chair, including a thorough agenda, pointed questions during the meeting, and, occasionally, ground rules for board discussions.

The agenda can be a powerful tool. As discussed in Chapter Seven, items should be as succinct and explicit as possible. A director presented with a vague agenda item such as "organizational issues" would have no idea what the chair had planned. He or she would not have any way of preparing for discussion or thinking through major issues in advance.

On the other hand, a succinctly phrased item such as "alternatives to hiring a new creative director from outside" tells the board several things about the CEO's goals and needs. First, it says he or she sees obstacles to recruiting an outsider for that key post. Second, it encourages the director to mull alternatives *before* the meeting. Third, it acknowledges to directors an area of uncertainty—the company's ability to recruit a top-flight outsider for such an important job. And fourth, it enables the directors to reflect on ways to help eliminate that uncertainty.

The effective agenda allocates a time period to each topic. As discussed in Chapter Seven, the CEO should be generous in devoting time to important and interesting issues. This tells directors that they will be able to mull the matter in depth, and it encourages them to come prepared with their best thoughts and information.

The agenda should also offer guidance on the kind of discussion the CEO desires. Should directors come prepared to review issues and offer advice and counsel? To generate alternatives? To raise new issues? To solve problems or make new recommendations? Or simply to endorse a proposed management course of action?

Allowing Open-Ended Discussion

While leadership is crucial in the board chairman, that should not be construed as a mandate to overstructure meetings. Striving to contain and control every discussion is a common pitfall for inexperienced business owners. Many topics are better suited to open-ended conversation. Allowing an hour or so on the agenda to muddle through a topic can be highly productive, especially on broad questions about process or strategy. Such an open-ended discussion might not yield an organized framework or concrete ideas. But it can help sort through issues and facts in a way that speeds progress — especially if the chairman is listening closely and has someone taking good notes.

A muddling-through approach might be appropriate, for instance, if a business owner is stalled on how to begin thinking about choosing a successor. "I'm concerned about this, and I know I should be concerned," he might tell the board. "But I don't even know enough about it to manage the conversation. What are your thoughts on defining the succession process?"

Open-ended discussions can blossom into full-blown brainstorming sessions. As discussed in Chapter One, brainstorming can be useful in tackling new or particularly knotty problems.

Most CEOs find it helpful to set ground rules: "OK, this is a brainstorming session. Let's just throw out all the ideas we can and not worry about whether they're relevant to my business or not."

It is particularly important that the chair resist overexplaining or becoming defensive during a brainstorming session. While rejecting some ideas with "We've already considered that" or "That would never work in my business because . . ." may come naturally, these responses can shut down creativity.

Although it may be most difficult for the CEO, he or she should follow the ground rules, fielding all ideas neutrally and waiting until later to evaluate and winnow them.

Sparking Productive, Creative Discussions

Once the ground rules are clear, how can the board chairman help spark the kind of freewheeling, candid interchange most likely to yield helpful results?

Let us take a look at some techniques that many business owners have found helpful.

Avoid the long windup. Listening to a long-winded preface to each agenda topic can leave the board confused about the direction of the discussion and turned off on the subject. Most directors prefer to have introductory material in writing in advance, so they can dive into the question without delay at the meeting.

A related problem is too-long presentations by managers. While management briefings can be important and valuable, many tend to ramble. Some CEOs lay ground rules before the meeting, limiting the time allowed for presentations and excusing the managers from the board room afterward.

Start impartially. Few things squelch a lively discussion more quickly than a leader who introduces the topic with a firm statement of opinion. "I'm sure the answer is . . . ," as an opening line, will choke off a debate in moments.

Many CEOs invite open, spontaneous discussion by introducing an issue impartially. "I see this as a tough decision. Here are some of the pros and cons," the chair might say. Or, "I'm torn between two alternatives."

Describing a real or hypothetical situation that raises the issue in concrete terms can be effective as well. "I'm going to pose for you a situation. But I'm going to try not to let you know my thinking at this stage, because I'm really not sure," the CEO may begin.

Challenge your own thinking. Another step in this process is for the CEO to challenge his or her own thinking up front. "I'm having some second thoughts about our direction on this. What do you think?" is a possible opener. The CEO might also seek specific objections to a plan: "Here's where we are with this. What are the weaknesses in what I've just laid out for you?"

Appoint a devil's advocate. Some business owners take aside one director before the meeting and ask him or her to act as a devil's advocate on a particular topic.

"Jill, I know you've had a lot of experience in this area. Before we get too far, I'd like you to try to poke holes in the discussion and challenge my assumptions," the CEO might say. Most directors appreciate these techniques as honest requests for help and respond with the best they have to offer.

Split into smaller groups. If the board is at loggerheads, the CEO might ask directors to break up into smaller groups, brainstorm for a while, and return to the full board with joint recommendations. The smaller size of the groups, coupled with the different decision-making character of each, can yield new insights and ideas that may get the discussion rolling again.

One board of a privately held commercial storage concern resolved a knotty problem this way. Directors were stuck on the question of how to structure the company to protect corporate assets from legal liability associated with trucking, warehousing, and other relatively risky aspects of the business.

On the one hand, dividing the company into several smaller corporations would insulate one part of the company from liability for, say, a truck accident or a warehouse fire in another. On the other hand, forming and maintaining all those separate corporations would be complex, expensive, and confusing to management.

The board was split. Rather than forcing the issue to a vote, directors broke into subgroups to brainstorm their way out of the trap. The result: a fresh approach to the problem.

Why not isolate the liability-prone businesses in one small corporation and maintain the rest in a single large one? one group of directors suggested. While seemingly simple, the solution had not occurred to the full board because it was lodged on the horns of a two-sided dilemma—the issue of one versus many units. The full board united behind the new alternative.

Do not hesitate to defer major decisions. The CEO should not hesitate to defer a board decision on an important issue to the next meeting, particularly if the question has come to an impasse. This may mean that the CEO has to deflect pressure for quick action from company insiders or others. But it almost always yields a better result. Time can be of tremendous value in calming emotions and clarifying disputes.

One company faced a thorny shareholder dispute over an annual compensation package for family shareholders who worked in the company. Management was pressing the board's compensation committee to recommend action at the full board's January meeting, so that incentives and other financial issues could be settled early in the year. But tensions between family managers and shareholders not employed in the company were running high, and committee members knew the full board was split on the issue.

Rather than forcing the dispute to a head, the compensation committee deferred the matter until its April meeting. The result: The family held a meeting in the interim and reached a peaceable resolution that averted future problems. In this case, the benefits of waiting clearly outweighed the risks.

Despite pressures to the contrary, most board issues are the kind that *can* be deferred for a few weeks or months without damage to the company. Many CEOs find the risks of a delay far less significant than the long-term damage that can be done by hasty, ill-considered actions.

Make it fun. Many CEOs recommend trying to make the board experience rewarding and fun for directors. Many directors "look forward to meetings. They get a chance to be on the other side of the desk and to do to me what's being done to them by somebody else," says Mr. Mathile of the IAMS Company. "They can say, 'If I were running this company, this is the way I'd do it.' You have to make them feel that their opinion is important."

Pointing out specific signs and examples of the board's impact on operations and management is gratifying to directors as well. Few things are more rewarding than seeing how one's thoughts or ideas have had a constructive impact.

Limit participation by outside advisers. The best efforts of the CEO to get the board debate rolling can be damaged by the presence of too many visitors—particularly consultants or other paid advisers. While experts' input can be valuable, most CEOs find it best to invite them one at a time. Otherwise, groups of paid advisers have a remarkable ability to coalesce on an issue — to find a way to agree on an answer, regardless of the merits, so that each of them comes out looking good.

As discussed in Chapter Six, professional advisers may have a conflict of interest in board matters. They may be intent on preserving their relationship with the client at all costs. This risk is compounded when more than one adviser is present at a board session, creating a potential obstacle to effective board-room debate.

Know Your Directors

Few things are more helpful in guiding board discussion than a thorough knowledge and understanding of each director. Many business owners try in preparing for board meetings to remain mindful of directors' personal strengths, weaknesses, personalities, and preferences. The following suggestions show how this can be useful in reaping the full benefits of the board and in averting unproductive conflict.

Tap individual directors' strengths and experience. While general board discussion can be a powerful tool, some individual directors have far more to offer on certain topics than others. Some CEOs ask directors with specialized knowledge to prepare in advance to address the board on certain topics. Others find it helpful to write down for their own reference follow-up questions on important agenda items, marked with the initials of the person best suited to answer.

The same techniques can be used to capitalize on the diversity of a board's experience. One CEO was enthusiastic about the popular idea of starting a quality assurance program at his manufacturing concern. But while hanging up banners and giving lip service to the idea was easy enough, he was wrestling with the question, "How does this translate into action at *my* company?"

In a novel move, he asked each director to come to a meeting prepared to describe his or her own company's quality program and how it had been implemented. By the end of the presentations, it was clear that there was no single right answer to the question; to be effective, each company's quality program must be tailored to the company's unique needs and characteristics. The result: a concentrated board effort to help customize the manufacturer's quality program.

Avoid setting up conflicts. While healthy disagreement among directors can be productive, it usually pays to avert deep divisions on the board. One CEO, if he senses a potential dispute, discusses the issue with directors before the board meeting. Asking the views of the dissidents ahead of time can calm tensions, he finds. It also enables him to weigh various courses of action. If a board discussion on the matter seems likely to be counterproductive, he reframes or defers the issue.

Avoid unleashing windbags. A single director can cast a pall on an entire board by monopolizing the discussion. This poses a challenge to the chairman, who must curb that person's verbosity without squelching a healthy interchange.

Many CEOs find it helpful in such cases to introduce discussions by saying, "Let's just go around the table, and I'd like each of you to offer your thoughts." If that tactic proves too subtle, the chairman can follow up with a tactful, "Thank you for your thoughts, George. I'd like to hear what other people think about this now."

Offer Feedback to Directors

Everyone appreciates feedback, even the most seasoned director. The CEO-director relationship requires a different approach to giving feedback than the CEO-subordinate relationship, though. Here are a few techniques business owners have found helpful.

Include a minimum of one contribution per director in the minutes. Many CEOs like to acknowledge at least one contribution by each director, by name, in the board minutes. This helps directors feel appreciated and encourages further effort.

It also has the indirect benefit of making the CEO conscious of each director's value to the board as a whole. It should not be difficult to identify one contribution per member, per meeting. If it is, the CEO might want to reassess the board and consider making a change.

Recognize extra effort. The CEO should take time to express appreciation for any extra effort offered by directors. If the CEO asks one person to speak on a topic or attend a management meeting because of his or her expertise in a specific area, for instance, that person's effort should be recognized.

"I hope you didn't mind my asking so much of you," the CEO might say, "but I really wanted the benefit of your experience. It is so valuable to us."

Take responsibility for your job. Many directors appreciate periodic reassurance from the CEO that he or she is taking full responsibility for managing the company. Effective directors do not want to feel as though they are running the business. They chafe at any inkling that the CEO is unquestioningly implementing all their ideas. Many directors fall silent in such an atmosphere, fearing that anything they say will be taken too literally.

The CEO should make clear that he or she relies on the board only for advice and counsel. While this may seem obvious, it can prevent misunderstandings and help sustain open, honest interchange.

Summarize the board's impact. At least once a year, many CEOs like to review for directors the fruits of the board's labors. An update on major board topics during the year, a summary of the personal and professional benefits gleaned from the board, and a simple "thank you" from the chair can be of great value to directors.

"I want you all to realize how much I appreciate you, and how much I've gained from this board," may be the heart of the message.

Reviewing the year's board work is also good discipline for the CEO and opens to discussion the general topic of board performance. As discussed in Chapter Seven, the result can be helpful in evaluating the board.

Watch for Trouble Signs

Some early warning signs can help alert the business owner to potential problems on the board. While many factors can cause a board to function poorly, they typically fall into three categories: the unimaginative agenda, the inflexible individual, and the contested board.

The Unimaginative Agenda. Several developments can signal the need for a more imaginative, challenging agenda. If board meetings seem to drag, it is a trouble sign. Members of effective boards typically report that their meeting time flies.

If meetings seem comfortable and predictable, the CEO probably is not posing challenging or important enough questions. As unappealing as it may seem, the CEO should *expect* to feel uncomfortable and on edge for at least part of every meeting.

If directors begin arriving late and leaving early, it is a sign that they are bored, poorly managed, or unsuited for their jobs. The CEO should quickly explore the reasons for their apparent lack of interest.

Another danger sign is the recurrence of the same agenda topics, over and over. Any sense that you are recycling the same topics from meeting to meeting or year to year is an indication that the board is performing routine functions rather than serving as a forum for advice and counsel.

As discussed, a prevalence of management reports and other operating recaps reflects a backward focus inappropriate for the board room. This is a signal that the business owner is not stretching him or herself to anticipate future issues and questions and present them to the board. In most cases, reporting can be structured so it takes less than one-fourth of total meeting time, leaving as much as three hours at each meeting for critical issues.

Some CEOs fall into the trap of using their boards merely as a source of information. This is a natural tendency, particularly on the part of entrepreneurs who are used to managing subordinates rather than peers. But it misses the opportunity to plumb the board's fullest potential, and it makes directors feel diminished as well.

Also, the CEO might be wary of any tendency by directors to rely too heavily on formalistic rules of procedure. Meetings should not be sloppy or unbusinesslike; there is nothing wrong with a director suggesting that the group adhere to the topic at hand. But an overreliance on Roberts Rules of Order can reflect a need for more stimulating, challenging agenda topics.

It might also be a sign that the CEO needs to soothe tensions or otherwise improve the board-room atmosphere and trust level. An obsession with declaring each other out of order or challenging each other's motions can be a clear sign that directors are bogging down in interpersonal conflicts.

The inflexible individual. Another set of warning signals can indicate the presence of a member ill-suited for his or her position. One of the most common problems among individual directors is inflexibility. Sometimes, a director is so wedded to a set of assumptions that he or she perceives all issues in black and white. This person is a prisoner of his or her experience.

"Until you improve your production efficiency, you're never going to get anywhere on any of these issues," the director might say — over and over. Or, "My experience proves that none of these trendy ideas about creative financing are any good."

Such an attitude compromises one of the principal sources of board creativity — the ability to tap "flexible frameworks," or different viewpoints on the same problems, as discussed in Chapter One. Even though the director's viewpoint may be partly correct, it becomes an impediment rather than a stimulus to problem solving.

A similar problem is the tendency among some directors to relate every topic to their own businesses. While sharing information from one's own business is often helpful, the director must be sensitive to the fine line between being helpful and haranguing. Ideally, the director can offer relevant experience but engage in analogous thinking as well — stretching to apply his or her knowledge to the specific issue at hand.

Perhaps most disappointing are instances in which individual directors simply fail to fulfill their promise. The third-generation business owner from an industry bristling with problems analogous to your own, for instance, might seem the ideal director for your third-generation family business. But in practice, the person may simply lack the depth and thoughtfulness required of an effective director, and he or she may hamper rather than help board discussion.

As discussed in Chapter Eight, most business owners find a candid and direct solution the best in these situations. Relieving an effective director of his or her duties in a straightforward but appreciative and empathic way is usually the best course of action for all concerned.

"If one director continues to agitate in a negative way, and people don't like working with that person, that's unhealthy," says Bernard J. Hale, a vice-president of Bergen Brunswig Corporation and an experienced director. "In the long run, it can create cliques and power groups, or people banding together to get even with someone. Directors can lose sight of what they're supposed to be doing, which is helping the enterprise in a positive fashion. . . . It's better if the CEO simply 'disinvites' that person."

The contested board. Sometimes, problems spring from shareholder politics or from tensions among directors. Some directors tend to view themselves as representatives of certain constituencies, such as a shareholder group or an employee group. "Well, I've talked to all the nonemployed shareholders, and I want to tell you, they all feel the same way," such a director may say. These directors may withdraw into their constituency viewpoint so frequently that they force other directors to take opposing points of view, fractionalizing the board. This poses a major threat to the board's functioning.

This can be a tough problem to resolve. If a shareholder dispute is the source of the tensions, some CEOs try loading the board with shareholders—a remedy that seldom works.

Another method is to hold a family or shareholder meeting to discuss shareholder differences. As discussed in Chapter Ten, this can presage the formation of a family council, which can serve as a permanent forum for shareholder issues. Other CEOs allow the board to serve that purpose and form an advisory council of independent outsiders to get the advice and counsel they need.

Engaging a consultant or expert in organizational behavior to conduct a group consultation also can help improve group dynamics on the board or improve the board-management relationship. An experienced adviser can help the board, management, and shareholders better understand their working relationship and use the information to improve the effectiveness of the board (Alderfer, 1988).

Special Uses for Directors

Many business owners find unique and special ways to involve outside directors in their businesses. Here are a few examples of duties directors can usefully undertake:

- Interviewing key recruits, not only to assess the candidate but to sell the recruit on the company
- Interviewing recent hires to gather first impressions from a fresh perspective
- Attending corporate ceremonies, such as groundbreakings or ESOP days
- Meeting with lenders regarding a major refinancing or other transaction
- Addressing occasional management meetings on special or timely topics
- Sitting in on important strategic-planning sessions relevant to the director's expertise
- Acting informally as mentor to a successor or next generation of management

Another idea growing in popularity is holding directors' retreats to probe major issues and build effective relationships between directors and management. While directors' retreats are most common among large companies, some smaller private firms use them as well. These two- to four-day sessions at a resort or other comfortable private site typically include two or more formal board sessions, usually in the mornings. Afternoons are reserved for informal activities and recreation.

One company invites key professional advisers and suppliers to a morning retreat session to give a state-of-the-world address to directors and managers. In this session, the company's insurance broker, banker, accountant, industrial psychologist, and others were each asked to summarize recent changes in their industry or profession and predict how those changes would affect the company.

Finally, each participant was asked to recommend ways they might be of greater service to the company, such as by providing asset reappraisals, risk analyses, and so on. At the same session, the company's management made a brief presentation on its strategic direction and developments in its industry — again, to help its advisers and suppliers prepare to serve its needs.

Larger companies sometimes use retreats to explore strategic issues in depth. The day-and-a-half to three-day sessions can enable directors to tackle complex issues that cannot be addressed in regular half-day meetings. They also allow more time for management presentations and tend to heighten participating managers' confidence and trust in the board.

Retreats can be expensive, perhaps doubling the company's annual board expenses in some cases. But many companies that use them for well-planned business purposes — not as a perk — believe the benefits outweigh the expense.

Summary

For the business owner, every meeting with a new outside board can be an adventure, an exploration into the unknown.

The dynamics of effective boards can spark breakthrough thinking — insights and ideas exciting to all involved that transcend the capabilities of any individual participant.

The role of the board chain is to tap a unique and powerful resource common to effective boards: a shared eagerness among members to tackle tough issues. This can require some unfamiliar skills, including an ability to let directors know what is expected of them, to permit open-ended discussions, and to encourage creativity and spontaneity among members.

At the same time, the open, rigorous interchange of the board room can pose a challenge, and even an emotional threat, to the entrepreneur or business owner unaccustomed to working in a forum of peers.

Running an effective board also demands a degree of candor unfamiliar to many business owners. It means being an asker and listener rather than the one who controls the flow of ideas. It means managing respected peers rather than subordinates. And it means hearing feedback—lots of it. Acknowledging these new pressures and demands and finding suitable ways to cope with them is an important part of managing a board.

Effective CEOs also find ways to tap the best in individual directors, as well as in the board as a group. They remain mindful of directors' individual strengths and weaknesses and periodically offer constructive feedback to the board. They watch for trouble signs, including any failure on their own part to challenge the board. Perhaps most important, they give themselves permission to appear indecisive, fallible, or uncertain sometimes and allow themselves the freedom to reject advice and counsel offered by the board.

9

How Directors
Can Contribute
to the Business

Few positions in business are as potentially intimate, challenging, or complex as that of the outside director. The effective board member may play roles ranging from statesman and sage to oracle, arbiter, friend, and confessor. He or she may be a teacher one day and a critic the next, a source of emotional support one week and a philosopher the next.

All this for a director's honorarium? "You have to enjoy it," says John R. "Ted" Kennedy, an experienced director and retired head of a Federal Industries unit in Toronto. "If you see it as a job, it will be a pain in the neck."

Serving in the ambitious roles discussed in this book can raise some unfamiliar issues for directors. This chapter is addressed to them, and to those who may be considering invitations to serve. The chapter aims to help in evaluating board opportunities. It provides a framework for asking effective questions. It describes some appropriate ways to show interest in the business and to support the CEO. And it discusses some of the special issues facing the director in the family-owned business.

What Should I Consider Before Agreeing to Serve?

Many people say yes too quickly when asked to be a director. "It's usually flattering to be invited," says Bernard Hale, a vice-president of Bergen Brunswig Corporation and an experienced director. "But you really ought to investigate the offer as much as possible. You need to know the leader, the values, and the culture of that particular organization."

The following are some general issues of concern raised by seasoned directors.

Does the Business Owner Really Want Help? To offer a real opportunity to directors, the business owner should genuinely be seeking help and objective advice.

"Some CEOs don't really want a board, and if they have one, they treat it sort of like a mushroom," says Ronald Taylor, president of the DeVry Institute, an Evanston, Illinois, educational concern. "Some do that in a very sophisticated way. They tie the board up in presentations and formalities."

The owner should be able to articulate a constructive purpose for the board. "The director has to ask himself whether the climate is right to make a contribution," says William Nance, a former executive of Vlasic Foods. "Is management just window-dressing for political purposes? Do they have a serious financial problem?"

Shirley Brinsfield, an experienced entrepreneur and business owner, generally likes to avoid the boards of two kinds of business owners: the "empire builder" and the "maintainer." The empire builder, he explains, regards his business as a kingdom that he or she runs. "He may not worry too much whether he is creating value" for constituents. The maintainer, on the other hand, is most interested in sustaining the status quo. This is antithetical to the highest purpose of an effective board.

Is the Business Owner Reasonably Candid About the Company? The owner should be forthcoming with information about the company's finances, culture, and strategy. "If he's not absolutely specific, that worries me a little," Mr. Hale says. "If I become a member of the board, I really need to know those things."

Directors should have a high regard for the company's management and owner and should feel certain that they are of the highest integrity before agreeing to serve. They should be proud of the association. They should feel comfortable that the company does not face any prohibitive threats of liability. They should also respect the corporate mission and philosophy.

Clayton Mathile, president of the IAMS Company, a Dayton, Ohio, pet food manufacturer, adds intellectual honesty to his list of criteria. "If that owner isn't willing to deal with the issues, I'm not there any more," he says.

Will the Board Structure Permit Meaningful Input? Many directors take steps to make sure the business owner has established the right mission for the board; they want at all costs to avoid being treated as a rubber stamp or window dressing. Many directors also look for a certain critical mass of outsiders on the board. "I avoid the family tea party, where the wife and cousin and aunt are on the board and I'm the only outsider, making a nuisance of myself," says one experienced director.

What Are My Nonfinancial Costs of Serving? Many directors weigh the opportunity costs of any board position. What am I giving up in order to accept? the candidate should ask him or herself. If the cost in terms of professional or personal pursuits is too high, the board position is likely to yield more frustration than anything else.

Board service should not conflict with the director's primary career responsibilities; some executives review invitations with colleagues or superiors at their own companies before accepting. It should not demand too much time away from family responsibilities. Nor should it pose conflicts of interest, of course, as discussed in Chapters Four and Six.

Can I Really Make a Contribution? Sometimes, the director candidate is in a better position than the business owner to decide whether he or she has enough to offer. "If you can't help them, don't accept," advises Irving L. Blackman, principal in a Chicago accounting firm.

Mr. Brinsfield gauges the owners' expectations against his own capacity and willingness to serve. "In some situations, they're looking for more than they're paying for," he says. "I'd like to have some chance of exceeding their expectations."

Does It Look Like Fun? The bottom line, directors agree, is that any board position should afford the board member pleasure, rewards, and an opportunity to learn.

An affinity with the business is an important prerequisite. "I wouldn't want to be involved as a director in any business that I wouldn't want to be in myself," says Walter Horwich, an experienced adviser. "If you can't see yourself in that business, don't accept." The personal chemistry should be right. "You have to like the CEO," Mr. Mathile says. "You have to want to help him and see him be successful." The director should find other board members interesting and potentially stimulating as well.

Finally, Mr. Brinsfield takes a look at the whole ownership and management team. "Assuming possible failure, are these people I would like to go down with?" he asks himself. "I don't want to go down with a bunch of jerks. I'd strongly prefer to go down with people I respect."

Assuming the invitation meets all these criteria, the board member stands on the threshold of a provocative, challenging, and potentially gratifying experience. How can a director be most helpful? What advice do seasoned board members offer on supporting the CEO, showing interest in the business, and helping to resolve sensitive issues?

Ask Effective Questions

One of the greatest contributions a director can make is to identify, and sometimes challenge, deeply held assumptions on the part of management. This requires the board member to maintain his or her intellectual distance from management. To truly serve the company, the director must avoid slipping unconsciously into the same patterns of thinking as those who own and run the company.

The most effective way for the director to accomplish that is to ask good questions. Inquiries that unearth the assumptions and decision-making habits at work in the business can be enlightening for all concerned. On familiar topics, the right questions to ask are often obvious to the director. Other times, even the most experienced directors rely, sometimes unconsciously, on a conceptual framework for questioning that enables them to examine unfamiliar subjects with rigor and discipline.

Essentially, they ask the same *kinds* of questions about different topics, tailoring each to suit the subjects at hand. Let us take a closer look at this conceptual framework for good questioning.

What Process Was Used? No director can address a management budget or plan with the same level of expertise and knowledge as the CEO or other managers who prepared it. But every director can raise important questions about the process used to prepare the document. These "how" questions can expose inadequacies or strengths in any plan.

How did you arrive at this budget? the board might ask the CEO. Was the process "top down" or "bottom up"? Is the budget sales-driven or financially driven? (That is, did you start by asking the sales group for revenue projections, or by asking your financial people what profit levels we should insist upon next year?) How credible are the numbers? What are your assumptions about the economy, interest rates, and other variables? Did you develop contingency plans should any of those variables change?

Or, in the case of a pension or profit-sharing plan, the board might ask: "How did we choose an investment adviser? How did we decide on our investment philosophy and risk-taking posture? How did that affect our choice, and how did we convey those values to the adviser? How much choice among investment alternatives do we want to offer employees? How should we present the plan and communicate our investment philosophy to employees?

Another good example is the succession issue. No board can decide for the business owner whom to choose as his or her successor. But directors can almost always help define and plan the process to be used in making the selection. When do we need to address this issue? directors might ask. How do we want to make the selection—by arranging a competition among candidates, conducting an open search, or designating an heir apparent well in advance? How do we want to communicate the process to the organization?

What Tradeoffs Are Involved? Another major category of effective questions aims to identify the sacrifices or tradeoffs inherent in any decision. If we make this choice, what spinoff effects will it have? directors might ask. Have you considered the impact on other constituencies, on the competition, on the community, and so on?

Pricing, dividends, and other major strategic and financial decisions inevitably raise tradeoff questions. What is the risk of holding down dividends to shareholders in order to keep our product prices down? Or, if we force down prices to our suppliers in order to invest in research and development, what might we lose in terms of supplier reliability and loyalty? Should we hold down employee wages instead? If we do, what consequences will that have?

Compensation is another area rife with tradeoffs. When presented with a compensation plan, the board might ask, If we reward our star salespeople by basing incentives on individual performance, what impact will that have on the morale of the rest of the sales team? (Or, conversely, if we measure only team performance, how much will we lose by discouraging the star performers?)

If we base our incentive plan on prevailing industry practice, how much will we lose in terms of attracting top-flight employees? If we compensate officers and managers well but hold hourly workers' pay below industry averages, what do we stand to lose in terms of worker performance and longevity?

Or, in the case of the company's philanthropic policy, the board might ask, What do we lose by allocating such a small (or large) proportion of our profit to charity? Are we missing an opportunity by failing to take into account employees' social or political concerns? Would we gain anything by tailoring our giving to reflect the nature of our business? (In the case of a food company, for instance, donations to hunger-relief campaigns might have both social and public-relations value.) Would we benefit more by making only a few large, noteworthy donations or by dispersing our giving among many recipients?

Shirley Brinsfield, an experienced director, entrepreneur, and business owner, offers another conceptual framework for addressing tradeoffs. In a question fundamental to the role of the effective director, he constantly asks himself, "Are we creating value for all our constituents?" This means "adding value" in all the markets the company serves, including financial, product, labor, and capital markets, as well as among suppliers and the community at large.

At the board level, this entails a constant reevaluation of how well the company is competing on all fronts. In the capital markets, for instance, the company should strive to secure funds at the lowest cost possible and put them to more productive use than anyone else. In the marketplace, the company should sell products at the highest price feasible. In the labor market, the company should be paying as little as possible without draining or exploiting its work force; this entails offering workers the opportunity for personal growth and nonmonetary rewards in addition to financial gain.

In the financial arena, owners should strive to build the long-term value of the company without making destructive sacrifices of short-term profit and dividends. "A good board member is constantly testing whatever is being proposed against the larger picture," Mr. Brinsfield says.

Addressing these tradeoffs conscientiously, he adds, can be "a very painful process. You have to open yourself up to being emotionally involved with your business, customers, workers, and investors. If you really do that appropriately, it's a stressful situation.

"The values you develop in one situation may not be applicable in another. Working your way through changing those values from issue to issue is a little like falling in and out of love," he says.

Do You Have a Contingency Plan? One of a director's most helpful and provocative functions is scanning the horizon for unforeseen events or trends that could disrupt or damage the business. What broad social, economic, political, or market developments might affect our company? These contingency, or "what if," questions, are a useful antidote for many managers' natural tendency to focus too intensely inward on the business.

What if our biggest supplier enters our business? the board

might ask. What if interest rates soar (or plunge)? What if we have a systems failure? What if a competitor gets really aggressive in our industry? What if a unionization movement develops in the company? How would we react if hit by bad publicity or a crisis of another kind?

Such questions from the board may seem nagging and worrisome, especially at first. But they serve a crucial function by encouraging the CEO to make a habit of contingency thinking — a discipline that can keep unpleasant surprises to a minimum. Exhibit 7 contains a further sampling of questions cited by experienced directors and business owners as particularly helpful.

Exhibit 7. Great Questions for Directors to Ask.

- What are the toughest ethical questions in this industry?
- How can we take advantage of this setback to accomplish something else, such as trimming fat?
- What impact would this decision have on other constituencies, such as employees or customers?
- How would this decision mesh with our strategic plan or corporate mission?
- What aspects of our corporate culture do you value most and see as most worth preserving?
- How can we better communicate the company's mission and philosophy to employees and other constituents?
- What aspects of our corporate history are most interesting or noteworthy, and how can we highlight those as important dimensions of our culture?
- Is this company meeting its potential? If not, what are the obstacles?
- Are we committed to growth or profit? When push comes to shove, will we opt for gaining market share or raising prices?
- Are we allowing the right amount of time for employees to devote to creative endeavors, such as the development of new products, new markets, and new ideas?
- What are we doing to ensure that we have the most predictable earnings in the industry?
- What is our cost of capital, and is it appropriate to our strategy and mission?
- What is the value of the company? How is it changing, and what does that tell us about management and strategic performance?
- Would this business be worth more in the hands of a different owner? If so, why?
- How vulnerable are we to swings in the business cycle, and what are we doing to prepare for the next one?
- Are we letting this problem or person become a scapegoat or an excuse for poor performance?

Exhibit 7. Great Questions for Directors to Ask, Cont'd.

- What are we trying to learn as an organization, and are those goals appropriate to our strategy and mission? How can we encourage learning?
- What new risks are we taking, and do they suit our strategy, mission, and culture?
- How should we communicate our risk-taking posture to the organization?
- Are we prepared for any contingencies that might arise—a strike, a spike in interest rates, a new-product flop, new competition, an industry consolidation, a recession, loss of raw-material supplies, the advent of new technology?
- What are we doing to fulfill our responsibility to the community as a whole?
- What can we learn from the experience of companies that have already gone through the crisis we face?

Show Interest in the Business

CEOs appreciate directors whose interest in the business goes beyond the board room. Few gestures are more important in this regard than doing one's homework. The business owner who can count on directors to prepare thoroughly for meetings has increased confidence in the board and tends to use it to the fullest extent.

A related demand is to listen carefully and patiently to management explanations and reports. As Exhibit 8 shows, one of CEOs' chief complaints about directors is that they become unwilling over time to listen to explanations of changes taking place in the company and the business environment (Heidrick Partners, 1989, pp. 16–18).

Exhibit 8. Chief Executives Assess Their Directors.

New Directors

What is your major satisfaction with new outside directors?

- Interest in and enthusiasm for the company.
- New perspective, not complacent.
- Eager, curious, good attendance.
- Ability to pick up quickly a number of aspects of a complex business.
- Good attitude, work hard.

Exhibit 8. Chief Executives Assess Their Directors, Cont'd.

- Some surprising insights, perceptions, and suggestions having substantial value.
- Force management to go back and reexamine corporate methodology.

What is your major dissatisfaction with new outside directors?

- Lack of historical memory.
- Sometimes too quiet, don't fully participate.
- Too quick to participate.
- If they can look at the broad picture, great. If they retreat within personal expertise, they are a pain.

Established Directors

What is your major satisfaction with outside directors who are no longer new?

- Loyalty to company.
- They have been called upon to exercise extraordinary courage. Each has met this test in exceptional fashion.
- Wisdom and knowledge they bring to board deliberations and the counseling they provide on important decisions facing the company.
- Intimate knowledge of organization and people.
- They stay enthusiastic, attentive, and involved.

What is your major dissatisfaction with outside directors who are no longer new?

- Some do not work hard enough.
- Some don't do homework, don't add value, cause meetings to lose focus.
- Some are just part of the woodwork. We are beginning performance evaluations before inviting reelections.
- Older, retired directors seem to be overly concerned with their liability as directors and less ready and willing to take prudent risks.
- If retired, less alert, less active, less knowledgeable.
- Unwillingness to listen to explanations of changes taking place in company and in the business environment.

Source: Heidrick Partners, 1989, pp. 16–18.

A very short note acknowledging materials received between meetings is appreciated by many CEOs. Others ask for advice or occasional private meetings with board members, a request directors should try to meet. Directors should also take advantage of invitations to visit company facilities and plants, whenever time permits. Exhibit 9 offers a sampling of other practical suggestions.

Exhibit 9. Some Do's and Don't's for Directors.

Do's

- Ask questions, either at or between meetings.
- Make your information needs known to the CEO.
- Bring up analogous situations from your own experience.
- Always offer advice or suggestions in a way that gives the CEO a graceful out, or means of refusing.
- Suggest, don't command.
- Support the CEO to the extent honestly possible.
- Do your homework, allowing enough time between meetings to study board materials for warning signs.
- Express your opinion.
- Share books, articles, and information about your company.
- Put the company on your business mailing list.
- Invite heads of departments, functions, or task forces from the company to visit your business.
- Call the CEO between meetings once or twice a year.
- Use "we" in discussing company issues.
- When visitors are present in the board room, agree in advance on boundaries of discussion.
- Make sure you know the CEO's goal in raising subjects for discussion: a vote, a consensus, brainstorming, clarification, endorsement, generating alternatives?
- Be available to the CEO between meetings.
- Try to acknowledge information you receive from the company between meetings, even if only with a very short note.
- Be punctual.
- Take the initiative to visit the company's offices and plants at least once a year.
- Use plant and facility visits to assess the company's business, show interest, and get acquainted with management.
- Attend an occasional company ceremony, such as a groundbreaking or party.
- Use social and ceremonial activities to gather information, assess managers' abilities, and make friends.
- Volunteer to be available to key employees at the CEO's discretion.
- Remain mindful of your obligations to all constituencies, not just shareholders.
- React constructively to surprises, problems, crises, or trouble signs.
- Urge the CEO to make proper and optimal use of the board.
- Be alert to any trouble signs in the CEO-board relationship, such as meeting cancellations or a lack of candor.
- Be alert to nuances in board discussions.
- Raise with the CEO any concerns about board performance in a discreet and constructive way.
- Know your legal duties and liabilities.
- Make sure any potential conflicts of interest are known to other directors and abstain from any related votes or discussions.

Exhibit 9. Some Do's and Don't's for Directors, Cont'd.

- Make sure your dissenting votes are recorded in the minutes, including your reasons.
- Be discreet and cautious in offering advice on family matters, such as succession and ownership issues.
- Respect the CEO's desire for confidentiality.

Don't's

- Don't serve on a board if you don't like the people who own or run the company.
- Don't serve only to gain prestige.
- Don't serve if you're unwilling to share the names of valuable contacts without embarrassment or concern.
- In board discussions, don't stay on one subject too long.
- Don't talk too much in board discussions.
- Don't raise the same question repeatedly.
- Don't allow yourself to be mired in petty family or shareholder concerns.
- Don't be shy about sharing your experience.
- Don't ask for information that isn't useful to your decision-making needs.
- Don't serve on too many boards.
- Don't feel the need to be right.
- Don't feel the need to be an expert on every subject.
- Don't disclose information that would damage the company's interests.
- Don't permit personal goals or interests to overshadow your obligation to the corporation.

Support the CEO

A major function of directors is to support the CEO whenever they can honestly do so. This can be especially important in the private business, where the CEO is also likely to be a dominant owner and may lack other sources of outside review and support. Here are some ways directors can be especially useful in this regard:

Help Monitor the Board's Performance. Individual directors can be of enormous help to the CEO in reviewing and evaluating the board. While some business owners name a consultant or individual director as a facilitator with formal responsibility for monitoring board performance, others rely on informal assessments.

Many CEOs appreciate constructive feedback from individual directors on the board's performance, the CEO's use of the board, the agenda, informational materials, or other aspects of board operations. This can be offered over lunch or in other private sessions, or during a board meeting if appropriate. As discussed in Chapter Seven, some chairmen find it helpful to set aside time during one board meeting each year for directors to appraise the board's performance and make suggestions.

Help the CEO Make the Best Use of the Board. Some business owners, especially those who lack experience with outside directors, make mistakes in dealing with their boards. Failing to keep directors informed, failing to consult with the board, and other tactical errors can damage the board's effectiveness and hurt directors' morale.

Many directors use such mistakes as opportunities to educate the CEO in the proper role of the board. If a business owner surprises the board with an agreed-upon acquisition or other *fait accompli,* Mr. Hale says, directors might say, "Look, we'd like to know more about this. Next time, why don't you use us *before* you decide? Let us help you ask the right questions, so you can avoid making possible mistakes."

In other cases, business owners may try to dodge problems. If the CEO starts canceling board meetings or talking sports instead of business, "that tells me there's a problem," Mr. Hale says. The director's role in such a situation, he says, is to "talk with the CEO, and figure out a way to do so that isn't threatening."

Defer Decisions When Appropriate. As discussed in Chapter Eight, most matters that come before the board do not have to be decided overnight. The board room is more hospitable than most business settings to deferring judgment. In fact, many issues become easier to resolve if allowed to rest between board meetings. Often, a board's deferral of a decision can be helpful to the CEO in deflecting shareholder pressure or simply sanctioning a cooling-off period to allow all concerned to think things over.

Offer Sensitive Advice in Private. Directors often have insights into sensitive business matters that cannot be addressed in the board room. Board members who enjoy a trusting relationship with the business owner can sometimes address these matters over lunch, on the golf course, or in another informal, relaxed setting.

One business owner was squelching the efforts of his designated successor — his son — without realizing it. The owner was proud of the young man and praised him privately to the board. But whenever the son reported to directors on his areas of responsibility, the CEO unconsciously fell into his old patterns as a father, preempting normal board discussion with pointed criticism that clearly damaged the young man's morale.

Sensing a problem that could damage the business, a longtime director asked the CEO out for a round of golf. "Look, Pete," he said, "I'd like to offer an observation, for whatever it might be worth. You said something to John the other day in our meeting that might be a little deflating to him, and I've noticed you've done that before, too. You might want to think about the effect that's going to have on his self-confidence and his ability to run the business someday."

The business owner was shaken but accepted the suggestion and thought it over. To his credit, he was able to change his patterns of board room behavior and begin treating his son in a more professional manner.

The Importance of Empathy. As discussed in Chapter Nine, working with an aggressive, candid board can be difficult for the business owner, particularly the entrepreneur who is unaccustomed to feeling out of control or being held accountable. Often, the observant director can help with an empathic remark, such as, "I haven't got all this figured out in my own business either, Ralph."

A simple acknowledgment may soothe the CEO smarting from board criticism. "I guess it's our day to beat up on you, Fred," a director might say. Or, "How does it feel to get beat up by a bunch of outsiders who don't know your business?"

A note of sympathetic humor can provide a healing touch.

When one CEO sought his directors' reactions to his idea of promoting an insider to a key post, he was chagrined at their negative response. "Everybody has to go outside from time to time," one director told the CEO.

Seeing the disappointment on the CEO's face, another board member remarked, "And every single time I've done it, it's been a pain!" The tension in the room eased amid a burst of laughter, and the CEO visibly relaxed.

Sometimes, the business owner may be embarrassed by his or her seeming inability to resolve a problem. "This is the third plan I've shown you," he or she may lament. The director might respond, "Well, I'm on my sixth one, and I'm not done yet!"

Avoid Putting the Business Owner on the Defensive. Whenever possible, the director should avoid making remarks so critical of the CEO that they lack productive impact.

One director recalls a situation in which a business owner and his investment manager were proudly describing to the board some successful individual stock picks they had made on behalf of the company. Notably missing, though, was an explanation of the team's overall investment philosophy or goals.

"I came driving in from left field and said, 'Wait a minute! What's the strategy?'" the director recalls. The discussion spun off the tracks as the CEO defended his choices, and the director knew he had made a mistake. "Great ideas tend to follow from a constructive approach, but I put the guy on the defensive," he says. "You shouldn't put people who have worked hard on something in the position of feeling threatened by your 'genius question.'"

Resist Board-Room Competition. Many boards, especially at first, have one member who is more outspoken than others. This can make other members feel they should step up their own contributions. In the worst case, it can create an escalating contest among directors trying to outdo each other.

Many directors find it helpful to remember that inequities among board members' contributions tend to even out in time as a variety of issues arise and members grow accustomed to working as a group. In a council of peers, competition should be nonexistent. No one should feel a need to prove anything; instead, all should feel free to offer questions, ideas, and suggestions at their own individual pace.

Ease Needed Board Transitions. Directors who become too attached to their board seats can cause a CEO deep discomfort. Few situations are more awkward for the business owner than dealing with a director's reluctance to resign or retire when asked. Some retain board members long beyond their usefulness, simply to avoid hurting the feelings of these longtime associates and friends.

The effective director is mindful of the board's role as a resource that must be tailored to the changing needs of the CEO and the business and tries to behave accordingly. When one young business owner first took over as CEO of the family business, a valued outside director took him aside.

With the previous CEO retiring, the director said, "I've given some thought to the idea that maybe it's time for me to go, too." The CEO was stunned: "I dropped my jaw," he says, and quickly set about persuading the director to stay.

Gratefully, the director agreed. "He just wanted to hear that I wanted him," the CEO says with appreciation. "He wanted to know that I believed he could contribute."

Special Issues for Directors
of the Family-Owned Business

Often, directors are asked to serve family businesses, including those with many second-, third-, or fourth-generation shareholders. These board members face some special challenges, particularly if the shareholder group is discontented or divided.

One is to help shareholders recognize that the seeds of certain issues are inherent in family business. While the owners may not see — or wish to see — the problems clearly, an effective director can often help the family address and resolve them. "If there's a family in there running things, part of the mission of the board is to help the family make it together," Mr. Black-man says.

Periodic social gatherings or fireside chats with share-holders can help foster good relations with family members and provide directors with the information they need to understand family-business dynamics. (This and other means of linking the family with the board are discussed in depth in Chapter Ten.)

Let us take a look at some specific issues that often arise for directors of family-owned businesses.

Drawing the Line Between Family and Business Matters. One of the most sensitive matters is helping the business owners balance family needs and the demands of running a healthy busi-ness. As the family business evolves over succeeding genera-tions, many owners must find outlets for family feelings, nostal-gia, and personal values to prevent them from interfering with the business. As discussed in Chapter Ten, one such outlet can be a family council or asset board.

The trusted outside director can help educate family mem-bers about the need to separate business and family issues. One family, for instance, agonized over the impending divorce of a son who was the designated successor to his father as head of the family business. When the father's hurt and disappoint-ment began interfering with his business dealings with his son, directors were uniquely able to define the issue.

"Look, you've got to draw the line here" between busi-ness and personal matters, one board member told the father. "I'm not here to tell you where the line is, but you have to de-cide. If you're going to throw your son out over a divorce you don't like, that's one thing. But if you want him in the com-pany, you've got to separate your personal feelings from busi-ness matters."

Serving As a Lightning Rod. Occasionally, the director can calm family conflict by listening to unhappy shareholders and guiding them toward an appropriate resolution. But direc-tors should be extremely cautious in this regard. No director should become the emotional dumping ground or leaning post for a disgruntled shareholder. In most cases, the director should seek ways to bring a shareholder's complaints out into the open so they can be aired and resolved in an appropriate way. This protects the director from being caught in the middle of a family triangle, acting as an intermediary between family members.

At the same time, the effective director can sometimes foster peace among factions by guiding them discreetly toward compromise. Sometimes, this means a sale of stock by dissidents; other times, the factions moderate their positions with the help of discussions with directors and each other.

Taking Sides in a Family Dispute. Directors should avoid taking sides in a family dispute. That almost invariably ends the board member's usefulness to the business.

In all cases, the director should make clear that he or she represents all stakeholders' interests, not just one constituency, and that the director's principal concern is business policy.

Sometimes, an outside adviser, such as a compensation expert or a family-business consultant, can be helpful in resolving disputes.

Returning Issues to the Family for Resolution. Some thorny issues wind up with the board when they should be thrashed out by the family. A director presented with a dividend dispute, for instance, might rightly ask the family to decide on appropriate debt and profit levels for the business. Once the family reaches consensus on that issue, dividend decisions should follow clearly and without controversy.

Anticipating Future Family-Related Business Issues. Part of the director's role in the family business is to help anticipate future family-related business issues. The director should take stock early in his or her board term of certain critical aspects of family-business health. Here is a sampling of questions the director might ask him or herself:

• Is the family articulating its philosophy and values for the business and putting them into effect?

- How strong is the family consensus on such key issues as dividends, profit performance, and shareholder liquidity?
- How much capital will be needed to satisfy shareholders' future needs and demands?
- Are any other issues looming that could fragment the shareholder base?
- If the shareholder base is already fragmented, are extreme actions needed, such as a management buyout, a public sale of stock, a buyout of the dissident shareholders?

Once the director understands the dynamics of the family business, he or she can be of great help in framing prospective issues—often by asking the "what if" kinds of questions described earlier in this chapter. The CEOs of family businesses with multiple owners or offspring, for instance, probably need to be thinking ten years or more in the future as they make plans. Does the principal owner's estate plan take into account the future needs of the business? Are fair buy-sell agreements in place in case another shareholder feels the need to sell? If a minority shareholder died, what would be the impact on the company? Does the stock valuation in buy-sell agreements fairly reflect the company's current value? These are only a few of the questions that can determine the welfare and survival of the family business.

Succession is another good example. One family-business board raises the questions of management, organizational, and ownership succession once a year. What if principal shareholders in the business die? directors ask. What will that mean, not only for the leadership and organization of the company, but also for ownership?

While these can be difficult issues, the director can comfort the owners by pointing out that they are nearly universal in family businesses. "These are problems and questions that every owner has to expect," directors might tell the business owners. "Businesses change over time, and there's no way you're going to look ten or twenty years from now the same way you look now. Some very normal changes have to occur."

Mentoring Successors. Many family-business owners ask directors to help educate and broaden members of the next generation of management. This can be rewarding for all concerned, providing the director has the time and takes pleasure in this nurturing role.

Here's how John R. "Ted" Kennedy, an experienced director and former head of a Federal Industries unit in Toronto, describes the mentoring role: "I look for opportunities to expose these young people to some of my other businesses. I look for ways to critique them and guide them, but not to push them in a heavy-handed way. I try to expose them to the thought processes, the analysis, the investigation and planning of strategy that's necessary to the executive.

"So often, they're ill-equipped to become president. They may have grown up in one segment of the company and their view of the business may be very narrow. My job is to broaden them a little, to stretch their experience and give them other ways of looking at things. In a nice way, I also expose them to a more modern and formal way of running a business — developing proper budgets, motivating employees, and so on."

Some Resources for Directors

Directors should not hesitate to reach out for advice, information, and support from various sources. The company's general counsel can be helpful to directors in understanding their legal duties. Outside consultants, while often useful, should be used sparingly, particularly by the small-company board. Many companies need the services of a compensation consultant from time to time. But others find prohibitive the $15,000 to $25,000 minimum fee charged by many such advisers.

Some directors like to attend industry seminars or conventions. Board members might also ask the CEO for key industrywide performance data and financial ratios to help in reviewing the company's performance. A subscription to the industry trade magazine can be helpful. The National Association of Corporate Directors, a Washington-based organization, also publishes newsletters and organizes membership programs for directors.

Any corporate history can be useful, as can such sources as *The Corporate Director's Guidebook,* published by the American

Bar Association. Directors should not neglect each other as resources, either. Many board members discuss board issues informally to test their perceptions and gather feedback on complex issues.

Summary

Serving as an effective outside director can raise some challenging and unfamiliar issues, even for experienced executives, entrepreneurs, and business owners. Directors should evaluate board invitations carefully before agreeing to serve. The integrity and sincerity of the business owner and the potential for making a real contribution are among the factors the candidate should consider.

Raising good questions is a central role of the director. While no one can possibly know as much about any business as its owner-manager, many board members rely, sometimes unconsciously, on a strong conceptual framework for effective questioning. This approach helps improve the quality of decision making at the company by examining the process used to make a decision, the tradeoffs involved, and the contingencies that might affect it. These "how," "who's hurt," and "what if" questions can encourage the CEO to internalize a rigorous, disciplined approach to decision making of all kinds.

The director can provide valuable support to the CEO in several subtle but important ways. He or she can help monitor board performance and encourage optimal use of the board. The director can provide empathic support to the business owner in difficult situations. The board member can also encourage productive discussions by resisting any urge to compete with other directors or to put the CEO on the defensive.

Directors in family businesses face some special challenges. Often, they can help shareholders decide where to draw the line between family and business issues. They can serve as a lightning rod in shareholder disputes, helping channel differences of opinion to the proper form. And they can help the business owner anticipate future issues that might affect the welfare and survival of the family business.

10

Linking the Family
with the Board

A common conception about family business in America holds that the first generation builds the business and later generations cash in — by selling the company or going public with most of the stock.

Now, powerful forces are disrupting that pattern. For more than a decade, a wave of hostile takeovers has sparked restructurings and layoffs, diminishing the appeal of publicly controlled status. At the same time, the growing emphasis in society on the value of both family and entrepreneurship has brightened the allure of private ownership as an alternative. As a result, more families than ever will likely try in the coming years to keep control of their businesses through the third generation and beyond. This raises some complicated new questions for business owners and directors.

As the shareholder base broadens and grows through the generations, managing shareholder relations becomes more important. Harnessing the power of a cohesive, committed family shareholder base can provide great strength to a company. Conversely, managing disparate family interests can sap management energy and distract the CEO from pressing business issues. And while an effective outside board can be of great help in perpetuating the family business, directors must enjoy the trust of family shareholders and communicate well with them in order to exercise the needed creativity and insight.

This chapter addresses these issues. It is designed primarily for business owners and directors interested in businesses in their second or later generation of family ownership, and for those desiring to reach and surpass that milestone. The chapter discusses linking family shareholders and the outside board. For owners of first- and second-generation family businesses, it offers help in resisting the temptation to create a family board — a natural tendency, but one that wastes the opportunity to draw on the wisdom and experience of outside directors. The chapter offers examples of how to build a separate family council instead, and how to encourage effective relations between it and the board. And it will discuss ways to negotiate some common obstacles in the path to perpetuating that good relationship.

Stages in the Evolving Family Business

Shareholder relations in the family businesses typically become more complex as the second generation of family owners grows older and their offspring approach the age at which they will assume an important ownership role. It may happen earlier in large families with in-laws involved. The ties binding the family sometimes loosen or fray at this point. Often, the cohesive influence of the founder or other early business leader is waning. The death of key first-generation family members may weaken the shareholders' sense of unity and common origin.

The emerging generation of shareholders may differ greatly in their expectations of the business. Cousins are usually not bonded as closely as brothers and sisters. They may demand greater financial freedom, including a liquid market for their shares. They may disagree on appropriate levels of dividends, debt, and profit for the business. Their expanding numbers may complicate the selection of future managers. They may have conflicting views on how family members should be employed and compensated in the business and other basic matters. In a growing business, the changing strategic needs of the company can complicate management at the same time, heightening capital requirements and sometimes demanding an entirely new style of management or even a new corporate structure.

All of these conflicts and hurdles are perfectly normal and natural. Yet failure to anticipate them can waste the opportunity to harness the power of an expanding, potentially committed shareholder base. At worst, it can lead to serious shareholder disputes, liquidity and capital problems, or management crises of the kind that profoundly affect the role of the board and even force many family businesses into extinction.

How can business owners and directors anticipate these hurdles and plan to surmount them effectively? The author's experience and study of evolving family businesses suggest that many pass through fairly predictable stages of development. While each family business is unique, many evolve at varying rates through three basic stages of ownership (see Table 4).

In stage one, the earliest or entrepreneurial stage, a founder or founding partners often commingle management and ownership. The primary shareholder issues are relatively simple. Protection for the spouse (or spouses) in the event of injury or death of the founder, estate planning, and succession and leadership transition typically take top priority. Little or no formal family organization is needed at this stage. Communication tends to be simple and spontaneous.

The interests of the family and business often overlap heavily at this stage, making it difficult to see where family members' business concerns end and personal ones begin. The business commands much or most of its owners' time and energy, often requiring great personal sacrifices.

In the second ownership stage, the shareholder base often takes the form of a family partnership among siblings. In this stage, maintaining teamwork and family harmony typically dominate owners' concerns. Again, family meetings are usually informal at this stage, with business conducted at periodic Sunday night suppers or other casual meetings. The interests of the family and business, while diverging somewhat, are still closely entwined.

Ownership concerns become vastly more complex in the third ownership stage, marking the beginning of the family dy-

Table 4. Ownership Issues in the Evolving Family Business.

Ownership Stage	Dominant Shareholder Issues
Stage One: The Founder(s)	Leadership transition Succession Spouse insurance Estate planning
Stage Two: The Sibling Partnership	Maintaining teamwork and harmony Sustaining family ownership Succession
Stage Three: The Family Dynasty	Allocation of corporate capital: dividends debt, and profit levels Shareholder liquidity Family tradition and culture Family conflict resolution Family participation and role Family vision and mission Family linkage with the business

nasty. As cousins, in-laws, and others without direct involvement in the business emerge as shareholders, new pressures arise. Allocation of corporate capital, including such issues as dividend policy, debt levels, and shareholder liquidity, becomes important.

New shareholder differences emerge. With many shareholders lacking the intense partnership involvement of their parents, the interests and identity of the family and the business often diverge at this stage. Family members who own stock but do not work in the company may wonder, "What's in this for me?"

At the same time, questions about the family's mission and role in perpetuating the business may arise. Resolving family conflicts may become more difficult, with some members placing high value on family tradition and culture even as others grow restless and desire greater financial and professional freedom. Managing family members' ties with the business may grow complex, confusing, and frustrating.

It is at this stage that many businesses enter crisis. Some

family members may demand to sell their shares, sometimes just as the business itself requires new capital. Dissident shareholders may grow frustrated with the performance of their investment or the direction of the company. Increasingly, managing shareholder relations may divert management attention and drain valuable corporate resources. One way or another, these issues must be resolved.

Feeling trapped or desperate, many owners respond by going public or otherwise divesting all or part of the company — no matter what their feelings may be about the value of perpetuating private ownership. An increasing number of family businesses, however, are developing formal, carefully structured family councils at this stage to manage the burgeoning array of ownership issues.

The Evolutionary Phases of Family-Business Management

Further complicating the picture may be the separate, but sometimes tandem, evolution of the *management needs* of the business through a series of equally predictable phases (see Table 5).

Table 5. Management Issues in the Evolving Family Business.

Management Stage	Dominant Management Issues
Stage One: Entrepreneurship	Survival Growth
Stage Two: Professionalization	Adopting professional management systems Revitalizing strategy
Stage Three: The Holding Company	Allocation of resources Overseeing investment portfolio Corporate culture Succession and leadership Performance of investment Strategy Shareholder relations

During the first management stage — entrepreneurship — the founder dominates management. The business often has no active board or, ideally, has an active board composed of the founder, outside directors, and perhaps a successor. Strategy for the company's single business is often relatively simple, driven by the need for survival and growth.

During the second management stage — professionalization — a sea change may occur in the strategic needs of the business. The founder and any partners in management may begin to feel overwhelmed. They may find that their hard work and immersion in management detail are no longer adequate to motivate and manage the company's 50–100 (or more) employees. New, professional management systems may be needed. At the same time, new competition and growth pressures may call for a revitalization of strategy.

At this stage, the board, if active, may be composed of outside directors plus two or more business partners with significant ownership stakes. This kind of mixed board can still be effective in grappling with the new challenges facing the business, particularly if a critical mass of well-qualified outsiders is present.

During the third management stage — the holding company phase — the successful family business grows considerably more diverse and complex. It often expands into separate strategic units, each with problems and challenges of its own. At this stage, managers may again feel overwhelmed as broad questions about the overall investment portfolio compete with individual business units' problems. Questions about the performance of the shareholders' investment and the evolution of corporate culture often join the usual issues facing the board.

At this stage as well, many businesses reorganize into a holding company overseeing a group of separate operating subsidiaries. This structure has several advantages. It tailors the corporate structure to the functional needs of its businesses. The separate subsidiaries afford flexibility in offering managerial opportunities to family members. The units also make room for varying levels of ownership, entrepreneurship, and risk by different family members, as well as by key nonfamily executives.

In very large, mature family businesses, each operating subsidiary might possibly benefit from its own separate, active board of outside directors. Guiding the whole may be a holding company board or, as it is sometimes called, an "asset board." This group oversees the family's investment portfolio, monitors the performance of all the subsidiary boards, and stays attuned to shareholder goals and needs.

Ideally, as shown in Table 6, the membership and structure of the active outside board evolved with the ownership and management demands of the family business. The table shows the kind of board most appropriate for the family business at each of the ownership and management stages discussed in this chapter. A pure board is one composed entirely of independent outside directors, plus the CEO and perhaps a designated successor. A mixed board is one composed of outsiders plus a few significant shareholders and the CEO.

As successful family businesses evolve through these stages of ownership and management, many will eventually reach the third stage in each category—becoming big, multi-unit holding companies overseen by numerous third- or later-generation heirs to the entrepreneur.

If that complex image is the shape of the future, what is the best way to perpetuate private ownership and ensure continued growth?

The Family Council

As discussed in earlier chapters, an active outside board can be invaluable in helping solve the problems of family businesses in all stages. But no board of directors, no matter how experienced and expert, can function effectively without the support and trust of shareholders. Any company must have a means of resolving shareholder conflict and communicating shareholder goals and needs to the board. And any business must be able to define the role and responsibilities of shareholders, in contrast with those that are entrusted to the outside board.

In the third, or "family dynasty," stage of the family business, a carefully structured family council is often needed to

Table 6. The Outside Board in the Evolving Family Business.

OWNERSHIP STAGE	MANAGEMENT STAGE		
	One: Entrepreneurship	Two: Professionalization	Three: The Holding Company
One: Founder	Pure board [a]	Mixed board	Not applicable [b]
Two: Siblings	Pure board	Mixed board	Mixed board [c]
Three: Cousins	Pure board	Mixed board	Holding company or asset board with several subsidary boards

[a] The ideal evolutionary pattern for the board is shown by the arrow. While a pure board is ideal at this stage, many businesses operate with no active board.

[b] Few businesses are simultaneously in the founding and holding company stage.

[c] Ideally, businesses that have evolved to the holding company or portfolio stage should already have replaced their mixed boards with a board structure more appropriate to the business's needs.

educate shareholders and help fulfill these purposes. Such a group can be invaluable as a vehicle for conflict resolution. It can help achieve consensus on capital and liquidity problems and other divisive issues without tearing the company apart or forcing such drastic moves as a public sale of stock.

The family council can also serve the more subtle but equally important purpose of imparting to the family a sense of identity and mission. It can give family members a collective sense of values and responsibility apart from each member's individual worries about dividends, the company's performance, and so on. "The family council allows the family to speak with one voice to the board. That's the hope," says Ivan Lansberg, a noted family business consultant.

At the same time, the family council can underscore the value of private ownership by manifesting the family's philosophy and values in the business and the community. And it can create new opportunities for family members, both in financing new ventures and in affording management experience in the existing business.

Here are some specific suggestions for organizing a family council.

Choose an Appropriate Structure. The family council can be structured in many ways, formal or informal. Many smaller families simply gather all members together for informal discussions. Others organize committees of family members to handle various matters and ask each committee to report annually to a meeting of the family as a whole.

Some large families organize their councils like a representative government body. Either members of the council can be elected at large, or branches of the family can each select a delegate to the council.

Most family councils meet two to four times a year. Some gather as often as monthly, depending on the size of the group and the business. Many combine business-related meetings and activities, such as plant visits, with recreation at semiannual gatherings at a resort or hotel. Some invite family business consultants or other outside experts to these sessions to address family members on current issues.

Some families arrange meetings around the board's schedule, in order to air family matters and views before directors meet. This gives the family a chance to communicate readily with the board. It also encourages family members who hold seats on the board to air personal feelings and opinions outside the board room, to avoid consuming board time with matters more appropriate to the family council.

The Role of the Family Council. The role of the family council is to find consensus on matters where the owners' wishes matter most, as well as to perform certain functions unique to the family. Ideally, it can provide family members with a sense of identity and mission that transcends their role as mere financial stakeholders in a business.

Some families establish bylaws to make the council's goals and membership clear to everyone from the beginning. Exhibit 10 offers a sample set of family council bylaws.

Exhibit 10. An Example of Family Council Bylaws.

Bylaws of the Smith Family Council.

Function

The Smith Family Council is established to nurture relationships among the members of the Smith family. It is intended as an additional forum for communication among shareholders and between family members and the board of directors of SmithCo. Initially, the purposes of the council are defined as follows:

1. To facilitate communication: exchange information; talk with each other.
2. To promote understanding: become better friends; promote fellowship; share good times; develop our relationships and learn from each other's experiences; deal with each other.
3. To provide family support: strengthen family bonds; build goodwill to overcome conflict, help each other when help is needed and sought; get recognition and appreciation.
4. To solve problems: address family grievances; make decisions on family matters; address common problems.
5. To provide continuity: initiate the next generation; be an example for the next generation.

Membership

For the time being, the membership of the Smith Family Council will consist of the five siblings in the second generation. The question of the membership of other family members will be readdressed in the future.

Meetings

Meetings of the Family Council will be held quarterly. The time and place of meetings will be set to accommodate members with children and will generally

Exhibit 10. An Example of Family Council Bylaws, Cont'd.

---

be held near Tampa, Florida, or Denver, Colorado. The members of the Family Council are committed to making the meetings productive and worthwhile to justify the time away from other family members.

Officers/Roles

The Family Council will not have officers per se. The following positions will rotate every quarter:

> *Meeting Organizer:* Responsible for determining where and when meetings will be held and arranging for conference facilities and social activities. Travel arrangements will be made by individual members.
> *Meeting Planner:* Responsible for arranging the speaker (if any), meeting topic, and agenda.
> *Secretary:* Responsible for preparing the meeting minutes and keeping the minute book.

The family council faces a variety of important questions. What is the family's philosophy of doing business? What is its mission, both within and outside of the company? How are members to resolve conflicts? How should family values be manifested in relation to the business?

Just as important is a long list of capital-related issues, such as dividend policy, liquidity, terms of liquidity, profit goals, and the character and risk of the corporate investment portfolio. What businesses should we be in? family members might ask. Should we do startups? Where should we invest most heavily? Do we want to be highly leveraged? Do we want to invest in high-risk businesses? (See Exhibit 11 for a fuller sampling of subjects that should concern the family council.)

The family council also can take responsibility for certain functions unique to the family. Preserving family traditions and values and educating family shareholders about the business are two important examples. Often, family education is crucial in helping members make decisions on such matters as appropriate debt, profit, and dividend levels for the business, the role of the shareholder, and other matters. "A significant effort needs to be made to educate shareholders about the rights, responsibilities, and privileges that come with ownership," Mr. Lansberg says.

Exhibit 11. Topics Important to the Family Council.

- Allocation of capital: appropriate dividend, profit, debt, and reinvestment levels for the business
- Liquidity for holders
- Family business philosophy
- Family tradition in the business
- Family history and its role in the business
- Family culture and its role in the business
- Family values and their role in business strategy
- Performance of investment
- Estate planning by owners
- Family mission
- Family members' role in the business
- Family members' participation in the business
- Role in society: philanthropy, civic activities, politics
- Family responsibilities as business owners
- Family visibility in the public domain
- The role of the business in supporting family members' goals
- Education of family members in all these areas

Even the process of selecting family-council members can be an educational one. Mr. Lansberg advises the family council to identify ideal attributes for council members to guide various branches of the family in nominating members, with the council making the final selection. He also urges the family council to help younger family members to acquire those attributes, such as knowledge of other companies' board operations or familiarity with other family businesses.

The family council can also help examine cases where "economic rationality bumps up against family values," Mr. Lansberg adds. A family of Jewish ancestry might veto any management initiative to do business with certain Palestinian groups, for instance, no matter how lucrative. Or a family that values equal rights for women in management might mandate rapid promotion of women, no matter how contrary that might be to prevailing industry practice. "The family council is the place where these issues are examined and the family articulates its values," Mr. Lansberg says.

Finally, the family council can cultivate among members a sense of cohesiveness and purpose completely separate from the goals of the business. Ideally, in a well-run business, the family council fosters among its members a sense of trust in managers and directors to oversee strategic objectives with only an appropriate level of involvement from shareholders. In turn, shareholders' energy can be channeled into more productive activities, helping transform suspicious or meddlesome family members into a collective source of energy and support for the business.

The Family Mission Statement. Many families write a family mission statement as part of their effort to articulate and fulfill these goals. This document is a kind of constitution of the family, telling the reader "who we are and what we stand for."

The mission statement describes the family's goals and values, its vision for the business, and its mode of operation and decision making. (Please see Appendix B for a sample outline.) It can be invaluable in conveying to directors and other constituents the family's commitment to the business and its posture on a range of important issues. Some families also produce a family history or background book to help educate directors and constituents about members' values, goals, and culture.

Nonbusiness Activities of the Family Council. Family councils also engage in a wide range of other functions. The council may have a budget and a secretary. Increasingly, family councils maintain an office away from the business, often staffed by a retiring founder or partner in the business.

The family might publish a newsletter to help keep members informed. It might act as investment banker for members. It may provide a network of contacts for members to use in their own businesses or careers. It may oversee collective holdings or projects, such as a family ranch or summer home or the purchase of tickets to sporting and cultural events. Large family organizations sometimes hire administrators to manage services to members, such as tax accounting, real estate management, shared investments, philanthropies, socials, and other matters.

Some families organize councils of older members, who

act as a kind of mentoring group for younger family members seeking advice, coaching, and feedback from adults other than their parents. Others keep a psychologist or counselor on retainer to the family to provide confidential help with personal problems.

Other families may name committees of members to deal with various nonbusiness issues, such as philanthropy, family history, family investment, and so on. Each committee may report to a gathering of the whole family at annual or semiannual family meetings or more frequently.

The Telemedia Example

The owners of Telemedia, a large Canadian media concern, provide a remarkable example of integrating the interests and goals of family and business without shortchanging either one. The big media and telecommunications group was founded in 1971 by Philippe de Gaspé Beaubien. His wife, Nan-b, cochaired the enterprise for many years and now heads the family organization and serves as a director of several family operations. Two of their three grown chidren work in the family businesses, and the third will join after completing business studies at Harvard University.

Together, the family has structured both a holding company to oversee the family-controlled businesses and their subsidiary boards and a forward-looking family council aimed at perpetuating the family's mission, goals, values, and business control.

The Holding Company. The board of the holding company, Gasbeau, oversees the family's burgeoning and diverse business operations. It monitors the separate boards of various subsidiary companies and allocates funds among the family's portfolio of investments.

To ensure the competitiveness and continued growth of the family operations, Gasbeau is "a meritocracy run on sound business principles for the creation of long-term value," Nan-b de Gaspé Beaubien says. Its board is charged with helping to maintain the family's control of its core business activities.

At the same time, the family's values and mission play a major role in Gasbeau's governance. Gasbeau's conceptual and strategic plan says the company will be built "on the twin foundations of a sound business philosophy and a strong sense of family aspirations and values.

"The commitment to growth, excellence, innovation and risk-taking which has marked the founder should as much as possible be embodied in the heritage" of Gasbeau, "so that those hallmarks of entrepreneurship and imagination continue to be a living part of its future activities."

The Family Council. The separate family organization, Fambeau, helps imbue the business with strong family values, in addition to dealing with philanthropic policy, family education, and other family matters. It also serves as a vehicle to retain and pass on family values to future generations. The family's five current members — the parents and their three children — comprise the current board.

Fambeau's purposes, summarized in its bylaws, include attending to the spiritual, social, and intellectual interests of the family and its descendants; preserving the honor and integrity of members; fostering cooperation and philanthropic activities; and providing opportunities for members to better themselves through education and training.

Fambeau meetings are conducted in a businesslike fashion, with agendas and minutes. Its bylaws establish clear, detailed procedures for board and annual member meetings, officer selection, and other corporate affairs.

The family stresses the significance of Fambeau's role and mission. "We're very concerned that everyone recognize the importance of Fambeau," Nan-b de Gaspé Beaubien says.

Open participation by all Fambeau members is encouraged. "One of the keys in any family is communication," she adds. "Our method of communication has been totally open from the start."

Links Between the Family and the Business. The family and holding-company organizations are linked on several levels. Under the bylaws, the CEO of Gasbeau (presently Philippe de

Gaspé Beaubien) is automatically afforded a seat on the Fambeau council, and the head of Fambeau sits on Gasbeau's board. Other family members are present on the Gasbeau board as well, but their voices are tempered by those of several outside directors. Four of the Gasbeau board's nine members are carefully selected, independent outsiders. "These people must be able to make a sound contribution to the business and share the family values as well," Nan-b de Gaspé Beaubien says.

Taking the Long View. At first glance, the de Gaspé Beaubiens' enterprises may seem to have little need of complex structures to ensure business perpetuation and shareholder harmony. But Nan-b de Gaspé Beaubien believes education of succeeding generations of shareholders is crucial to responsible corporate ownership. She also believes, as Gasbeau's conceptual and strategic plan states, that "it is important . . . to put the rules in place before they are needed."

While the company's first- and second-generation shareholders are cohesive and peaceful, the plan establishes clear "dispute settlement mechanisms" to facilitate liquidation of dissident individual shareholders under certain circumstances. It also specifies goals and procedures for return on equity, personnel development, the financial independence of subsidiaries, debt and dividend levels, and ensuring shareholder liquidity.

A strong respect for the disciplines of good business underlie all the planning. While Gasbeau companies are "free to hire any family member," for instance, such employment must be "only on the basis of merit." Clearly, the de Gaspé Beaubiens have laid a firm foundation for the fruitful, responsible perpetuation of the family business well beyond the second generation.

"The more one receives, I truly believe, the more one has to give back. And the more you give, the more you seem to receive," says Nan-b de Gaspé Beaubien. "If one receives shares in a company, it behooves one to accept the responsibility that goes with that. . . . Money can become a drug. It offers people a choice — a choice of becoming lazy. I think you must educate children about the meaning of ownership. 'How do I prepare myself to do something of value with it?' is a primary question."

In focusing on these issues, she adds, "I'm hoping that we can make our part of the world a little better."

Getting from Here to There

The ideal governing structure — an outside board functioning smoothly in tandem with a family organization — can be difficult to achieve. Many family businesses follow the path of least resistance instead, keeping strategic planning and decision making "all in the family" and packing their boards with shareholders. What if your family business has no outside board and no vehicle for addressing major shareholder issues — and your shareholders are deeply suspicious of either idea? Here are some suggestions.

Plan Ahead. As the family business evolves, many owners add more and more family members to the board. The result is often an oversized, family-dominated panel ill-suited to grapple with the problems of a growing company.

As ownership of the company becomes more fragmented, as discussed above, the logic of involving shareholders on the board breaks down. The presence on the board of a second-generation owner with a 25 percent stake does not mean that his or her five children with 5 percent each should all be directors too! This often forces a painful downsizing of the board to involve outsiders and make it more effective. (The case study below provides an example of how one family accomplished this.) Many business owners, such as the de Gaspé Beaubiens, find it helpful to begin shaping family members' expectations about the board as early as possible. Involving outside directors in the first or second generation of family-business ownership and separating family and board issues then, before the family shareholder group grows too large, can avert the need for a painful disassembling of the board later.

Begin Early to Link the Family with the Board. Many business owners find informal ways to involve younger family members with the outside board, helping educate them and prepare them for their responsibilities as future business owners at the same time.

Al Hoffman, owner of a Chicago locksmith-supply business, asked his three children who are working in the business to help choose the members of his first outside board. Then, he asked each to select a specific responsibility for board management, including preparing background packets, agendas, a corporate history, and so forth. "It's not *my* board. It's *our* board, and it's eventually going to be *their* board," he says.

Communicate Openly with Family Members About Planned Changes. The idea of separating family members from the board can be difficult for some shareholders to accept. In the process, the family will lose some influence, and helping family members accept that fact requires careful education and planning.

Many business owners find it helpful to expose family members to the experience other family businesses have had with outside boards, perhaps through social gatherings arranged by a mutual acquaintance.

It helps to emphasize the positive. The CEO might stress to shareholders the added value outside directors can bring to the business and to the family's investment. The opportunity to secure such resources, experience, and expertise at a relatively low cost may appeal to the shareholders.

Stressing the importance of the family council to the continuity of the business can help alleviate family members' sense of loss or resentment at losing board seats. This often requires some family education about the importance of the issues the family council must tackle—allocation of corporate resources, the shareholder mission, and so on. Family business experts can be engaged to help in this task.

Phase In the Restructuring. Many family business owners find restructuring the board and organizing a family council too big a change for shareholders to accept all at once. Some phase in the changes over five to ten years to make them more palatable.

One family with ten family members on its board began

by inviting outsiders as observers to board sessions. By the time older family members retire, chances are good that these outsiders will have won enough trust and respect that the remaining family members will feel comfortable inviting them to assume full directorships.

Another family agreed that an outside director should replace one of the family members on the board, but no one volunteered to step down. The family drew straws to pick the resigning member.

Others who find restructuring the legal board too difficult simply leave the family-dominated board in place and form an advisory council, a separate group of outsiders who can provide advice and counsel, as discussed earlier in this book.

Consider Compensating Family Members for Lost Directors' Fees.
Many oversized, family-laden boards have been formed largely to funnel tax-advantaged income to family members in the form of directors' fees. Unlike corporate dividends, which are taxed at both the corporate and personal level, directors' fees are taxed only once, as income to the recipient.

Predictably, family directors are often reluctant to give up these fees for the sake of restructuring the corporate board. Many business owners try to find alternative forms of compensation, such as gifts to minors. Some bite the bullet, converting the directors' fees to dividends and paying the additional taxes.

Again, if no acceptable alternatives can be found, other business owners simply leave the family-dominated board in place and create an advisory council instead.

Permanently Restrict Family Membership on the Board.
Ideally, board membership in the mature family business is limited to outsiders, plus the CEO and perhaps a designated successor. This is not always possible, especially in cases where branches of the family with a significant owership share want board representation. Allowing a few seats for family members is often necessary.

Ideally, these directorships should be structured in a way that stresses an educational and communications role for family board members. Many families arrange for family members to rotate into board seats at one- or two-year intervals, to increase the family's exposure to the board's deliberations. Others permit family members to act as observers on the same basis.

This has the advantage of making clear that family members' role is *not* to have a voice in the strategic discussion, but rather to help maintain good communications between the family and the board.

Remaking the Family Board: A Case Study

Balancing family control with effective management of a business can demand some unusual personal growth and sacrifice.

One fast-growing family business had twelve family members as directors when some knotty ownership and management issues led the family to a difficult decision. Concluding that they needed outside help, family members decided to shrink and remake the board.

Eight family members would step down, the family decided, making room for three outsiders. Four family members would retain seats, including the chairman and president of the company (the founder and one son) and two others selected by family vote. To ensure that no one felt cheated, *all* the family members gave up their directors' fees—those who remained on the board as well as those who did not.

For the outside directorships, the CEO generated a list of a half dozen candidates with the help of a consultant. "At that time, the family was still nervous about it," he recalls. He assuaged those fears in part by inviting the candidates to visit the company before selections were made. "It was important to the family that they got to meet these strangers."

Some family members were concerned about the loss of influence associated with giving up their board seats. "They were uncertain that their voices would be heard," the CEO says. Planning annual gatherings where directors and family members meet and mingle helped ease their concerns, he says.

"It has become a nice tradition," the CEO says. The family typically rents rooms at a resort for two days, with board and family meetings scheduled for the first day and social and recreational activities for the rest of the time. "I think it's very important for the family to know there's a forum to express their positions on different issues," he says.

He also told directors that family members might call them from time to time with questions or information. "If [family members] had felt they were going to be locked out, I don't think the board would ever have been formed," the CEO says.

Now, many of the ownership-related issues that had been plaguing family members have been put to rest "in a fair way, so everyone is pretty satisfied," he says.

Many family members are glad for the board's help with "some touchy situations. It was a relief to have the board in place so that these issues wouldn't destroy our family. We had always been pretty close and able to overcome our differences."

Meanwhile, the family receives minutes and agendas from board sessions. The family's regular quarterly meetings typically are scheduled just before the regular board sessions, to facilitate communications. Philanthropic policy, ways of voting shares, education on business performance and plans, and other ownership matters dominate the family meetings.

The family also organized a committee to preserve the traditions and culture of the family business. The group is creating scrapbooks and a family history that can be passed on to successive generations.

"That ties in with our pride in the company, too. You've got a founder that everybody loved, and you want that to be preserved and passed on," the CEO says. "Those things become especially important" as the business grows and embraces professional management systems.

The family's extraordinary efforts to cope peacefully with the demands and responsibilities of business ownership will yield far-reaching rewards, the CEO believes. Members of the third generation look forward eagerly to family gatherings, which provide compelling examples of shared decision making and conflict resolution.

"For an anniversary once, we all wrote in an album what our parents meant to us," the CEO recalls. "I remember writing about my father that he always taught me by example, and that's really how our children are learning. They're seeing how we handle situations. We are sharing that we can be mature, and yet be human as well — having disagreements and then getting back together again. That ability speaks well for our family, and I hope it would perpetuate itself with our children and their children."

The Family Role in Selecting Directors

Family involvement in selecting the company's first outside directors is crucial in building trust between shareholders and the board. Many companies form a committee of family members, with each member perhaps representing one branch of the family. This panel might select the first outside board from candidates nominated by family members, the CEO, or a professional adviser.

Naming a family nomating committee is preferable to allowing the CEO to pick a slate. No matter how honorable the CEO's intentions, some family members may suspect that he or she is trying to pack the board with directors favorable to his or her personal interests. The CEO should avoid at all costs creating the impression that directors will inevitably side with management.

It is crucial that family members be comfortable with the board selections. Each family member or branch of the family should have veto power over nominees. If even one branch or member objects to a candidate everyone else thinks is well qualified, that person should be rejected without argument.

At the same time, no branch or shareholder group should be allowed to force its candidate on others, or to bargain with another shareholder group for support of its own choice. As discussed in Chapter Seven, the result may be a constituency board, with individual directors feeling obligated to shareholder factions rather than to the interests of the company as a whole.

The screening process can be conducted in several ways. Smaller families may actually meet with candidates in person. Other families circulate candidates resumes and ask for feedback or objections at family meetings.

After the outside board is established, many family businesses turn the nomination process over to a committee of two to three outside directors. As directorships fall open, this panel (which might also include a senior family member) offers a slate of carefully screened candidates for shareholder approval.

Throughout this process, the family mission statement is especially important. The family can use it both as a tool to educate candidates about their expectations of the board and a device to monitor the board's adherence to family values and mission.

The Role of the Board in Perpetuating Family Control

Once outside directors are in place, they often can help perpetuate family control and leadership of the business, as discussed in Chapter Two. Among other things, the board can aid in the succession. Directors can evaluate and act as mentors to potential successors and provide peers for the younger generation of family members. They can assist widows during the succession process. They can help the older generation decide when to step aside. Directors can also assist in setting fair compensation levels for family members in the business, as well as dividends and benefits to inactive family members. Perhaps most importantly, directors can help improve strategic planning and thinking, increasing the business's competitiveness and survival chances.

In more subtle ways, directors can also help the family monitor the stability and cohesiveness of the shareholder base. They should try continually to monitor the strength of the family consensus regarding the business. If a director detects a deterioration of the family mission, he or she can sometimes discreetly help family members address and resolve the matter.

While family education is the family's job, directors can sometimes encourage the family to educate successor generations about the privileges and responsibilities of business ownership. For example, some directors participate by making presentations to family members on relevant areas of their experience. Board members can also encourage business owners to undertake responsible personal estate planning that will help avert financial problems for the business.

And if directors detect any significant deterioration in the shareholders' commitment to the business, they can begin to address related issues of concern in the board room. If shareholders are headed toward serious conflict that might force some to liquidate their shares, for instance, directors might want to examine alternatives for raising capital. Any issue that affects the long-range financial plans and capital needs of the business demands the directors' attention.

Directors sometimes recommend that families locked in shareholder disputes retain outside advisers to help sort out the issues. "This clearly is the domain of the family council, but I can see that it is causing some members a lot of difficulty," the director might say. "Have you considered hiring somebody to help the family with this?"

Many times, a simple display of interest by outside directors encourages family shareholders to conduct their affairs in a more organized and responsible way. Directors' requests for information, for instance, may be afforded more respect than similar requests from family members. A shareholder might see another family member's question about his or her long-term commitment to the business as meddlesome or irrelevant. The shareholder may legitimately ask, "Why is it so important that you know my intentions?"

But when a respected outside director asks the same question, shareholders may listen to the explanation with greater respect. "We'd like to make ten-year commitments for the business," the director may respond. "If several of you want out in the next five years, we'll amend our thinking. But if you're committed to staying in the business, we'll be able to make different plans for the company's capital."

A trusting relationship between family members and the outside board is essential. The board must retain the prerogative on crucial business issues, including responsibility for strategy and corporate performance. Essentially, family members must recognize that they are not as qualified as outside directors to oversee such matters.

Directors must sometimes help educate shareholders not involved in the business about their appropriate role. Directors should not allow themselves to be misused by shareholders demanding information or challenging specific decisions. Sometimes, other family members or the family council must step in to prevent uninvolved shareholders from badgering directors.

"We want you to enjoy all the benefits of business ownership and membership in the family," a family member might advise the offender. "But the board is a precious group of people who are basically serving as volunteers. If you can't feel comfortable with their role and leave them alone, then you will have to sell your shares."

Staying the Course

Once the outside board and family council are established, how should their relationship be managed?

A consistent flow of information from the board to family members is crucial in sustaining trust. Shareholders should receive board agendas and minutes, as well as background on each director and information about his or her views. Some families send out bimonthly information updates to all shareholders.

Some families plan meetings in a way that encourages effective family-board interaction. Some hold family meetings before board meetings, airing ownership issues and then, when appropriate, having a family member report to the board on ownership-related issues. Fireside talks, coffee hours, and social gatherings between family members and directors can help foster trust and give directors crucial information to help in making decisions that affect shareholder interests. Occasionally, individual directors might attend family gatherings as well. All of these activities are best held in an informal, family-style setting, helping to give family members a sense of reassurance and comfort.

Some families delegate the task of finding consensus on major issues to a special task force and then have a representative report the group's conclusions to the board. Others name a family ombudsman, whose job is to gather opinions from family members on crucial issues such as shareholder liquidity, the validity of the family mission statement, and so on. (A professional adviser can play the same role.)

The Rewards

The rigors of sustaining good board-shareholder relations during and beyond the third stage of family business ownership may seem burdensome indeed. But many family businesses with long experience find the rewards well worth all the work.

"There may be disagreements in our family about how a business decision ought to be made, but there are never disagreements on the basic values of the business," says Paul Lehman, a president of Fel-Pro, a large, fourth-generation automotive-parts concern. "Appreciating and sharing the values we received from our parents, and translating them to our kids, has really been a rewarding thing. . . . That's not to say there aren't tensions and pressures. You really have to work hard to keep family harmony. But at the heart of it is total consensus on the business values and mission. And that's a nice thing."

Summary

Driven by a growing awareness of the value of family ownership and entrepreneurship, more families than ever are trying to retain control of their companies through the third generation and beyond. This raises some complicated new issues for owners and directors. As the shareholder base expands and diversifies through the generations, it often fragments and tears at the very foundation of the business.

As discussed throughout this book, an outside board can help with the strategic challenges of maturation and growth. But private company directors need effective, clear ways of communicating with shareholders as well. Many maturing family businesses structure family councils to manage shareholder concerns.

In some ways, the role of an effective family council is to ensure that the business is run with the same kind of responsiveness to shareholders that characterizes a good public company. The council helps foster consensus on such important matters as the family's mission and role in the business, dividends, profit and debt levels, and other matters. Ideally, it functions in tandem with an effective outside board, speaking with a clear, cohesive voice on shareholder issues.

Achieving this ideal governing structure for the mature family business usually is not easy. It often requires sacrifices of family members, including giving up some family seats on the board as well as directors' fees and a degree of influence in board matters. Advance planning can be of great help in shaping family members' expectations about their role in the business and in separating family and business issues. Once shareholders are organized into a family council; deliberate efforts are necessary to link the council with the board and foster trust and good communications between them. Ideally, the family council eventually takes on a life of its own, perpetuating itself through its members' common sense of mission.

The rewards can be great. The family council can assume a crucial role in perpetuating family ownership and manifesting family values in the business and the community. At the same time, the active outside board can vastly enrich the family's experience and fortunes by helping to chart a sound strategic course for the business.

11

The Challenge for Owners and Boards: Perpetuating the Private Enterprise

When speakers from a Fortune 100 conglomerate and Steelcase, one of the nation's largest and most successful family-owned firms, shared the program at a recent strategic-planning conference, Paul Lehman was struck by the contrast in their messages.

The executive from Steelcase described his company's mission as providing high-quality products and services to all constituents, with a strong emphasis on citizenship in its community and its role as a responsible employer. "I remember thinking that we had many things in common," says Mr. Lehman, president of Fel-Pro, a large automotive parts maker in its fourth generation of family ownership.

But when the Fortune 100 man's turn on the dais came, he droned on and on exclusively about his company's profit performance, Mr. Lehman recalls. When he remarked on the contrast later in a private conversation with the Fortune 100 executive, the man's only response was a disparaging remark that Steelcase's financial results probably were not as good as they seemed.

"My mouth fell open, and I said to myself, 'These are the kind of people who would destroy our business real fast,'" Mr. Lehman recalls. Managers with such a short-term, quick-results orientation would likely slash the long-term human resources programs valued so highly by companies like Fel-Pro and Steelcase, he surmised. At Fel-Pro, "we want to be able to make decisions about our mission ourselves. We want to be masters of our own destiny. And we want to be able to preserve what we think is good about our company for our children and our community."

Forming an outside board, inviting objective criticism, grappling with board-shareholder relations — these suggestions and many others offered in this book may seem daunting indeed to the business owner already meeting the day-to-day challenge of running a company.

Is perpetuating private ownership really worth all the trouble?

The answer to that question, of course, is every business owner's personal choice. But many owners — those looking back on generations of family control or many years of independent, private ownership — say that it *is* worth it.

The rewards of perpetuating private ownership, in fact, often surpass any imagined by the entrepreneur in the early years of struggling to build a young business. The payoff may be a gratifying sense of personal purpose and responsibility, as well as significant benefits for the economy and society as a whole.

The Value of Continuity

The desire to leave a meaningful legacy — to achieve immortality in some sense — is innate in most people. The opportunity to pass on an institution of one's own creation can be a rich reward, as well as a powerful motivation to make that institution as strong, honest, and efficient as possible. Research shows that smaller, privately owned businesses often practice and espouse higher levels of ethics and social responsibility than larger bureaucracies.

Many business owners choose to pass on their company to family members, key managers, or employees — the people who helped make the business strong. This makes the business an excellent vehicle for perpetuating concepts and values fundamental to free enterprise, such as sacrifice, saving, investment, and risk.

Suppliers, customers, consumers, and the community at large can benefit from the stability of committed private business owners. These longstanding relationships encourage honest and responsible dealings that have spinoff value for the entire community.

Private ownership makes a difference in the nature of business investment as well. Free from the pressure to satisfy Wall Street with appealing quarterly returns, the private business owner can make a stronger commitment to building the underlying value of the enterprise over the long term.

He or she has greater latitude to deploy "patient capital"—staying with a promising investment through tough times, when those with lesser commitment, or a greater need to generate short-term profit, might back off. The private company also has greater freedom to take a chance on creative ideas that might languish in a more restrictive or bureaucratic environment.

A Sense of Stewardship

In the early years of most businesses, the struggle to survive and grow so consumes the owner that it often becomes an end in itself. But as the business matures and questions about its long-term future arise, many owners face a kind of personal crisis. While many look to the conventional path of selling the business when the market peaks and retiring early, or perhaps starting yet another business, they may wonder privately, "Is this all there is?"

At this point, a search for further meaning can engender a new sense of stewardship. As the business owner looks beyond the short-term rewards of wealth and influence, he or she may experience a new sense of purpose. The opportunity to serve society and future generations through an institution of one's own making takes on new meaning.

For those who accomplish the transition from entrepreneurship to stewardship, the idea that ownership is a privilege conferring responsibilities, as well as rights and rewards, becomes more important. Business owners at this stage often become interested in the idea of "doing right" with the power afforded by ownership. They become more aware, for instance, of their role in the community and their obligation to behave in a socially responsible way that will help sustain the quality of life there. At this point, many also seek the counsel and guidance of an outside board — a powerful aid in the effort to exercise the privileges and power of ownership in a balanced and responsible fashion.

Stewardship of a large company is "a lot of responsibility," says Fred Ruiz, second-generation owner and CEO of Ruiz Food Products, a Tulare, California, food concern with more than 800 employees, who recently established an outside board. "A lot of people here rely on me to make the right decisions."

Maintaining a Pluralistic Society

Pluralism — the distribution of power among scores of independent units — is a crucial underpinning of democracy. Private businesses can be a powerful contributor to a strong, diverse, and pluralistic society. They not only help maintain power in the hands of small units such as families, but they foster the innovation and personal freedom necessary to sustain a vital and prosperous society.

"I believe that business has a community role to play. That's where strong family culture and values can help the company," says Nan-b de Gaspé Beaubien, co-chair of Telemedia, a large family-owned media concern based in Montreal.

A thriving private business community enables its owners to manifest many diverse value systems forcefully and constructively. Conversely, it short-circuits the homogenizing effect of corporate mergers.

The presence of potent private businesses can greatly strengthen the social fabric of their home communities. The wealth and stability they create can foster personal vitality and growth all around them, particularly if the business owners take responsibility for civic leadership and philanthropic activity.

The pride of ownership can encourage this kind of pluralism. One's name on the door of a productive, respected business can foster a potent sense of personal or family pride and identity. This sense of esteem and self-awareness is a further incentive to provide high-quality products and services and to deal honestly, fairly, and generously with people — including all of a business's constituencies. This motivation often fades in the more anonymous management structure of the public company.

For the Lehman, Weinberg, and Morris families of Skokie, Illinois, owners of Fel-Pro, private ownership has been a powerful incentive to foster the vitality and growth of all the company's constituencies. Family members think of the 2,000-employee company as "very customer-oriented, very service-oriented, and very family-oriented. We are also very much aware of the community in which we operate," Paul Lehman says. "The principal value is, not only are we family-run, but we think of the company in a larger sense as family." Half of Fel-Pro's employees have a relative working in the company. A remarkably generous employee benefit package provides strong support for workers and their families, including on-site child care and a summer camp facility. The owners' policies have fostered an open and cooperative attitude between employees and management.

The reward: seventy-two years of growth and market leadership, coupled with intense employee loyalty and a public image as a good corporate citizen and a desirable place to work.

"We value being able to do the kinds of things that make good business sense and good people sense, with a lot of freedom," Mr. Lehman says. "If we were publicly held, I don't think we would have the same kind of freedom to experiment and to do things that make good gut sense."

APPENDIX A

A Sample
Board Prospectus

Board of Advisers

We seek a board of advisers — an outside, informal, independent source of stimulation and ideas — to help us manage the future of our successful business. We believe our business and industry will face more complex issues and challenges than those we have confronted before. We believe a board of advisers to be an invaluable resource to aid us as owners and managers. The following describes our company and the role and purpose we envision for our board.

Our Business

We are the largest organization of our kind in the metropolitan area. We have ten (10) locations and a significant investment in real estate through three (3) real-estate holding companies. We have several separate but related businesses. In all, we are a $5 million enterprise with 75 employees.

We provide the highest-quality and broadest line of high-price products and services to our customers. We are proud to have recently received the very first "Excellence" award our industry has ever conveyed. We reach our customers through a valued 100-year-old reputation and very active public relations. Market reputation in this business, however, can be dangerously harmed by only a few years of slack performance. Therefore, we depend critically upon our management's ability to meet the tremendous variety of customer needs spontaneously and flexibly and to orchestrate a complex set of services rapidly.

We are a family business, owned and operated by three brothers. We are dedicated to the highest standards of ethics and quality. We wish to see our children earn and inherit the ownership and management of the firm.

The Need for a Board

Our local and traditional market potential has matured. The changing attitudes of the public to our industry are forcing us to adapt. Recent federal legislation will greatly affect the structure of our industry and how firms compete. We must invent new ways of doing business and challenge conventional industry thinking. We must find new growth opportunities in the next few crucial years. We will need to evaluate several innovative, experimental new ventures recently undertaken. We will need to consider new sources of private capital. Our personal goals and desires are changing. We must prepare for management and ownership succession.

The expertise and counsel of an outside board will help us face these new opportunities and challenges. We need to assure ourselves, our families, and our employees that we will have a successful future.

The Purpose of the Board

The primary purpose of our board will be to help guide us as managers of a business. We will greatly benefit from highly successful people whose *only* interest is what is best for the business.

- First, we hope the board will help us evaluate and think through the key issues and decisions facing our business. The board will offer us a forum, a sounding board, to talk out our ideas. A board will bring with it a fresher perspective that will encourage us to consider more alternatives and to challenge our reasoning.
- Board meetings will generate for us and our management

the discipline to regularly review our operations and commitments.

- In time, our board will aid us as we evaluate the development and potential of our management successors.
- Finally, the board provides added assurance to us, to our families, and to our employees that caring people with a good, general grasp of our business are available for counsel in times of critical need.

The Nature of our Board

We expect that our board of advisers will include three (3) active business executives who have (collectively) already experienced much of what we face. Our board will formally *meet three times per year* at a morning meeting. We hope our board members will be available for occasional phone discussions and an infrequent lunch between board meetings. We will work diligently to keep you fully informed of our financial and strategic progress. We do not view you as decision makers or operating managers—only as concerned counselors on our future. Over time, we will introduce you to our management and our families. We will ask for your comments on our strategic plan, succession plan, and administrative policies and systems.

We hope your experience assessing our circumstances and considering our needs will be stimulating and useful to you as you manage your own firm. Surely we cannot materially overvalue the contribution you will make. We hope an annual retainer "honorarium" of $3,000 will express to you our commitment and some of our appreciation.

Conclusion

We believe an independent, outside board of advisers will help us be better managers and create a better future for all those who depend on our business. We will be proud if a few successful and talented people will care enough and believe enough in our future to serve on our board of advisers.

APPENDIX B

A Family Business Mission Statement

I. Preamble
- Statement of Resolve and Commitment
- Rationale or "Precepts"
  - Values to cherish as a family
  - Societal changes that affect our family and values
  - Requirements or supports necessary for future success
  - Role of owning enterprise to aid hopes and support values
  - Why are we so fortunate to have this opportunity?

II. Vision
- Number of business units
- Role of new business formation
- Relationship or interdependence among businesses
- Ownership structure
- Family role in business leadership and new business entrepreneurship

III. Constitution
- Participation Policy in Business and in Family
  - Preparation
  - Exits
  - In-Laws
  - Departure
- Family Leadership and Governance Plan
  - Family leadership succession
  - Role of family "council"

- Relationship defined between council and Board of Directors
- Plan for Family Education, Communications, and Trust
  - Education in business and progress and issues
  - Development of human relations skills for family strength and harmony (listening, communication, conflict resolution, etc.)
  - Policy to communicate family compensation and ownership and inheritance plans
  - Monitor everyone's personal goals, needs, and expectations
- Plan for Involvement and Meaning
  - Pride through history, testimonials, PR
  - Steps to institutionalize our culture and traditions
  - Meaning of family and "love" to us
  - Development of family code of understanding or "creed"
  - Roles for everyone (philanthropy, civic involvement ombudsman, industry future, and family leadership)
- Plan for Broadly Shared Benefits
  - New venture support
  - Liquidity and personal freedom
  - Personal assessment, education, and development
  - Family perks
  - Community contacts
  - Philanthropy
  - Shared resources
  - Contingency plan for those "in need"
  - Family "fun"
- Plan to Administer to Family Function
  - Office and resources
  - Budget and funding

IV. Planning for the Continuing Family Agenda
- Topics
- Schedule and venue
- Responsibilities and preparation

REFERENCES

Alderfer, C. P. "Understanding and Consulting to Family Business Boards." *Family Business Review,* 1988, *1* (3), 249–261.

American Society of Corporate Secretaries. *Meetings of the Board of Directors and Its Committees: A Guidebook.* (2nd ed.) New York: American Society of Corporate Secretaries, 1986.

Anderson, C. A., and Anthony, R. N. *The New Corporate Directors.* New York: Wiley, 1986.

Bennett, A. "Hot Seats: Board Members Draw Fire, and Some Think Twice About Serving." *Wall Street Journal,* Feb. 5, 1986, p. 1.

Cardinal Meat Specialists. *The Philosophy of Cardinal Meat Specialists.* Mississauga, Ontario: Cardinal Meat Specialists, 1986.

Committee on Corporate Laws, American Bar Association. *Corporate Director's Guidebook.* (Rev. ed.) Chicago: American Bar Association, 1978.

Danco, L. A., and Jonovic, D. J. *Outside Directors in the Family-Owned Business.* Cleveland, Ohio: The University Press, 1981.

Goozner, M. "Lack of Successor Called Peril to Firms, Jobs." *Chicago Tribune,* Nov. 16, 1989, Sec. 2, p. 1.

Greenberg, J. W. "Current Trends in D&O Insurance." *Director's Monthly,* 1989, *13* (9), 1–7.

Heidrick Partners. *Orientation and Education of Outside Directors: A Survey of the Practices of 200 Leading Industrial and Non-Industrial Corporations.* Chicago: Heidrick Partners, 1989.

Melloan, G. "Business World: A Good Director Is Getting Harder to Find." *Wall Street Journal,* Feb. 9, 1988, p. 22.

Minnesota Mining & Manufacturing Company. *Our Story So Far.* St. Paul: Minnesota Mining & Manufacturing Company, 1977.

Parco Foods. *Corporate Mission Statement.* Blue Island, Ill.: Parco Foods, 1987.

Schipani, C. A., and Siedel, G. J. "Legal Liability: The Board of Directors." *Family Business Review,* 1988, *1* (3), 282.

Solar Press. *Corporate Mission Statement.* Naperville, Ill.: Solar Press, 1988.

Tillman, F. A. "Commentary on Legal Liability: Organizing the Advisory Council." *Family Business Review,* 1988, *1* (3), 287–288.

Vance, S. C. *Corporate Leadership: Boards, Directors, and Strategy.* New York: McGraw-Hill, 1983.

Verespej, M. A. "Lawsuit Troubles Still Hound Directors." *Industry Week,* June 1, 1987, pp. 15–16.

Ward, J. L. "Perpetuating the Family Business." In C. E. Arnoff, R. B. Good, and J. L. Ward (eds.), *The Future of Private Enterprise.* Atlanta: Georgia State University Press, 1986.

Ward, J. L. *Keeping the Family Business Healthy.* San Francisco: Jossey-Bass, 1987.

Ward, J. L., and Handy, J. L. "Survey of Board Practices." *Family Business Review,* 1988, *1* (3), 289–308.

Weber, D. "The Directors and Officers Liability Insurance Crisis—Is There a Solution in Sight?" *Marsh & McLennan Commentary,* 1986, *5* (4), 1–3.

Whisler, T. L. *Rules of the Game.* Homewood, Ill.: Dow Jones-Irwin, 1984.

Wyatt Company. *Directors and Officers Liability Survey—1989.* Chicago: Wyatt Company, 1990a.

Wyatt Company. *Special Directors and Officers Liability Peer Group Report for Small Businesses—1989.* Chicago: Wyatt Company, 1990b.

INDEX